**THE POWER OF PARTNERSHIP
IN OPEN GOVERNMENT**

INFORMATION POLICY SERIES
Edited by Sandra Braman

The Information Policy Series publishes research on and analysis of significant problems in the field of information policy, including decisions and practices that enable or constrain information, communication, and culture irrespective of the legal siloes in which they have traditionally been located as well as state-law-society interactions. Defining information policy as all laws, regulations, and decision-making principles that affect any form of information creation, processing, flows, and use, the series includes attention to the formal decisions, decision-making processes, and entities of government; the formal and informal decisions, decision-making processes, and entities of private and public sector agents capable of constitutive effects on the nature of society; and the cultural habits and predispositions of governmentality that support and sustain government and governance. The parametric functions of information policy at the boundaries of social, informational, and technological systems are of global importance because they provide the context for all communications, interactions, and social processes.

A complete list of the books in the Information Policy series appears at the back of this book.

THE POWER OF PARTNERSHIP IN OPEN GOVERNMENT

Reconsidering Multistakeholder Governance Reform

SUZANNE J. PIOTROWSKI,
DANIEL BERLINER, AND ALEX INGRAMS

The MIT Press
Cambridge, Massachusetts
London, England

© 2022 Massachusetts Institute of Technology

This work is subject to a Creative Commons CC-BY-NC-ND license.

Subject to such license, all rights are reserved.

The open access edition of this book was made possible by generous funding from the Lois and Samuel Pratt Program for Freedom of Information at Rutgers Law School and the Institute of Public Administration at Leiden University.

The MIT Press would like to thank the anonymous peer reviewers who provided comments on drafts of this book. The generous work of academic experts is essential for establishing the authority and quality of our publications. We acknowledge with gratitude the contributions of these otherwise uncredited readers.

This book was set in Adobe Garamond and Berthold Akzidenz Grotesk by Westchester Publishing Services. Printed and bound in the United States of America.

Library of Congress Cataloging-in-Publication Data

Names: Piotrowski, Suzanne J., 1973– author. | Berliner, Daniel, author. | Ingrams, Alex, author.
Title: The power of partnership in open government : reconsidering multistakeholder governance reform / Suzanne J. Piotrowski, Daniel Berliner, and Alex Ingrams.
Description: Cambridge, Massachusetts : The MIT Press, [2022] | Series: Information Policy Series / edited by Sandra Braman | Includes bibliographical references and index.
Identifiers: LCCN 2022007845 (print) | LCCN 2022007846 (ebook) | ISBN 9780262544597 (Paperback) | ISBN 9780262372084 (ePub) | ISBN 9780262372091 (PDF)
Subjects: LCSH: Transparency in government. | Administrative agencies—Mexico—Management—Case studies. | Organizational change. | Organizational effectiveness.
Classification: LCC JC598 .P56 2022 (print) | LCC JC598 (ebook) | DDC 352.8/8—dc23/eng/20220630
LC record available at https://lccn.loc.gov/2022007845
LC ebook record available at https://lccn.loc.gov/2022007846

10 9 8 7 6 5 4 3 2 1

To our families

Contents

List of Illustrations *ix*
List of Tables *xi*
Series Editor's Introduction *xiii*
Acknowledgments *xvii*

1 INTRODUCTION *1*
  The Question of Impact *5*
  Our Argument: Two Pathways to Impact *17*
  Contributions *30*
  Plan of the Book *32*

2 PUBLIC MANAGEMENT REFORM IN A GLOBAL PERSPECTIVE *35*
  The Roots of the Open Government Movement *36*
  Open Government Reforms in Practice *41*
  Competing Visions of Public Management Reform *51*
  The Fate of Public Sector Reform *58*
  Conclusions *67*

3 THE OPEN GOVERNMENT PARTNERSHIP AS AN INTERNATIONAL INSTITUTION *69*
  Multistakeholder Initiatives and International Institutions *70*
  The Origin Story *77*
  Overview of the Open Government Partnership *100*

4 PATHWAYS OF CHANGE *119*
  Evidence of the Direct Pathway of Change *120*
  Evidence of the Indirect Pathway of Change *148*
  Conclusion *173*

5 A CASE STUDY: DIRECT AND INDIRECT PATHWAYS OF CHANGE IN MEXICO   *177*
Methodology and Case Selection   *179*
Background and Context   *181*
Mexico's Open Government Partnership Membership: Initial Phases   *183*
Government Surveillance and Civil Society Withdrawal   *200*
Subnational and Legislative Developments   *206*
Summary and Evaluation of the Direct and Indirect Pathways of Change   *213*
Conclusion   *219*

6 EPILOGUE: LOOKING FORWARD   *221*
The Future of Open Government   *222*
Building on Prior Work   *227*
Wrapping Up   *233*

Notes   *235*
References   *239*
Index   *271*

List of Illustrations

Figure 1.1 Impact pathways for international institutions *17*
Figure 2.1 Public management reform and associated risks *58*
Figure 4.1 Direct pathway of change *122*
Figure 4.2 Performance of commitments over time *128*
Figure 4.3 Matrix of four types of commitment *130*
Figure 4.4 The indirect pathway of change *151*

List of Tables

Table 1.1 Open Government Partnership member countries as of January 2019   *15*

Table 1.2 Relationships between institutional design features and prevalent causal mechanisms potentially associated with the impact of membership   *19*

Table 1.3 Summary of direct and indirect pathways of impact of institutional organizations   *28*

Table 2.1 Examples of open government initiatives   *43*

Table 3.1 Open Government Partnership total funding from private foundations and bilateral aid agencies, 2013–2021   *101*

Table 4.1 Predicted effect of country processes on commitment success   *125*

Table 4.2 Open Government Partnership commitment statistics (2011–2019)   *127*

Table 4.3 The Global Open Data Index top 20 countries (2013–2016)   *154*

Table 5.1 Summary of Mexico's National Action Plan commitments   *214*

Table 5.2 Summary of evidence from Mexican case for process-driven mechanisms   *217*

Series Editor's Introduction
Sandra Braman

It is easy, these days, to be discouraged about political matters. Agreements—say, on climate change—are signed, but goals are not achieved. Ambitions are committed to publicly—say, on improving protections for human rights—but fully effective means of ensuring such protections have not yet been found. When it comes to openness in government, the international Open Government Partnership (OGP) has been criticized for failing, so far, to achieve all that it set out to do. In *The Power of Partnership in Open Government*, though, authors Suzanne J. Piotrowski, Daniel Berliner, and Alex Ingrams offer an alternative, more optimistic view via their original theoretical lens on indirect pathways of change rather than the direct pathways that have long been the standard approach of policy analysts.

The Open Government Partnership, launched alongside the United Nations General Assembly in 2011, is an effort to move those governments that commit toward further openness, what the authors note President Obama referred to as "the essence of democracy" in the launch speech. Rather than going the formal route of a treaty with its attendant obligations, the OGP seeks to embody "lean dynamism" in an effort to maximize flexibility and local tailoring in a multistakeholder manner that includes civil society organizations with full parity of representation and innovative models of cocreation between governments and their citizens. The terminology is not used, but this can be understood as a form of adaptive policymaking, with two-year cycles of iterative decision making to reset commitments and the processes that will be undertaken to achieve them in response to developments that had taken place up to that point. Rather than enforcement mechanisms, there are evaluative tools. The bargain, as the authors put it, is exchanging flexibility and weak enforcement for participation and iteration. Eight governments were committed at the launch moment, with leadership shared by the United States and Brazil. By 2019, seventy-seven countries were actively participating, as were several subnational governments, although some countries withdrew from their commitments along the way.

Direct pathways to policy impact are familiar. They focus on commitments made—the authors introduce the delicious concept of a formal policy as a "commitment machine"—and assume that the only thing that matters is the fulfillment of commitment goals as achieved through formal administrative processes. The direct causal chain in the case of the Open Government Partnership included joining the partnership, making commitments, implementing commitments, evaluating direct successes and failures, and repeating the steps. The Open Government Partnership commitments themselves are discrete reform projects that vary enormously in kind, from digitizing public service delivery to using mobile technology devices in schools and on. Critiques of Open Government Partnership direct pathways to change include failures to achieve goals, the assertion of trivial or already-accomplished commitments, and reliance on ambiguous claims that cannot be evaluated.

Indirect pathways involve not the things of commitments but the processes through which commitments are made and acted upon. The policy impact of indirect causal chains includes building new networks and coalitions, contributing to normative changes, and creating new opportunities and power resources for reformers both inside and outside of government. It is the argument of *The Power of Partnership in Open Government* that it is the indirect pathways that have the greatest potential for impact on public sector reform—even if it is much more difficult to evaluate such effects. Successes of the Open Government Partnership indirect pathways to change include clarifying, legitimizing, and globalizing new ways of achieving public sector reform and the mainstreaming of open government as a major theme for other institutions. Civil society actors have been empowered in new ways.

There has been standard-setting for how governments treat data and transparency in government procurement practices. New principles have been introduced, such as beneficial ownership transparency to prevent the use of shell corporations for money laundering, tax avoidance, and corruption. Numerous linkages have been built with other international organizations and initiatives, with policy networks crossing not only the public and private sectors but also issue area boundaries.

This book uses the Open Government Partnership as its case, but the analytical approach presented is valuable for those working with any type of policy issue. A number of concepts used in discussion of the Open Government Partnership have been around for a while, such as multistakeholderism, policy networks, and legal globalization (harmonization of laws and regulations across national boundaries irrespective of differences in political and/or legal systems). Here, they usefully coalesce within the more comprehensive theoretical framework the authors offer. In an interesting way, the authors reverse the causal directions embedded in international regime theory. In the influential formulation by Stephen Krasner, policy regimes arise out of agreements—whether formal or informal, explicit or implicit—on underlying principles, norms, rules, and decision-making procedures for policymaking in a specific issue area that develop before formal law is put into place. In the case of the Open Government Partnership, according to these authors, there are commitments to formal laws and explicit government practices that came first but have had their most valuable contributions in the building of a global open government regime, a reversal of the causal flows of international regime theory. There is also a surprising resonance, although at quite another level of analysis, with Gilbert Simondon's theoretical work on how influence flows interpersonally in ways quite other than those visible in the networked relationships that currently receive so much attention. And the authors recognize that the real world intervenes, with deep appreciation for the contingencies that create policy windows in which successes are achieved as a result of a particular confluence of factors that could not have been controlled deliberately but can be taken advantage of when they occur together. The detailed analysis of the origin story is fascinating—would that we had the same for the Internet Governance Forum.

Much to their credit, the authors take on the challenge of thinking through what may happen to the successes of the indirect pathways given the rise of tyrannical populism in four of the eight original signee governments and given the pervasive consequences of the COVID-19 pandemic. On the populism point, the authors suggest that there has as yet been no pushback on Open Government Partnership–related initiatives by such rulers because the diffusion of norms via indirect pathways has been so successful. An alternative reading might be that they haven't bothered because there has been so little success via direct pathways that it hasn't been considered worth their trouble to intervene. Open Government Partnership–related initiatives have looked at informational matters related to the pandemic, but it is argued here that it is too soon to tell what the long-term impact on openness commitments of this health crisis may be.

With its seminal insights, this book is rich for those who already have scholarly or policymaking depth in the areas of policy reform and international policymaking and should, from this point on, be considered foundational. At the same time, it is so thorough and clearly written and does such a good job of introducing major strands in the diverse literatures brought together in this interdisciplinary work that it is also a primer for those new to open government and to public reform. The authors offer large intellectual moves that we have needed as we struggle to understand how to most usefully analyze and make policy in what continue to be turbulent times.

Acknowledgments

This book could not have been written without guidance, inspiration, and sound advice from many people in the authors' academic communities, researchers and policy professionals in the field of open government, the MIT Press, and family and friends.

The generous and continuing financial support of the Lois and Samuel Pratt Program for Freedom of Information at the Rutgers Law School made this project possible. This funding enabled all aspects of the project, including research assistance, travel, writing workshops, copy editing, and support for open-access publishing.

The research assistance we received from numerous outstanding students associated with the Transparency and Governance Center at Rutgers University was invaluable. Our thanks go to Fangda Ding, Rebecca Porter, Gabrielle Rossi, Kayla Schwoerer, and Claire Newsome for all their help. Jonathan Wexler served as an able, and at times entertaining, copy editor and reader on various chapters and the book proposal.

The Global Conference for Transparency Research is an energetic and stimulating venue for discussion about the most pressing topics in transparency research around the world. The idea for this book emerged from conversations among the authors at this conference and was informed by the rich environment of enquiry and debate at subsequent ones.

The authors' own academic institutions supported us throughout the research and publication process—the School of Public Affairs and Administration, Rutgers University Newark; the Department of Government,

London School of Economics; the School of Politics and Global Studies, Arizona State University; the Institute of Governance, Tilburg University; and the Institute of Public Administration, Leiden University.

We appreciate our colleagues who provided feedback on the original idea for the work, commented on individual chapters, or offered various types of support along the way, including Sandra Coliver, Alice Evans, Joseph Foti, Stephan Grimmelikhuijsen, Frank Hendriks, Mathias Koenig-Archibugi, Milli Lake, Ranjit Lall, Charles Menifield, Abraham Newman, Tom Pegram, Greg Porumbescu, Alasdair Roberts, David Rosenbloom, Gregg Van Ryzin, and Stavros Zouridis.

We had many vital and fascinating discussions with the individuals we interviewed for the research and who made it possible for us to uncover our insights about the direct and indirect pathways of public sector reform and to make connections between ideas and processes taking shape among different sectors of society and among different countries and transnational stakeholders. We appreciate them taking the time to speak with us and sharing their insights.

This book is dedicated to our families. Suzanne is especially grateful for Richard, Douglas, and Simon Heap's patience and unwavering support while this book was being written.

Finally, we would like to thank all of those individuals associated with MIT Press who helped usher this project along. The anonymous reviewers were exceedingly thorough and constructive with their critiques. The final product is undoubtedly better because of their thoughtful feedback. Texas A&M University's Prof. Sandra Braman serves as the Information Policy Series editor. This project would not be the one it is today without her high level of professionalism, insightful assessments, and always helpful guidance—and we thank her for it.

1 INTRODUCTION

On September 20, 2011, at the UN General Assembly meeting in New York City, eight founding governments launched the Open Government Partnership. Representatives from Brazil, Indonesia, Mexico, Norway, the Philippines, South Africa, the United Kingdom, and the United States each endorsed a declaration of shared principles and presented action plans containing their governments' specific commitments. The new multilateral initiative aimed to harness the recent wave of attention and energy surrounding open government to "secure concrete commitments from governments to promote transparency, empower citizens, fight corruption, and harness new technologies to strengthen governance" (Open Government Partnership, n.d.).

The Open Government Partnership boasted several unique elements for an international institution. Although initiated largely by joint efforts between the United States and a collaboration of foundations and aid agencies, more than half of the founding governments were in the Global South. Brazil served alongside the United States, both as inaugural cochairs. The Open Government Partnership embraced multistakeholder participation, giving civil society organizations full parity of representation on its Steering Committee and promoting innovative models of cocreation between governments and their citizens. The partnership eschewed one-size-fits-all standards, instead encouraging governments to make flexible, voluntary commitments that fit local context and could generate a "race to the top" (Weinstein, 2013). The Open Government Partnership also sought to avoid the lumbering bureaucracy of many traditional international institutions, aiming instead for a lean dynamism often explicitly compared with a start-up company. The combination of these features was appealing: As of the official launch, thirty-eight new governments had announced intentions to join, committing to develop their own action plans.

And so, with great fanfare and a speech from US president Barack Obama calling open government "the essence of democracy" (White House, 2011), the Open Government Partnership was officially launched.

But the new movement was not welcomed by everyone. Despite having an original approach and influential leaders to ring in its arrival, from the start, there were many eyebrows raised by the prospect of such a lightweight outfit being able to live up to the hype. The *Economist* (2011a) described the initiative as "really nothing new or major" and said "its launch seemed rushed" (2011b). Transparency experts said that the move smacked of "cyber-optimism" (Rooney, 2013) and asked: "Can we expect the OGP to be anything more than feel-good window-dressing?" (Michener, 2011b).

Indeed, several years later, this prognosis appeared to have been borne out. One could easily think that the Open Government Partnership was a failure—particularly in the founding countries. It appeared that in many of the founding countries, the reform movements for transparency and accountability had begun to lose their way, with other forces in government and society having more powerful, opposing effects on governance. Examples of founding countries behaving cynically in contradiction to the principles of openness seemed to abound. Indeed, many of the open government policies billed as new or inventive were just the continuation of traditional transparency programs (Piotrowski, 2017).

Of the Partnership's eight founding member countries, six would see major democratic disruptions over the next several years. These included the election of populist leaders in the Philippines, the United States, Brazil, and Mexico; national-scale corruption scandals in Brazil, Mexico, and South Africa; and episodes of governance dysfunction like the handling of Brexit in the United Kingdom. Only Indonesia and Norway generally seemed immune from these trends.

Reasons for skepticism could also be found in the initiative's structure and goals. Member countries commit to no set standard of action; instead, they design their own National Action Plans composed of individual commitments whose number, scope, focus, and design are up to individual governments. Many governments made commitments that were minor, vague, irrelevant, or concerned policies already underway. Further, as long as countries adhered to the formal procedural guidelines, there was no express requirement that the commitments be implemented. Even the goals of open government itself were criticized for their ambiguity, with Yu and Robinson (2012) arguing that "the term 'open government' has become too vague to be a useful label," creating risks that "governments may be able to take credit for increased public accountability simply by delivering open data technology" (182). Many individuals involved with the Open Government Partnership raised concerns over the prevalence of commitments that seemed to value flashy technology over real progress toward accountability. Other analysts criticized the open government movement for its apparent neoliberal tilt (Bates, 2014; Pozen, 2018) or as a "back-door strategy for democracy-promotion and opening markets" (Michener & Bersch, 2013, 240). Meanwhile, disagreements over the relative merits of reforms based on open data or freedom of information (Noveck, 2017) threatened to open rifts in the open government advocacy community.

The inclusion of civil society organizations in the Open Government Partnership's governance structure led to growing tensions between them and governments both globally and in specific countries, especially around issues of freedom of association and other human rights. The membership of certain countries became controversial, and after civil society groups successfully demanded more stringent membership rules and sanctions, several governments announced their withdrawal—including Tanzania, formerly a Steering Committee member. Tensions erupted within countries as well, with civil society coalitions in both Mexico and Guatemala announcing their refusal to continue cooperation with their governments in the cocreation process. According to Civicus (2016), the participation environment for civil society organizations was seriously undermined in nearly a third of all Open Government Partnership members in 2016.

Surveying this landscape in the late 2010s, one might see the Open Government Partnership, and the open government movement overall, as a failure, rife with internal conflicts and overwhelmed by a world turning toward illiberalism, populism, unrepentant corruption, and hypocrisy around transparency. One might see the Open Government Partnership as another traveler on the well-worn path of so many international initiatives toward empty rhetoric, window-dressing action, and ultimate irrelevance.

However, this is not a book about the failure of the Open Government Partnership. Instead, this is a book about the often-overlooked ways that voluntary, flexible, participatory, and iterative international initiatives *can* shape domestic public sector reform. Looking beyond the headlines and beneath the surface, we argue that existing approaches neglect the full breadth of mechanisms through which an institution like the Open Government Partnership can have meaningful impacts.

Should the partnership be understood as a commitment machine, impactful only to the extent that it induces member governments to commit to meaningful reforms and actually follow through on them? This commit-and-comply focus is the standard approach in most research on international institutions and, indeed, in how many stakeholders have sought to assess the Open Government Partnership. We call this the direct pathway to impact.

But we argue that this approach is too narrow and that instead, we must understand the Open Government Partnership as involving participants in a *process* that both evolves over time and has its own causal effects, even independent of commitments themselves. This indirect pathway to change is composed of process-driven mechanisms and is distinct from the direct pathway of change that comprises more traditional compliance mechanisms.

In this book, we show that while the direct pathway of change has received the most attention, its mechanisms have been frequently stymied or have yielded disappointing results. Yet we argue that the indirect pathway instead highlights the most promising potential to drive reform and is, in many ways, the most instructional for understanding new processes by which international actors influence the ideas and practices used in the quest to transform government.

Our book is motivated by the question of how international initiatives can and do shape domestic public sector reform. We study this question in the contexts of a specific initiative—the Open Government Partnership—and a particular arena of governance—the cluster of transparency, accountability, participation, and technology-based reforms known collectively as open government. In the remainder of this chapter, we introduce the reader to these specific contexts and then review the relevant pieces of literature, crossing usual disciplinary boundaries between international relations and public administration. Finally, we present our argument, emphasizing the importance of the indirect pathway of impact, and discuss the types of evidence we draw on in this book to demonstrate.

THE QUESTION OF IMPACT

Can a voluntary international initiative have a meaningful impact on public sector reform? We seek to answer this question in the case of the Open Government Partnership, given its novel institutional design features, rapid growth in membership, and clear centrality to a new reform movement focusing on open government. Indeed, this is a daunting question in light of the design of the Open Government Partnership and the existing literature on both international institutions and public sector reforms.

The Open Government Partnership is an unusual international initiative, combining a largely voluntary, flexible, and nonbinding soft institutional design (Abbott & Snidal, 2000) with an unprecedented level of civil society participation within the organization and an iterative process that repeats every two years. There are several characteristics that make the partnership stand out as a novelty in the world of international institutions.

First, the Open Government Partnership sets no binding standard to which members must adhere; rather, it encourages flexible commitments driven by local needs and interests. The range of commitments across issue areas and policy types is enormous, including new legislation, open data portals, new venues for participatory policymaking, and sectoral transparency efforts across domains, including budgets, natural resources, foreign aid, and public service delivery. At best, this flexibility encourages innovation and alignment with local priorities. At worst, it allows countries to opportunistically make commitments that are narrow, superficial, or irrelevant to the goals of open government.

Second, the Open Government Partnership also sets a relatively low bar for membership. Although it always had eligibility criteria, these have allowed many nondemocratic countries to join the partnership, such as Azerbaijan and Jordan.

Third, the Open Government Partnership features only limited enforcement mechanisms. For the first several years, sanctions (such as being rendered inactive) could only be imposed for failing to adhere to the formal National Action Plan process and not for any broader features of open government or democratic rights in member countries. Furthermore, for the first several years, there was no penalty for governments failing to implement any of their commitments as long as National Action Plans were on time and met formal criteria for civil society collaboration.

Finally, the Open Government Partnership was initially launched as a lean, start-up model of global initiative that aimed to avoid what its founders saw as the slow, inefficient bureaucracies of traditional international institutions. Yet this model faced difficulty managing the Partnership's complex activities and diverse stakeholders.

However, the Open Government Partnership also featured an unprecedented level of formal inclusion of civil society organizations in its governance structure. Its Steering Committee features full parity between government and civil society representatives, with one cochair from each. The partnership also encourages deep civil society participation at the domestic level through consultation and cocreation in the National Action Plan design and implementation processes. Not only are civil society organizations encouraged to formally participate within the organization and throughout the action plan development process, but the Open Government Partnership also encourages domestic reforms focusing on public participation broadly defined to include not only civil society but other actors, like companies, citizens, associations, and so on. However, while these two types of participation are closely related, in the context of this book, when we mention "civil society participation," our intended emphasis is on the governance structures that emphasize partnership with civil society organizations. In chapter 3, we also describe many examples of public participation initiatives that member countries undertake as part of their broader open government reform efforts.

Finally, the Open Government Partnership also features an iterative process similar to—and, in fact, predating—the pledge-and-review model of the Paris Climate Agreement. Governments make new National Action Plans on a two-year cycle, informed (at least in principle) by experience and by the review and evaluation by the Independent Reporting Mechanism. This iterative process necessitates repeated interactions among stakeholders, continuous expectations of new commitments, and opportunities for learning and ratcheting up.

Importantly, these design features of the Open Government Partnership represent a bargain of sorts between naturally reticent governments and reformers in civil society groups, donors, and some government officials. This bargain consists of *flexibility* and *weak enforcement* in exchange for *participation* and *iteration*. For reticent government leaders and officials, the design of the Open Government Partnership is appealing on account of the flexible nature of commitments and the relatively narrow and nonbinding monitoring and sanctioning mechanisms. These same features have often been the target of critiques by reformers, especially among the more skeptical civil society actors.

In exchange for accepting these features, the Open Government Partnership was able to include the innovative design features of participation and iteration, which reformers and open government advocates hoped would be worthwhile. Yet both of these innovative features had little in the way of track records, and it remained to be seen if they might serve to counteract the possibilities for opportunism and window-dressing created by the Open Government Partnership's flexibility and weak enforcement provisions.

How would this institutional design bargain play out in practice? Can an initiative like the Open Government Partnership serve as an effective driver of meaningful reform?

Insights from existing literature on both international institutions—our independent variable—and public sector reform—our dependent variable—would suggest skepticism toward the potential for the partnership to lead to meaningful reform. We review these here.

Insights from the International Institutions Literature

Research on international institutions is often concerned with why states do (or do not) participate in international institutions and initiatives and why they comply (or not) with their commitments to them. Considering the Open Government Partnership's unusual institutional design in the context of this literature, one would have many reasons to be dubious. Indeed, skepticism runs deep in the field of international relations. Many critiques expect international institutions to accomplish nothing that would not have happened otherwise, or that does not serve the interests of powerful states (Mearsheimer, 1994). Others understand governments' participation in international institutions as driven purely by a logic of self-interest, sometimes cooperating when long-term benefits predominate but more often behaving opportunistically except where limited by hard mechanisms of monitoring and credible enforcement (Keohane & Martin, 1995; Simmons, 2010).

Even more optimistic theoretical approaches still see states' willingness to accept international rules as limited by sovereignty costs—the "loss of authority over decision making in an issue-area" (Abbott & Snidal, 2000, 436). In particular, states tend to resist agreements marked by greater hard law characteristics: obligation, precision, and delegation (Abbott & Snidal, 2000). Many scholars see a tradeoff in the design of international initiatives between stringency and membership (Bernauer et al., 2013; Prakash & Potoski, 2007)—as they incorporate more hard law characteristics or stronger monitoring and enforcement provisions, fewer states will be willing to join. But, simultaneously, a less stringent and easier membership threshold may come with negative consequences, such as slower decision making and less credibility.

Although the original design of the Open Government Partnership sought to escape some of these traditional tradeoffs, they nonetheless emerged as subjects of contention and as limits on some actors' willingness to join. For example, although India was initially one of the founding participants in the discussions that produced the Open Government Partnership, it withdrew several months before the official launch, citing sovereignty concerns and qualms over external monitoring (Bhaumik, 2011; Dey & Roy, 2013; McIntosh, 2011).

Studies of state compliance with international institutions often conclude that membership has no true impact, given processes of self-selection and screening (Downs, Rocke & Barsoom 1996; von Stein, 2005). Studies of the impact of international institutions on measurable outcomes across economic, environmental, and human rights issues often conclude that the impact of membership is zero or even negative, as states instrumentally take advantage of "window-dressing" institutions (Hafner-Burton & Tsutsui, 2005).

These perspectives would lead most observers to have decidedly low expectations of an initiative like the Open Government Partnership, given the myriad of opportunities created by its institutional design for member governments to take only window-dressing actions while nonetheless burnishing their reputations on the world stage.

Other theoretical perspectives, however, see the potential for soft institutions, particularly in conjunction with processes of learning, normative change, or mobilization of nongovernmental actors (Abbott & Snidal 2000; Newman & Posner, 2016; Ruggie, 2007). Constructivist approaches focus on normative changes (e.g., Finnemore & Sikkink, 1998) and the potential for both interactions and institutions to change stated preferences (Bearce & Bondanella, 2007) or activate learning networks (Ruggie, 2002). Liberal approaches focus on pressure from below by civil society (Simmons, 2009) and domestic constituencies (Dai, 2005) as well as transgovernmental interactions among bureaucrats themselves (Bach & Newman, 2010; Slaughter, 2009). Managerial approaches (Chayes & Chayes, 1993) suggest that most countries follow most of the rules most of the time and view problems as arising from lack of capacity or knowledge and difficulty of implementation or coordination.

Much research has been devoted to understanding whether such mechanisms can operate and under what circumstances. We build on these past efforts while also offering focused new evidence and extending past arguments to this new type of international institution and to processes that are *outside* direct compliance pathways.

Insights from the Public Sector Reform Literature

Our expectations for what successes the Open Government Partnership could achieve are also informed by research on the impacts of earlier management reforms and how they attempted to change the way the public sector functions. How successfully a transnational initiative achieves its goal of reforming the public sector depends, to a large degree, on how well the initiative can use novel ways to address public sector obstacles that prior reforms have tried to grapple with.

Scholars have studied public sector change for hundreds of years and observed a virtually continuous procession of new reform visions and fashions (Light, 1998). New ideas of reform can be distinguished by differences in the means, leadership models, and ultimate values (e.g., efficiency, equality, economic growth, democracy, etc.) of the reformers (Osborne, 2010a). For example, perhaps the most influential reform idea of the twentieth century was New Public Management, which emerged in the 1980s and drove a public sector reform process of privatization, decentralization, and citizen choice designed to deliver more efficiency and effectiveness in the public sector. These policies have been shown to directly impact the implementation of transparency related public sector programs (Piotrowski, 2007).

Although New Public Management lost its preeminent status as a global public sector reform movement in the early 2000s (Pollitt & Bouckaert, 2011), it continues to stand as a vital reference point for reformers because of its global reach and its powerful impact on many subsequent public sector reforms (Greve, 2015). Today, New Public Management's impact is under scrutiny. Its rise was characterized by hopes for improvements to government efficiency and effectiveness that have not turned out as intended (Hood & Peters, 2004; Osborne, 2010a). The experience of New Public Management has been borne out repeatedly in subsequent reforms: It constantly fell short of its goals because it was treated as a panacea for an impossible range of different bureaucratic problems (Hood, 1991).

The Open Government Partnership vision of reform would seem to fit this mold of over-optimism. Compared to New Public Management, the partnership aims for a different set of reform values, such as transparency, accountability, and participation, but there is a similar tone of optimism in open-government promulgations such as Obama's Open Government Directive (Coglianese, 2009).

It may be too early to say if the kinds of public sector reforms advanced by the Open Government Partnership will suffer the same fate of New Public Management—rising rapidly before going into decline. Some scholars would place open government alongside a raft of post–New Public Management reforms that try to correct the failures of that model (e.g., Dunleavy et al., 2006), while others would identify open government reform with the same streak of privatization and limited government (e.g., Catlaw & Sandberg, 2014). The reality that policymakers face is that there are many competing visions of public sector reform currently jockeying for position, and none has provided policymakers with a model of management reform that can fill the space left by New Public Management (Lodge & Gill, 2011). The Open Government Partnership faces a tough reform environment in a mix of competing reform visions offering answers to the problems of New Public Management.

We will explore whether the Open Government Partnership's process approach offers a plausible new way forward. Looking back on public sector reform history as well as considering some of the inherent characteristics of the open government idea, there are good reasons to be pessimistic.

Public sector reform literature suggests that reforms face an often-impossible task of reconciling the demands of different interest groups and their competing visions of what should be prioritized. Hood (1991), one of the leading scholars of New Public Management reforms, argues that public sector reforms contain a panoply of mutually inconsistent ideas and conflicting values that are difficult to accomplish simultaneously. Open government reform is itself a marriage of categories of public sector values that clash in problematic ways.

The first episode in the modern chapter of open government started with the freedom of information movement. Today, the kind of public sector reform championed by digital government reformers such as Beth Noveck (2009) seeks to make public agencies not just transparent but also open in the sense of agencies interacting dynamically in the internal and external exchange of information. The unification of these transparency and participation visions that Meijer, Curtin, and Hillebrandt (2012) called vision and voice are indeed powerful in theory, especially when combined with the communication and interactive platforms of Web 2.0 technologies. But they would seem to multiply problems of clashing values and supporters, too—perhaps in even more unpredictable ways than other reform movements (Berliner, Ingrams, & Piotrowski, 2018).

Though the existing literature on international institutions and public sector reform all cast doubt on the Open Government Partnership's potential for impact, the literature also highlights the Partnership's importance as a case to investigate in-depth, and there is a shortage of available literature on how transnational multistakeholderism influences the fortunes of national government reform efforts. Given the high-profile failures of open government around the world, what impacts should we expect from the Open Government Partnership?

What is open government?

The bundle of reforms pushed by the partnership is referred to as open government. Open government is often used interchangeably with *transparency*, but open government is more than transparency. The term *open government* gained currency in the 1950s in the lead-up to a global wave of legislation regarding access to information (Ingrams, 2018). Philosophically, freedom of information acts also connected such procedures to the principles of free speech and public deliberation necessary to inform and educate the public in the exercise of their democratic rights (Curtin & Meijer, 1995). These legal reforms in transparency and public deliberation spread through democratic countries over the next several decades. These reforms were, and still are, very popular but do have clear tensions at times with other public sector values such as privacy, secrecy, and efficiency (Piotrowski, 2010).

In fact, while not called *open government*, public laws passed earlier in history were harbingers of open government ideas. The first freedom of information act was passed in 1766 by Sweden, where it was called the Press Act. The Swedish case was an outlier in the history of freedom of information acts. However, the Press Act suggests that, despite the wave of freedom of information act reforms in the mid-twentieth century, open government ideas have a much older history (Banisar, 2006). The philosophy of information access, public accountability, and public deliberation is evident in the work of nineteenth-century scholars such as John Stuart Mill and Jeremy Bentham, particularly in Bentham's concept of publicity (Birkinshaw, 1997). There was another fundamental shift in our understanding of open government at the start of the twenty-first century, as open government advocates started to dedicate more attention to public participation in addition to transparency. Sharing information with the public was one thing, but the ability for the public to use the information to talk back to government is conceptually so wrapped up with the idea and purpose of public information that information access and public participation are essentially two sides of the same coin. Meijer, Curtin, and Hillebrandt (2012) called these two dimensions *vision* and *voice*, respectively.

The added element of public participation marked a radical change in the idea of open government. The interactive perspective of Web 2.0 and the idea of government as a platform, where the power of the crowd—interested citizens contributing ideas, expertise, or suggestions—could be used to make better policy decisions (e.g., Lathrop & Ruma, 2010), gained momentum. This interactive aspect of open government emphasizes public participation and collaboration. Like the information access and transparency dimensions of open government, specific laws could enshrine principles of public participation—for example, in e-government laws requiring public consultation with stakeholders (McDermott, 2010). Public participation in open government also resurrected traditional public participation methods that have been around for centuries by giving them new channels, including the use of online tools such as e-petitions where citizens put forward policy proposals that gather signatories (Lindner & Riehm, 2011); hackathons, where citizens win prizes for creating novel public service solutions with digital technology (Michener & Ritter, 2017); and technology-based tools for localized reporting of public service problems (Mergel & Desouza, 2013).

Popular interest in open government is rising, often closely linked with the rise of open data (Ubaldi, 2013) and freedom of information legislation. And yet, the term itself is often not specifically defined. We define *open government* as a public sector management reform movement focusing on three primary values: transparency, accountability, and participation. In many individual reform initiatives, technology plays a prominent role in the advancement of these values but is not a requirement. Open government policies can incorporate any one of the values or any combination. Technology is a driving tool in open government policies, but new technologies are not a necessary component of open government policies. For example, an open government policy can include the value of participation without new technologies (e.g., the public comment section of a traditional open public meeting). Alternatively, it can consist of the value of participation coupled with new technologies (e.g., an online government petition website), or it can include multiple values, such as participation and transparency, coupled with new technologies (e.g., a website that posts proposed regulations and allows the public to comment).

The Open Government Partnership

The Open Government Partnership is a transnational multistakeholder initiative founded in 2011 by eight governments: Brazil, Indonesia, Mexico, Norway, the Philippines, South Africa, the United Kingdom, and the United States. As of January 2019, seventy-seven active countries were participating in the partnership, as well as several subnational governments involved through a pilot program. Table 1.1 shows a list of which countries are members, when they joined, and their status in the partnership. For countries to become members of the Open Government Partnership, they must meet four eligibility criteria (requiring minimum levels of civic engagement, access to information legislation, fiscal transparency, and public asset disclosure), pass an Open Government Partnership values check assessment, endorse a declaration of open government, and commit to delivering action plans cocreated with civil society and to being assessed on their progress. As noted in the table, some countries joined as members but later decided to withdraw, while others have been made inactive either for civic space violations or for repeated failure to even produce a National Action Plan. Since 2015 (von Bertele, 2015), the Open Government Partnership has also included subnational members through its Open Government Partnership Local initiative—including Scotland, provinces like Jalisco in Mexico, and cities like Seoul in South Korea.

The action plans that governments produce center on a list of commitments that, if designed well, focus on improving transparency, accountability, participation, and innovative use of technology. Yet these commitments vary in their scope, ambition, and focus, potentially covering a wide range of issue areas related (and sometimes not) to open government. Concerns about these commitments have sometimes led to criticisms of "openwashing" (e.g., Alonso, 2011).

Table 1.1
Open Government Partnership member countries as of January 2019
Founding members:
Brazil, Indonesia, Mexico, Norway, Philippines, South Africa, United Kingdom, United States
Later in 2011:
Albania, Armenia, Azerbaijan,* Bulgaria, Canada, Chile, Colombia, Croatia, Czech Republic, Denmark, Dominican Republic, El Salvador, Estonia, Georgia, Greece, Guatemala, Honduras, Israel, Italy, Jordan, Kenya, Latvia, Lithuania, Malta, Moldova, Montenegro, North Macedonia, Paraguay, Peru, Romania, Slovak Republic, South Korea, Spain, Sweden, Tanzania,† Turkey,* Ukraine, Uruguay
2012:
Argentina, Costa Rica, Finland, Ghana, Hungary,† Liberia, Netherlands, Panama
2013:
Australia, Ireland, Malawi, Mongolia, New Zealand, Serbia, Sierra Leone, Trinidad and Tobago
2014:
Bosnia and Herzegovina, France, Tunisia
2015:
Cape Verde, Cote d'Ivoire, Papua New Guinea, Sri Lanka
2016:
Burkina Faso, Germany, Jamaica, Luxembourg, Nigeria, Pakistan
2017:
Afghanistan, Kyrgyzstan, Portugal
2018:
Ecuador, Morocco, Senegal, Seychelles
*: Inactive (Azerbaijan, Turkey) †: Withdrawn (Hungary, Tanzania)

However, the Open Government Partnership Articles of Governance also place expectations on governments that serve to guide the action plan development process. Thus, governments must develop their action plans in consultation with civil society, must be ambitious and go beyond their current practices, and their commitments must be relevant to one of four principles (transparency, accountability, public participation, and technology and innovation). The Articles convey that the civil society consultation process should be timely, transparent, and serious about dialogue and should take the form of a forum enabling "regular multi-stakeholder consultation on OGP implementation" (Open Government Partnership, 2015b, 19).

In theory (while not always practiced), each member produces a new action plan every two years, leading to a cycle of policy commitments and, in some cases, policy fulfillment that pushes the open government agenda forward. Local country researchers, overseen by the Independent Reporting Mechanism, assess progress made on the commitments in the plans. The Independent Reporting Mechanism, a component of the Open Government Partnership, selects a local country researcher based on their research expertise and gives the researcher special training on how to carry out the review of their country's action plan. The review is typically wide ranging and draws on broad consultation with governmental and civil society actors who are involved in implementing or monitoring the action plan. At the end of this process, the researcher produces a country progress report, ostensibly enabling learning, benchmarking, and accountability both within countries and globally.

At the global level, the Partnership's leadership rotates, with both a country chair from government and a civil society chair, normally not from the same country, leading the Steering Committee at any one time. The Steering Committee is made up of an equal number of government and civil society members. The Open Government Partnership Support Unit is staffed with a permanent secretariat that works with the Steering Committee. The Support Unit's goals are to "maintain institutional memory, manage Open Government Partnership's external communications, ensure the continuity of organizational relationships with Open Government Partnership's partners, and support the broader membership" (OGP Support Unit, n.d.). In 2017, the Open Government Partnership's budget was over $9.5 million. Funding for the partnership comes from private foundations, bilateral agencies, and some member governments (Open Government Partnership, ca. 2018). The Hewlett Foundation, Hivos, Omidyar Network, Ford Foundation, and Open Society Foundation are among the major nongovernmental funders, but member governments also donate modest amounts. A major forum for organizational planning and development is the annual (except for 2014 and 2017) global summit, usually hosted by the rotating country chair, where governmental representatives, academics, funders, civil society members, and advocacy organizations gather to address the Open Government Partnership's progress and future challenges. A further discussion of the mechanics of the Partnership is found in chapter 3.

OUR ARGUMENT: TWO PATHWAYS TO IMPACT

We argue that an assessment of the Open Government Partnership specifically and of the potential of international initiatives to shape domestic governance reform more broadly must distinguish between direct and indirect pathways of transnational impact on domestic governance reform. These pathways build on ideas that we earlier developed in Berliner, Ingrams, and Piotrowski (2021), with a more specific focus on compliance models and their alternatives. In this book, we have elaborated those ideas further and developed them to be more generally applicable. We summarize these in figure 1.1. A direct pathway follows a causal chain from eligibility and enforcement rules, to commitments to policy change, to compliance with commitments. For the Open Government Partnership, this comprises the

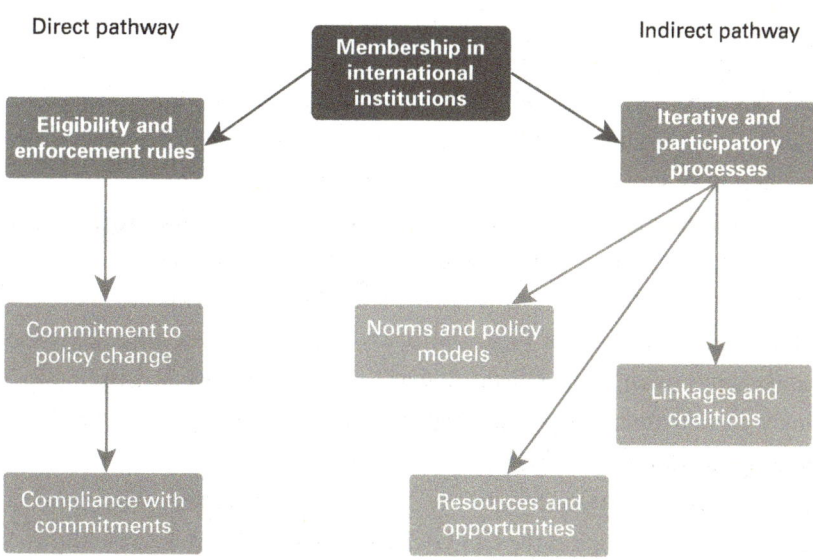

Figure 1.1
Impact pathways for international institutions.

actions of joining, making commitments, implementing those commitments, evaluating their direct successes and failures, and then iteratively repeating the process through subsequent rounds of National Action Plans.

An indirect pathway, however, focuses on broader mechanisms driven not by government commitments themselves but rather by the processes set in motion by membership. These include contributing to normative changes, building new networks and coalitions, and creating new opportunities and power resources for reformers inside and outside of government.

We argue that for voluntary and flexible initiatives like the Open Government Partnership, direct pathways of change will often be limited, context dependent, and superficial, especially in the short term. Yet the process-driven mechanisms of change of the indirect pathway have the potential for greater breadth and depth of impact on public sector reform, even if in ways that are often difficult to evaluate. Nonetheless, these broader mechanisms themselves crucially rely on participatory and iterative processes for impetus and sustainability—suggesting that these dynamics will be apparent to a greater extent in some initiatives than others.

The participation of nonstate actors opens new political opportunities and creates new sources of influence, particularly for civil society groups, and brings together actors within and across countries who have often not worked together previously. The formalized iteration of reform procedures also creates a repeated demand for new ideas and models, and opportunities for new norms and patterns of behavior to emerge over time.

This framework provides a useful conceptual tool for tracking the types of complex global innovation and diffusion processes that characterize modern public sector reforms. While we focus on these arguments in the context of the Open Government Partnership, we suggest that these arguments also generalize to other, similar institutional forms in which governments increasingly participate and that may become more common features of global reform agendas in the future.

For example, transnational multistakeholder initiatives (Raymond & DeNardis, 2015), such as the UN Global Compact and Extractive Industries Transparency Initiative, are more frequently participatory and iterative than more traditional organizations. There are also organizational parallels in the decentralized network developments that are shaping internet governance and the role of the state (Mueller, 2010; ten Oever, 2019). Yet we also see these procedural elements as variables, present to differing degrees across all institutions. Tallberg and colleagues (2013), for example, show wide variation and increases over time in the accessibility of international institutions to nongovernmental organizations. Recent work on global experimentalist governance (De Búrca, Keohane, & Sabel, 2014), the UN's Universal Periodic Review (Milewicz & Goodin, 2016), and the Paris Climate Agreement "pledge-and-review" system (Hale, 2016) also points toward the wider prevalence and increasing importance of iterative features.

In table 1.2, we summarize the broader relationships we hypothesize between institutional design features and the relevant causal mechanisms potentially linking membership with impacts on domestic governance. A focus on the direct pathway of change emphasizes variation in the horizontal dimension of this table and suggests that institutions with weak monitoring and enforcement provisions are unlikely to see compliance-driven mechanisms of impact at work. The indirect pathway of change, however, emphasizes the vertical dimension: For institutions with iterative and participatory design features, we expect to see process-driven mechanisms at work.

Our focus in this book is on the Open Government Partnership, which falls into the bottom-left quadrant, with relatively weak monitoring and enforcement provisions but unusually iterative and participatory processes. Past research, instead, has focused primarily on institutions in the top row, which are weak cases for process-driven mechanisms.

Table 1.2
Relationships between institutional design features and prevalent causal mechanisms potentially associated with the impact of membership

		Expectations of the direct pathway of change	
		Weak monitoring and enforcement	Strong monitoring and enforcement
Expectations of the indirect pathway of change	Low iteration and participation	No impact	Compliance-driven mechanisms
	High iteration and participation	Process-driven mechanisms	Both compliance- and process-driven mechanisms

Direct Pathway of Change

The direct pathway of change focuses on outcomes driven by the commitments governments make to international institutions either in joining or in their explicit action plans. For the Open Government Partnership, National Action Plans form the most important element of this and the most straightforward route for partnership membership to ostensibly lead to successful reform: Governments commit to meaningful reform efforts in their National Action Plans and subsequently carry them out, with resulting impacts on measurable outcomes. Yet each part of this pathway raises questions and has demonstrated severe limitations.

Most importantly, Open Government Partnership commitments are overwhelmingly discrete reform projects, such as the adoption of legislation, the creation of an online portal, the incorporation of citizen participation into a process, or a specific capacity-building effort (Piotrowski, 2017). The Independent Reporting Mechanism encourages specificity of commitments. Even at best, when commitments are both ambitious and fully implemented, they necessarily constitute only piecemeal fragments of a more holistic and long-term reform process (Fox, 2015; Michener, 2019). Consider, for example, an access to information law (in different contexts also referred to as a freedom of information law). Even if the legislation is designed according to international best practices and fully implemented and resourced in practice, it remains an open question how much impact this reform will have on outcomes such as good governance, corruption, and economic efficiency. Rather, such a law can potentially be an important piece of the puzzle of changing public sector institutions in concert with civil society, the media, reformers in government, independent accountability institutions, and an engaged public.

At worst, commitments may not be implemented at all or may be narrow, irrelevant, or mere window dressing intended to tick the boxes of the checklists of international and domestic stakeholders while accomplishing little of substance. According to the Open Government Partnership's record of commitments successfully implemented, 447 of 2,883 commitments made between 2011 and 2016 were fully completed, and a further 526 were at least substantially completed. This represents a fully or substantially completed proportion of only around one-third.

Of the commitments that do get completed, many involve applications of information technology in narrow ways, such as launching a government Twitter account, using mobile technology devices in schools, or digitizing public service delivery without any clear connection to transparency or public participation. In fact, the data show that "e-government" is the single most common theme of commitments. (As a point of reference, a few of the other themes are public participation, capacity-building, and records management.)

Many commitments that are implemented are not actually new initiatives but rather reflect governments taking credit for efforts that were already underway. While this rebranding of old work as new might have benefits, such as galvanizing the government's own efforts to complete projects, bringing greater public attention, or generating synergies with other commitments, it also may give the leaders of those governments unmerited credit.

Over time, the iterative process of the Independent Reporting Mechanism has yielded improvements in some areas. More recent National Action Plan rounds have yielded commitments that are more ambitious and more relevant than those in the Partnership's early years. This iterative process of action followed by evaluation, learning, and updating is an important strength of the Open Government Partnership's direct pathway of impact and resembles recent trends toward "problem-driven iterative adaptation" in development (Andrews, Pritchett, & Woolcock, 2013) and "experimentalist governance" in global policy (De Búrca, Keohane, & Sabel, 2014). It also bears many similarities to the pledge-and-review model adopted by the Paris Climate Agreement, by which governments make flexible, voluntary commitments toward reductions in CO_2 emissions that are subject to review every five years, and to the European Union's open method of coordination (Radaelli, 2003; Zeitlin, 2009).

More recently, the Independent Reporting Mechanism and the Support Unit have placed greater emphasis on the ambition of commitments, encouraging governments to refocus their National Action Plans on fewer commitments but with more transformative potential and to focus more on measurable outcomes rather than project-based outputs (Vossler & Foti, 2018). Yet these same efforts also risk undercutting the potential for impact by placing greater priority on measurable results achieved within a set timeframe rather than on true transformative potential.

Open Government Partnership commitments are also dependent on domestic political context. Leadership changes in many countries have left the partnership process with an absence of political energy and halted or even reversed progress on commitments. Elsewhere, as in Mexico, national governments lose interest as relationships with civil society turn from collaboration to conflict. Contrarily, the Open Government Partnership process can thrive where political conditions are favorable, such as in moments when substantial political attention and resources are focused on governance reform. Ukraine, for example, had made and implemented several ambitious commitments in the years following its post-2014 political transition.[1] Yet, in these contexts, it is also difficult to evaluate the impact of the Open Government Partnership itself, as many of these reforms would have likely happened anyway.

Another direct pathway of change for the Open Government Partnership is through its eligibility criteria for new members, which requires minimum levels of civil liberties, access to information legislation, fiscal transparency, and public asset disclosure. While the majority of members were already eligible at the outset and joined in the Partnership's first year, roughly a dozen countries were not initially eligible and thus engaged in processes of reform *prior* to joining. In some cases, these reform processes were unlikely attributable to the Open Government Partnership itself, such as the political transition in Tunisia that culminated in democratic elections in 2011. But in others, the desire to join the Partnership was an explicit driver of reform, such as in the adoption of access to information legislation in Morocco (OGP Support Unit, 2018). In such instances, the direct impact of the Open Government Partnership came prior to membership yet was nonetheless real.

Skepticism toward the Open Government Partnership has come primarily from considerations of its direct pathways of impact. Many observers have expressed skepticism over the nature of commitments (e.g., Marczynski, 2018; Steibel, Alves, & Konopacki, 2017), the extent to which they have been implemented (Fraundorfer, 2017), and the seeming absence of a link between policy output and meaningful policy outcomes (Adler, 2015; McKenzie, 2014). We agree with most of these critiques and yet argue that they miss the point. The limitations of the Open Government Partnership's compliance mechanisms are fundamental to the inherent dilemmas of its institutional design and the tradeoffs that made the Partnership possible in the first place.

If one considers a scenario where some core element of the Open Government Partnership's design was altered, then for every new potential that might be gained, something else would be lost. Possible methods exist by which the Partnership might crack down on members' subpar commitments, poor implementation, or problematic civil liberties records. Yet, if these enforcements went beyond the incremental steps the Open Government Partnership is already taking, the likely result would be member governments departing in droves, leaving behind a mere club of the already high-performing. Further, reduced flexibility in the National Action Plan process might undercut the opportunities that do exist for creativity, innovation, collaboration, and learning.

In summary, we conclude that the direct pathway, in the short term, can indeed matter in important ways sometimes and under certain circumstances, but it is more often limited, context dependent, and superficial. However, the longer-term, iterative process of repeated National Action Plans and Independent Reporting Mechanism cycles with gradual ratcheting up of expectations has the potential to shape the direct pathway into a more effective force for change. We now turn to the indirect pathway for impact, which we argue deserves greater attention.

Indirect Pathways of Change

By process-driven mechanisms, we mean those impacts delinked from the formal chain of eligibility rules, commitment to policy change, and compliance with commitments of international institutions. Indirect impacts may be difficult to measure, causally complex, emerge over longer timeframes, and be visible only in certain cases. Yet the processes associated with membership, even independently of commitments and compliance, can produce fundamental changes in the ideas, interactions, and opportunities of key actors involved in public sector reform at both domestic and global levels.

We consider indirect pathways of impact in three overarching categories: new norms and policy models of reform, new resources and opportunities for reformers, and new linkages and coalitions. These mechanisms pertain to actors involved in public sector reform both inside and outside of government and at domestic, global, and transnational levels.

Norms and policy models

First, the Open Government Partnership has contributed to defining, legitimizing, and globalizing new policy models of public sector reform. As described at length in chapter 2, the concept of open government ties together several more specific reform agendas—including transparency, participation, accountability, and technology—into a broader model of how government ought to work. While this process of defining open government as a distinct model had already begun in the United States, the Open Government Partnership played a role in contributing to and cementing that process of definition. Beyond that, the Partnership played a key role in globalizing the concept, promoting it vis-à-vis other international institutions, and imbuing open government reforms with a sense of normative legitimacy, as something that governments ought to do. As with global normative developments in other arenas, such as human rights and the environment, this sense of normative legitimacy sometimes manifests as window-dressing reforms that decouple form from function yet nonetheless speak to the powerful legitimacy of the new model.

Evidence of this pathway of impact can be seen in the mainstreaming of open government as a major theme in global institutions like the Organisation for Economic Co-Operation and Development (OECD), in the creation of new global indices like the Open Data Barometer and the Open Data Index, and in the rapid global proliferation of reforms like open data portals and forums for policy cocreation (Ingrams, Piotrowski, & Berliner, 2020). Importantly, it can also be seen in the increasing institutionalization of open government models in national and subnational politics, even beyond the formal remit of the Open Government Partnership itself. For example, in Mexico, a subnational open government initiative modeled after, but not formally linked with, the Partnership took root with a majority of states participating, including governors across three major political parties. This initiative continued in operation even after the collapse of national-level collaboration in Mexico's Open Government Partnership process.

The Open Government Partnership also served as a platform for the emergence of new subsidiary norms linked with open government. Advocates used Open Government Partnership working groups and meetings to develop and launch new standards like the Open Data Charter and the Open Contracting Partnership and to mainstream new principles like beneficial ownership transparency (to combat the use of shell corporations for money laundering, tax avoidance, and corruption). As the Open Government Partnership catalyzed the supply of new norms, the iterative process of making new National Action Plans every two years also drove the demand, and governments rapidly began making commitments focused on these new areas.

Resources and opportunities

Second, the Open Government Partnership has led to new resources—both material and symbolic—and new political opportunities for reformers both inside and outside of government. Most importantly, the Partnership has empowered civil society actors—both domestically and globally—in new ways. These include a formal seat at the table, seen both in the unprecedented formal parity between governments and civil society in the Open Government Partnership's global governance structure and in national-level consultation around National Action Plan design and implementation. But beyond the formal representation, these mechanisms also empower civil society groups with new forms of informal power through networking, information provision, and agenda-setting. Additionally, the formal inclusion of civil society groups can give them structural power through their implicit threat of exit. While this threat was exercised by civil society from the national-level Open Government Partnership process in Mexico, it has been threatened in other places such as Croatia (Montero & Taxell, 2015) and is latent at the international level, giving weight to civil society concerns over other institutional design issues.

The impacts of these new forms of power can be seen both at the global level, as civil society has taken advantage of its newfound empowerment to ratchet up the institutional design of the Open Government Partnership itself, including a broader scope, expanded capacity, and increased ability to monitor and sanction member governments, and at the domestic level, as civil society coalitions in many countries have successfully used their new role to obtain long-demanded policy concessions. In Mexico, one civil society representative even said that the Partnership was "like steroids for civil society."[2]

The Open Government Partnership also empowers reformers *inside* of government. Rather than focusing on more traditional diplomats and foreign ministries, the Partnership has sought to focus on line ministries, midlevel bureaucrats, and local governments, thus serving to provide resources, support, and models to current and potential future reformers in government. The result is that it is easier for government reformers to launch new open government projects when and where such reformers emerge and seek to leverage these international opportunities.

Linkages and coalitions

Finally, the Open Government Partnership has created new linkages and coalitions among public sector reformers inside and outside of government as well as with other types of actors. These linkages enable new forms of learning, diffusion of innovation, and strategic coordination, in addition to helping the open government movement find new allies across ideological divides. Transgovernmental linkages, from bureaucrat to bureaucrat across countries, spur the sharing of both innovative reforms and strategies for pursuing reform agendas. Linkages among civil society groups that were previously more isolated have led to flourishing regional networks, particularly in Latin America.

The Open Government Partnership itself has formed important linkages with other international organizations and initiatives, contributing to the gradual emergence of a regime complex (Keohane & Victor, 2011) for open government. For example, the Partnership has forged partnerships with the Extractive Industries Transparency Initiative to help coordinate mutual efforts and partnered with the World Bank to form a trust fund to support innovative reforms.

Perhaps most importantly, the Open Government Partnership has encouraged the creation of new coalitions that span disparate issue networks and cross ideological boundaries. Among civil society at both global and national levels, the Partnership has brought together organizations and issue communities that often did not work together previously, including human rights, media, anticorruption, environmental reform, good governance, and even business groups, often with very different ways of working with governments. Such developments have also played out within countries. In Mexico, for instance, the Open Government Partnership spurred a shift toward a new culture of collaboration among civil society groups, even bringing together groups focused on human rights and those focused on business competitiveness into a coalition focused on shared goals. However, these new coalitions have not always been without friction, as evidenced by the tension that often emerged between access to information and open data advocates (Berliner, Ingrams, & Piotrowski, 2018).

Importantly, this ability of the Open Government Partnership to build cross-ideological coalitions has also helped in several cases where national participation *did* endure across political transitions. These include transitions from Susilo Bambang Yudhoyono to Joko Widodo in Indonesia, from Cristina Fernández de Kirchner to Mauricio Macri in Argentina, from François Hollande to Emmanuel Macron in France, and from Felipe Calderón to Enrique Peña Nieto (at least initially) in Mexico. Crucially, these include cases of major ideological transition as well as cases where Open Government Partnership participation had been a signature issue of the outgoing leader and thus tempting to undermine as a sign of change. Most strikingly, the partnership process in the Philippines has survived the stark transition from Benigno Aquino to Rodrigo Duterte, as the new government saw the potential to pursue its own goals through the Open Government Partnership process, including improving performance on global competitiveness rankings, obtaining concessions from extractive industries, and broadening citizen participation in rural areas (though, as will be seen in chapter 4, this has sometimes been in unsettling ways). Certainly, in many other cases, political transitions have been major challenges for the Open Government Partnership process, including setbacks in Croatia and the United States.

In table 1.3, we summarize the key features of the two different pathways of impact of international institutions and the mechanisms they highlight.

Table 1.3
Summary of direct and indirect pathways of impact of institutional organizations

Pathways of impact	Key institutional design features	Key mechanisms	Key actors
Direct	Monitoring and enforcement; eligibility requirements	Government compliance with commitments; eligibility requirements.	Central government decision makers
Indirect	Iterative and participatory processes	Changing norms and policy models; new resources and opportunities for reformers; new linkages and changing coalitions	Central government decision makers, individual politicians and bureaucrats, civil society organizations, policy experts

Evaluating direct and indirect pathways

How do we evaluate an argument that focuses on the indirect pathway and its iterative and participatory processes of change? Often, previous research seeking to evaluate the effects of membership in international treaties or initiatives has focused on evaluating the average effect in a framework focused on causal inference. For such an approach, the self-selection of states into membership offers the greatest challenge (e.g., Von Stein, 2005). Simply comparing the behavior of members and nonmembers is insufficient, as members may join an initiative in order to take credit for actions that they anticipated undertaking anyway. It is difficult—indeed, often impossible—to assess the counterfactual scenario in which members did not actually join.

This inferential challenge applies to the Open Government Partnership and makes any attempt to quantitatively evaluate the impact of partnership membership complex and highly suspect. First, membership is nonrandom, as governments decide whether to join (or not to, as in the cases of India and Russia). Second, eligibility is governed by a set of criteria that can, in some cases, motivate reforms ahead of time to make membership possible (such as in Morocco).

Finally, it is unclear what the appropriate outcome variable in a quantitative analysis would be, given the scope and ambiguity of open government itself. There are no satisfactory crossnational measures of meaningful government transparency toward citizens in practice, and common indices of corruption and democracy are far too broad-brush and stable over time to capture even the most optimistic sorts of effects that might be expected of the Open Government Partnership. Desirable outputs of Open Government Partnership membership might include the passage and implementation of a well-designed whistleblowing law, the creation of a functional and easy-to-use portal for government data, or the institution of participatory decision-making bodies. Open government, similar to transparency, is frequently linked to issues of ethics and corruption (Piotrowski, 2014). Yet it remains a separate question, and beyond the scope of the present work, whether these types of reforms would, in turn, lead to measurable changes in broader outcomes like corruption and democracy.

Our focus in this book is slightly different. We are interested in the processes and mechanisms that might link international initiatives to meaningful public sector reform, even if those pathways cannot characterize the average effect of membership. We are focused more on a proximate dependent variable of meaningful public sector reforms themselves, even if it remains an open question whether or not those reforms, in turn, lead to movements on commonly measured outcome variables such as corruption and democracy indices. Our distinction between direct and indirect pathways is thus orthogonal, or crosscutting, to the question of "causal or not causal?"

Our evidence is primarily qualitative, not quantitative, and primarily concerns characterizing the nature of processes at work rather than measuring the outcomes they achieved. We approach these tasks at two separate levels of analysis: the international and the national. The international level focuses primarily on the historical development of the Open Government Partnership and the broader transnational open government reform movement over the period since 2011. At the national level, we offer thematic evidence drawn from an array of member countries and global settings, as well as a more focused case study of Mexico. Our evidence is collected from interviews, official documents, secondary data analysis, media reports, and participant observation.

At both levels, we trace how the Open Government Partnership contributed to new norms and policy models of reform, created new resources and opportunities for reformers, and forged new linkages and coalitions between different types of actors. We take care to bear in mind the question of counterfactuals: Would those same dynamics have taken place even in a world without the Open Government Partnership? Although such a question is often impossible to answer definitively, we highlight cases where the changes that took place were specific to partnership operations, processes, and relationships; were instigated by Open Government Partnership activities; or could not have plausibly occurred independently of the partnership through other causes.

CONTRIBUTIONS

To reiterate, we argue that the Open Government Partnership has had important impacts on public sector reform—but not necessarily in the ways that might be obvious and not necessarily in the ways to which the initiative itself gives the most attention. Impacts from commitments and compliance alone have been limited, frequently leading to discrete projects that, while worthwhile, are likely to be narrow in their potential impact—if they are implemented at all. However, indirect pathways of impact, including shaping policy models, empowering new actors, and forging new connections, have more transformative potential, even if they are more difficult to observe and measure.

Yet we do not suggest that the direct pathway has failed in the sense that it ought to be yielding more substantial impacts. Rather, we suggest that its limitations are fundamental to the basic tradeoffs that made the Open Government Partnership possible in the first place—between membership and stringency, participation and credibility, and flexibility and accountability. This series of fundamental institutional design dilemmas creates limits for what any membership-based international initiative can hope to achieve, and the Open Government Partnership is operating at or near the frontier of what is possible. What the Partnership's direct pathway has produced in terms of impact is what one ought to reasonably expect at this stage in the initiative's existence. Iterative learning from experience resulting in small tweaks to the National Action Plan and Independent Reporting Mechanism processes may yield more substantial results in the future, but the gains will likely be incremental. Importantly, one of the most pressing threats to this process comes from expectations themselves, as the Open Government Partnership and its proponents have created expectations of more transformative impact from the National Action Plan-Independent Reporting Mechanism process that is unlikely to be realized, thus setting themselves up for perceived failure.

Crucially, we also do not argue that the Partnership's direct pathway ought to be abandoned. Rather, we see its participatory and iterative National Action Plan–Independent Reporting Mechanism cycle as the engine that powers and makes possible the indirect pathways of impact. The cyclical, iterative process keeps government and civil society stakeholders in dialogue, creates demand for new models of governance reform, and ensures that opportunities for new actors to have influence will continue to open. The repetitive nature of the process transforms the status-quo option for member countries. Even if governments seek to opportunistically claim credit for membership while doing nothing, they still need to go through the formal motions of holding consultations, drafting a National Action Plan, making commitments, and cooperating with the Independent Reporting Mechanism—even if no commitments are implemented. This creates a new situation where governments need to keep running just to stand still and so, perhaps, will find it worthwhile or easier to simply move forward. These requirements force governments to continue engaging with civil society and other domestic, transnational, and international actors, thereby creating new opportunities for change. The National Action Plan process also creates a focal point for new coalitions to work together and for new models of governance reform to emerge and take root.

The Power of Partnership in Open Government is a book that adds to both the public administration literature on public sector management reform and the political science literature on international institutions. By the nature of the subject, it also pushes our understanding about the Open Government Partnership and international reform initiatives generally. We push the public sector reform field to consider open government as an aspect of reform and to take international and transnational influences seriously but critically. We push scholars within the international relations field to rethink how the impact of membership-based institutions works. For the Open Government Partnership itself, our research and analysis point to a broader scope for the evaluation of organizational outcomes and impacts than a commitment-based one alone. Finally, our research points to iterative and participatory processes as key design features for international reform initiatives.

PLAN OF THE BOOK

This introductory chapter introduces the reader to the central participants and ideas in the story of the Open Government Partnership and the set of problems and questions posed by its rise to prominence and puts forward the key contours of our arguments and the plan of the book. In chapter 2, we go over the theory and practice of public management reform. This is primarily a chapter to set out the key debates about how scholars and policymakers have grappled with the challenge of making public governance fair and effective. It traces the visions, values, and concrete tools and programs that have characterized the quest to transform the function and operation of the public sector. The main takeaway from this chapter is that there are a host of lessons from history guiding us to be skeptical of the claims of reformers.

In chapter 3, we situate the creation and design of the Open Government Partnership in the international relations literature and put into place many of the innovative ideas and institutional features of the partnership that we empirically investigate later. This chapter also sheds new light on the origin story of the partnership, leveraging interview and documentary evidence to tell this story in greater detail than has been publicly written to date. We emphasize how the creation and design of the Open Government Partnership exemplify *both* old dynamics of political contestation and new dynamics of flexibility and collaboration. This chapter also offers an overview of the structure and functions of the Open Government Partnership to lay the groundwork for the empirical evidence that follows.

Chapter 4 focuses on marshaling the empirical evidence and testing and debating the impacts that the Open Government Partnership has had on open government reform. A range of examples of direct and indirect impacts of the partnership are analyzed and presented. We assess whether its novel methods have had any of the desired results, and we conclude that the direct impacts from the Open Government Partnership have often been disappointing, while at the same time, indirect pathways of change have often created powerful new forms of partnership and opportunities in ways that we would not have expected.

Chapter 5 uses an in-depth case study of the Open Government Partnership in Mexico to explore and demonstrate the pathways of change in more detail from the perspective of both the direct and indirect pathways. We review both the overall chronology of Mexico's membership in the Open Government Partnership and evaluate specific contributions made to public sector reform both through a direct pathway of commitments and compliance as well as through more indirect pathways. Indeed, although commitments themselves have often been limited, we see substantial evidence of broader effects of the Open Government Partnership in Mexico. These include new policy models, new patterns of collaboration, new opportunities for reformers, and several specific moments of leverage for civil society groups.

Chapter 6 concludes the book by highlighting the implications and lessons of our research for the scholarly literature on both public management and international institutions, for the open government policy community and the Open Government Partnership itself, and, finally, for other multistakeholder and transnational reform efforts around the world.

2 PUBLIC MANAGEMENT REFORM IN A GLOBAL PERSPECTIVE

In this chapter, we give readers an in-depth insight into the open government movement.[1] We describe where it comes from, what is meant by *open*, how the movement configures alongside other public sector reform movements in terms of its goals and principal supporters, and what chances it has of changing the public sector for the better.

Government is the political apparatus given authority to govern a defined area or community of people. Like any public sector reform movement, open government seeks to change the way government works in terms of the inputs, processes, and outputs that structure government activity, focusing on two components of government organization—information management and public interaction among actors. This is a two-fold approach to public sector organization that emphasizes information *out* and participation *in*. Processes for publishing, information sharing, and digital platforms for public data go *out* into the public sphere, while feedback from a broad range of public actors, such as citizens and the private sector, comes *in* to internal decision-making systems. Meijer, Curtin, and Hillebrandt (2012) have called these two components of open government *vision* and *voice* to capture the relational character between government organizations internally and the public externally. In other words, the public not only obtains a greater vision about what government does but also gains more voice as opportunities to influence government increase.

While vision and voice capture the essential normative orientations of open government, in policy terms, the open government movement supports a range of different types of policies and programs. While these policies and programs have slowly taken shape and consolidated into the open government movement in the twenty-first century, the normative components of open government and the idea of openness in government itself are much older and draw from the rich soil of public administration theory.

In this chapter, we will uncover the origins of the idea of open government and analyze its development and potential future trajectories—ranging from a short-lived fad to far-reaching systemic change. We will trace the roots of the open government reform approach—both in scholarly paradigms and in their realization in specific policies and programs—and try to gauge what we are dealing with: a reform movement with inherent flaws, a government transformation, or something somewhere in between. In order to do this, we will situate open government in an analysis of prior public management reform trends and their related public administration theoretical paradigms. By analyzing the origins of the open government movement, its key ideas and actors, and its place among other competing models of reform, we will develop several propositions as to the future of open government public management reform. We pay particular attention to one of the most significant reform movements of the twentieth century, New Public Management, which preceded and triggered the contemporary search for new models of reform. While open government is part of this post–New Public Management search, it has essential characteristics of its own.

THE ROOTS OF THE OPEN GOVERNMENT MOVEMENT

The open government movement is a label given to a set of actors who seek changes to the way the public sector operates. However, the ideas and beliefs that characterize the movement are much older than the explicit open government movement itself. In this section, we trace clear precedents in philosophical and political history going back to the time of the Enlightenment that have influenced the open government movement of today.

The Enlightenment

While open government as a reform movement with a specific set of policy ambitions emerged in the twenty-first century, the roots of open government lie much earlier in Western political philosophy, notably in the scientific principles of rationalism and social egalitarianism from the Enlightenment and the liberalism of eighteenth-century moral and political philosophers.

Open government has beginnings in the writings of Enlightenment philosophers such as Francis Bacon (1561–1626) and Jean-Jacques Rousseau (1712–1778), who gave human reason, empirical inquiry, and the notion of the natural state of human equality greater prominence in the leading social and political circles of Europe. The growing influence and wealth of mercantile classes and the idea of making public information available for self-governing citizens found a natural home in the rationalism of the Enlightenment.

After the Enlightenment period, European and North American countries recognized these public information principles by enshrining them in laws. Sweden passed the world's first freedom of information law in 1766. In 1775 and 1789, the United States and French revolutions, as well as the United States Constitution, which passed in 1787, gave further political power to republican values of tolerance, religious freedom, and equality. Public agencies started to print internal government information in newspapers and organize information. The publishing of laws and treaties became mandatory, as did the storage of documents in readily accessible ways (Jaeger & Bertot, 2010).

Of course, there is a big difference between these Enlightenment concepts of rationalism, science, and egalitarianism and the promulgation of open government in the modern sense of citizens regularly monitoring political leaders. What makes the Enlightenment important in the history of open government is the belief in democracy and the power of rule by an informed public of citizens rather than unquestioning belief in a monarchy or oligarchy. The earliest freedom of information laws and the new republican constitutions in France and the United States also gave expression to the idea that citizens are sovereign members in a democracy and that the direction of a government is guided ultimately by their beliefs and wishes.

Industrialization and Liberalism

The next stage in the history of open government comes during the industrial era and the emerging welfare state of Western governments. Liberal reformers at the end of the eighteenth century and throughout the nineteenth century continued to campaign for greater equality for citizens, especially for women and the poor. Free market principles and the right of individuals to pursue their economic self-interests went hand-in-hand with these changes. Simultaneously, the emergence of industrial working classes in Europe and North America meant that governments needed to invest further in public education programs. These programs were forerunners of the welfare state and social democratic policies aimed at broadening participation in public life and politics.

The writings of several important intellectuals captured the political and moral philosophies of the liberal age. Principles of open government exist in the theories of Immanuel Kant, who argued for a universal morality of human beings, and Jeremy Bentham, who supported a broader notion of political participation for all individuals because all individuals have the same right to pursue happiness and liberty (Hood, 2007).

In the United States, liberal principles began to apply not just to the political rights of citizens but also internally to the civil service. The Pendleton Civil Service Act of 1883, which aimed to make the civil service a meritocracy, followed the assassination of President Garfield. Garfield's killer was a disgruntled scion of a prominent family who felt unjustly overlooked for a government position. The Pendleton law made competitive examinations for civil service positions mandatory. While the Pendleton reforms restrained elite privilege, moneyed interests were more difficult to control, especially as the power of industrial manufacturing reached unprecedented levels in the United States. Scholar and soon-to-be president Woodrow Wilson, in his article *The Study of Administration*, argued that government needed to be open to public examination to prevent corruption and the abuse of power (Wilson, 1887). And one of the most memorable defenses of transparency from Louis Brandeis in 1914 is encapsulated in the famous phrase, "Sunlight is said to be the best of disinfectants" (Brandeis, 1971, 92).

Bureaucracy and the Modern State

In the twentieth century, the unraveling of colonialism and the arrival of mechanized societies created the modern bureaucratic state. Coupled with the growth of neoclassical economics and the ideas of philosophers such as Karl Popper (1902–1994), the post–World War II period was marked by Western governments undertaking reforms to widen access to economic and political opportunities. Popper viewed openness as a way to revive democracy and reinforce egalitarian norms that would be a safeguard against social exclusion and elitism in politics (Ingrams, 2020). Governments, then as now, are involved in an ongoing process of designing new policy initiatives for transparency that support the legal-normative authority of the state and liberal democracy. According to public administration scholar David Rosenbloom (2000), administrative laws, such as transparency laws, are a primary vehicle for the process of retrofitting administrative principles and processes to the legal authority of government constitutions.

These administrative principles of the bureaucratic state took the form of public information laws and policies. In the United States, this was achieved by making bureaucracies more rational and open to public scrutiny and democratic influence through laws (e.g., the Administrative Procedure Act of 1946) that regulate recruitment and appointment to the civil service. Government also used public information to create systems of performance measurement (e.g., the Clinger-Cohen Act of 1996) and defined the rights and responsibilities of public agencies and citizens for requesting information from the government (e.g., the Freedom of Information Act of 1966).

Increasing political pressure to make government more accessible and transparent emerged as a concept after the Second World War when public information activists challenged the secrecy of military and administrative records, which were growing in size (Yu & Robinson, 2012). Freedom of information acts were an important step in the history of open government. While, as already mentioned, Sweden had forged ahead with such laws in the eighteenth century, other countries increasingly followed. Freedom of information policies were enshrined in many country laws and constitutions in the second half of the twentieth century. Finland led this wave of freedom of information legislating in 1951, but the United States followed in 1966. In the United States, the Watergate scandal, a crisis of presidential privilege and secrecy, drove public outcry against lack of access to government information and led to a strengthening of the Freedom of Information Act. Between the 1970s and the 1990s, virtually every democratic country passed similar legislation recognizing that strict protocols and legal rules were needed to make sure that public access to government information was a legal right. In subsequent years, the freedom of information movement crossed every continent and found inroads even to nondemocratic or emerging democratic countries (Ingrams, 2018). The global spread of freedom of information laws was a vital plank in the open government movement, as it created a worldwide precedent in the legal apparatus needed for individuals to force their governments to be more responsive.

Human rights advocates increasingly became influential interlocutors in the open government reform movement, and several well-known information rights organizations pushed for reform in countries that did not have laws in place for freedom of expression and freedom of information. Article 19, an international human rights group founded in the UK, campaigned for political action around Article 19 of the Universal Declaration of Human Rights, the freedom of opinion and expression. Other organizations founded in a range of Western countries, such as the Centre for Law and Democracy (Canada), the Open Society Institute (United States), and Access Info Europe (Spain), became active in campaigning for greater adoption of freedom of information laws and more proactive uses of open data for transparency and accountability. These organizations were also active in collecting and disseminating quantitative data on the countries' degrees of openness. For example, the Open Society Institute's survey of right to information laws became the Open Government Partnership's indicator for establishing membership eligibility based on a country's access to information legislation.

Mass Media, Democratization, and the Internet

The impact of the internet on the open government movement has been profound and far-reaching. The nature of open government changed once organizational strategies and processes became dominated by the quantity and accessibility of online information (Kassen, 2014). Open government relies on an ecosystem of online-human systems whereby information actors share, receive, interpret, and act on information (Millard, 2015). For this reason, the internet has dramatically altered these information dynamics and put pressure on government information management systems.

A turning point took place in the early 2000s in mass participation on the internet and the adoption of Web 2.0 technologies by individuals and organizations. Major social media platforms were founded. Facebook launched in 2004. The contribution of digital technology activists was vital in turning the efforts of information rights and free speech organizations into a global political movement. Key players included technology entrepreneurs such as Tim O'Reilly; global philanthropic organizations such as the Open Society Foundations (formerly the Open Society Institute) and the Omidyar Network; and policy advisors such as Beth Noveck in the Obama White House and Tim Kelsey in Whitehall under David Cameron.

In the United States, Obama's presidency is seen as the turning point in the fortunes of the open government movement, as the ideas of transparency, accountability, and participation, bound together by the potential of new digital technologies, became a viable political movement at the highest level of the US government. Obama's presidential campaign was explicitly built upon the idea that his administration would be an open style of politics in contrast to the secretiveness of the Bush administration (Jaeger & Bertot, 2010).[2] Obama's first major policy statement as president was the Open Government Directive, an executive order to the heads of US federal agencies to begin proactively opening their internal information, to include the public's views more in decision making, and to harness the participative potential of new digital technologies. One of the first national open data portals, data.gov, was launched in 2009, and the Open Government Partnership was launched in 2011. For the first time in history, open government as a concept had global political currency for political and organizational reform.

OPEN GOVERNMENT REFORMS IN PRACTICE

Today, the open government movement is characterized by the convergence of four central qualities—transparency, accountability, participation, and technology—which have been encapsulated in the Open Government Partnership core values of *access to information*, *public accountability*, *civic participation*, and *technology and innovation for openness and accountability*. Of note, these four areas differ slightly from the ones presented in Obama's 2009

Open Government Directive. In this book, we rely on the issue emphasis adopted by the Open Government Partnership and the more global version of these agendas—including accountability separately and subsuming collaboration under participation. Having looked at the history of the ideas and policies of open government, these four terms remain very abstract and theoretical, though the movement developed a diverse set of different policy ideas. What do these ideas and practices look like in action?

Open government in practice covers a wide range of policy areas and includes multiple different approaches to organizational change. Within this section, we present three substantive areas of open government—transparency, participation, and accountability—as well as technology, a central supporting element of the open government movement, as we have described above. Table 2.1 presents a handful of examples grouped into these substantive categories.

Transparency Policies

Not only does the concept of transparency have intuitive appeal, but scholars have also long identified it as an important foundation of democracy, sound economics, and good governance. Historically, transparency was most often seen as a political ideal for conditions deemed necessary to give people self-determination. However, as it has developed over time, the concept of transparency has been applied in a wide variety of economic, legal, and managerial settings that emphasize different goals and dimensions and, in turn, have manifested themselves in different policy approaches.

First, transparency makes it difficult for public officials to hide. This political aspect of transparency has benefits for tackling corruption (Cucciniello, Porumbescu, & Grimmelikhuijsen, 2017). By equalizing the types of information accessed by actors from different sectors or organizations, transparency also can make decision making more efficient and effective. This communicative aspect of transparency (sometimes called information symmetry) has benefits for encouraging healthier economic markets where competition can flourish (Boone & White, 2015) and for sounder governance.

Second, the concept of transparency has also historically been associated with specific rights-based legal principles. Article 19 of the International

Table 2.1
Examples of open government initiatives

Type of Policy	Examples
Transparency	• Open data • Beneficial ownership initiatives • Fiscal openness • Freedom of information/access to information laws • Foreign aid transparency policies • Transparency around natural resources • Lobbying transparency policies
Participation	• Citizen science projects • Consultation or cocreation in policymaking • Crowdsourcing • Nonprofit and private sector engagement • Open education • Participatory budgeting • Smart cities • Open regulations
Accountability	• Anticorruption laws and regulations • Anticorruption agencies or courts • Electoral reforms • Media capacity-building • Public reporting tools • Whistleblower legislation and procedures • Open public procurement policies • Public-private contracting regulations
Technology	All of the above policies can qualify as technology policies insofar as they use technology to achieve their goals. Highly common technologies in open government include the following: • Open data platforms • Crowdsourcing • Hackathons • Wikis and application programming interfaces • Citizen reporting apps • E-forums and discussion boards

Convention on Civil and Political Rights enshrines the right of an individual to seek and obtain information. The charter of the United Nations and the European Convention on Human Rights refers to information access as essential to the organization's effectiveness. Principles of transparency also exist in many constitutions and laws in European countries (Curtin & Meijer, 1995).

Third, performance management regimes associated with the rise of New Public Management have used transparency theory to support managerial effectiveness. In this view, transparency involves the use of performance indicators and focuses on services and the public as consumers. This management approach contrasts with the legal approach, which focuses on sources of policy and administrative decisions and views institutions in terms of deliberation, democracy, and human rights (Clark, 1996).

Fourth, transparency policies such as freedom of information laws are also often part of anticorruption initiatives. Governments adopt these laws with the rationale that strict standards and better enforcement of public access to information are more likely to expose and reduce corruption (Cordis & Warren, 2014). In developing countries, initiatives were undertaken to reinforce existing freedom of information laws to better tackle corruption. Anticorruption initiatives focus on specific areas of public organizations where corruption is likely deterred by data monitoring, such as job descriptions and salaries of public officials (Bowman & Stevens, 2013). For example, when the public can see public salary and job description information, the number of no-show jobs (where individuals are paid for jobs they do not do) is reduced.

Finally, on the other side of the transparency legislation coin are laws designed to protect people's identities and privacy from *too much* transparency (Piotrowski, 2010). These laws aim to protect the right to personal privacy while simultaneously supporting openness (Hardy & Maurushat, 2017; Ingrams, 2017a).

Motivated by these different approaches—either individually or in combination—transparency reforms are today seen as driven by a movement (Birchall, 2011). However, the intuitive value of transparency to government also means that it is subject to numerous competing perspectives and demands. This can also create situations where politicians give external obeisance to the value of transparency rhetorically but have a wide berth for interpreting the implementation of transparency policies in practice. In such situations, transparency can become a "magic concept" that is applied to almost any policy problem (Pollitt & Hupe, 2011), even if inappropriately.

Participation Policies

Open government reforms not only aim to provide access to information but also usually have a participatory dimension—the "voice" component in Meijer, Curtin, and Hillebrandt's (2012) terminology. However, participation has sometimes received too little attention in open government research (Susha, 2015). Policymakers frequently use public participation—often leveraging information and communication technologies—in order to develop, implement, or evaluate policies (Bingham, Nabatchi, & O'Leary, 2005). Yet voice is not merely an administrative initiative; rather, it can also play political roles involving different levels of political engagement. In some cases, such as participatory budgeting, formal mechanisms give citizen participation a more decisive voice over what happens in government and policymaking, potentially creating a more legitimate allocation of tax funds (Harrison & Sayogo, 2014).

Participation in open government may be of several types. Wijnhoven, Ehrenhard, and Kuhn (2015) suggest four types of participation based on the level of political or administrative involvement by the members of the public and how focused the participation is on producing an innovative policy or idea. (1) *Citizen innovation* is a type of participation that is focused on better administration with innovative goals; (2) *collaborative democracy* is focused on political actions with innovative democratic models as the goal; (3) *citizen sourcing* is highly administrative in focus and is about seeking approval or support for an existing policy rather than innovation; and (4) *constituency support* is highly politically focused and, like citizen sourcing, is focused on garnering support rather than innovating new ideas.

Participation policies also try to leverage the contributions of many different types of actors in society, including ordinary citizens, civil society, private sector organizations, experts, and officials themselves. Examples of these can be seen in the policy area of education. Public education in schools has been an active focus area for public participation initiatives because education is a core public good in society. In elementary and secondary levels of education, educators' roles reach beyond school buildings to the education that takes place after school with parents, friends, or the general community. Policymakers thus try to promote excellence in education by improving collaboration. Education policymakers can use crowdsourcing to generate new ideas for delivering education, validate them through proof of concepts, and improve the implementation of new policies (Aitamurto &

Landemore, 2016; Mergel, 2015). Indeed, many open government theories consider collaboration—the proactive solicitation of citizen input—as a critical component of public participation (Grimmelikhuijsen & Feeney, 2017). But participation can also occur at a more organizational level through engagement with nonprofit or private sector organizations (Gonzalez-Zapata & Heeks, 2015). These organizations fulfill the need for a demand side for open data projects and intermediary organizations; therefore, participation initiatives frequently focus on strengthening these demand-side organizations (Fung, 2013; Ohemeng & Ofosu-Adarkwa, 2015; Piscopo, Siebes, & Hardman, 2017). Some popular types of open government technologies, such as those providing visualization, mapping, or information on politics, social benefits, and the digital divide, are especially useful for the nonprofit sector (Kassen, 2014).

Another focus of participation initiatives in e-government is smart city initiatives that integrate digital service streams with smart sensors and devices to improve the predictive capacity of local services in areas such as household energy use or neighborhood garbage collection. Smart cities employ a range of other data tools designed to allow nongovernmental organizations to gather services into city platforms to provide users with easy access to tools such as apps, information aggregators, open data repositories, and service platforms (Zuiderwijk & Janssen, 2014). But here, too, private and nonprofit participation also matters, including data clearinghouses that gather data from different organizations, interpret the data, and enable regulation and delivery of services to be controlled by algorithmically based instructions in a smart system. Smart city ecosystems also often rely on collaboration with business (Abella, Ortiz-de-Urbina-Criado, & De Pablos-Heredero, 2017) and open data management (Zeleti, Ojo, & Curry, 2016).

Accountability Policies

Accountability "involves the means by which public agencies and their workers manage the diverse expectations generated within and outside the organization" (Romzek & Dubnick, 1987, p. 228). In the public sector, accountability can be both a political and a public administration phenomenon. In the political sense, accountability, can be vertical (through elections [Manin, Przeworski, & Stokes, 1999]); horizontal (through official checks and balances and oversight institutions [O'Donnell, 1998]); or diagonal (through societal voice such as media, activism, and protest). In any form, however, accountability requires not just "answerability" but also "enforcement" (Schedler, 1999) in the form of some formal or informal sanction.

In public administration theory, the concept of public accountability has roots in financial bookkeeping practices whereby civil servants keeping records of public money would render an account of how money was being spent (Bovens, Goodin, & Schillemans, 2014). However, the concept received more attention in the 1980s with the growth of New Public Management (Bovens et al., 2014; Forrer et al., 2010) and is applied today to all areas of government action. Public accountability is both a system of governmental processes and a specific quality or status. It is a process in the sense of being an institutional mechanism of checks and balances and a status in the sense that public organizations or government actors may (or may not) have it but are widely seen as virtuous when they do (Bovens et al., 2014). As a process, by sharing information widely with all stakeholders, open government embeds government in a system of accountability. In the latter sense, the status of openness is equated with the status of being accountable because openness expresses the status of being forthcoming and taking responsibility.

Although accountability is closely linked to transparency (Bovens, 2007; Fox, 2007; Shkabatur, 2012), they may not always be "twins," as claimed by Hood (2010). Rather, they may mesh well in a governance system as matching parts, or they may only overlap partially and interact in disjointed ways as an awkward couple. While transparency can be sufficient to create a process of accountability, transparency is not necessary for accountability (Fox, 2007). That is, it is possible for accountability to be achieved without transparency, and it is possible to have transparency but no subsequent accountability in terms of consequences or punishments for those who breach the public's trust (Fox, 2007). For example, laws can be applied in an accountable way by delivering legal interpretations that rely on all available evidence and information, even if such evidence and information is not available to the public in general. In fact, the proprietary nature of such evidence is often considered vital for a fair legal process whereby investigators can be protected from adverse media attention and public scrutiny before delivering a verdict.

Although accountability is a more general concept, many specific types of open government policies aim to improve or enable it—often by drawing on elements of transparency, participation, and technology. For example, in addition to freedom of information laws, other areas of transparency that are especially relevant to fighting corruption are public hearings on proposed laws, public procurement and asset transparency, budget transparency, and revenue from natural resources and international aid (Murillo, 2015). Anticorruption policies also increasingly experiment with social media where users share information about internal government operations, thus creating a continual and collective monitoring mechanism of public officials (Stamati, Papadopoulos, & Anagnostopoulos, 2015). Fiscal openness policies have a similar goal—to mitigate corruption—but focus specifically on the problem of conflicts of interests between the assets of government agencies and the interests of citizens. They include asset disclosure laws forcing politicians to make clear what investments they have (Schnell, 2015) and disclosure standards on the divesting of state-owned enterprises (Guedhami & Pittman, 2011). Policy areas that involve lucrative industries, such as fossil fuels, minerals, and environmental impacts of businesses (Rashchupkina, 2015) or contacts with overseas governments (Winters, 2014), are key for fiscal openness policies.

The open government focus on accountability not only draws on many traditional uses of accountability but also has a number of unique features, especially insofar as open government marries accountability with technology. Open government policymakers increasingly try to use technological tools for better public accountability. Accountability in open government policies includes access to budget data, effective control by the legislature, and an effective role for civil society and other accountability advocates and watchdogs (Benito & Bastida, 2009; Piotrowski & Van Ryzin, 2007). Nonprofit and private sector public service providers see data about government spending and performance and adjust their efforts to obtain public sector projects. Openness in public procurement can both allow citizens and civil society organizations to keep a watchful eye on how public money is spent and further reduce information asymmetries between the government and nongovernmental organizations. As a result, the latter can market their products to the public sector more efficiently because they know more about the value of specific products and services and can understand their competition.

New digital forms of accountability aim to increase interaction between internal and external stakeholders rather than the traditional approach of procedures and rules for bureaucratic reporting (Schillemans, Van Twist, & Van Hommerig, 2013). Online notice and comment policies and spending transparency help accountability (Shkabatur, 2012). Some scholars have also argued that social media can play an important role in public accountability systems, especially as social media encourages outside political influences from civil society or the news media to become increasingly involved in discussing matters of public interest (Borge Bravo & Esteve Del Valle, 2017). Open data initiatives can also facilitate accountability by pooling data from diverse sources and giving a range of organizations permission to reuse the data (Janssen & Estevez, 2013), potentially by organizing and presenting the data in meaningful ways that encourage accountability-relevant goals (Schmidthuber et al., 2017; Weerakkody et al., 2017). For example, finance departments create interactive graphics with their data to demonstrate how funding allocations are being spent (Yavuz & Welch, 2014).

Technology Policies

We have described the three components of open government reforms and described several specific types of policy initiatives that characterize each. However, this picture of open government reform would be incomplete without more discussion of the technology dimensions of the reforms.

Almost all of the aforementioned policies rely on the innovative use of technology in one way or another. In the modern era, a type of technology-aided transparency called computer-mediated transparency emerged (Evans & Campos, 2013; Meijer, 2009; Welch & Wong, 2001). Similarly, Fung, Graham, and Weil (2007) argue that information and communication technology has led to a third wave of transparency policies that they call "targeted transparency" because the policies designed with transparency tools are tailored to achieving accountability with specific outputs or behavioral changes.

Some argue that open government is a similar type of electronic transparency initiative that should be considered an extension of e-government reforms that started in many governments around the world in the 1990s (e.g., Abu-Shanab, 2015; Hansson, Belkacem, & Ekenberg, 2015). On the other hand, open government initiatives clearly have their genesis in a long history of openness initiatives before the digital technology revolution, so there does not appear to be a strong case to the idea of limiting open government to the e-government sphere—though clearly technology does play an important role.

An important emphasis on technology is seen in many open government policies. Managerial openness in the twenty-first century has rapidly advanced by the application of new information communication technology products and services from the private sector. In the United States, President Bill Clinton's administration viewed technology as a way to improve the openness of government, such as with the creation of the Government Information Locator System (Lewis, 2000). The focus on transparency during the Obama administration was even further driven by applications of new digital technologies, such as social media, wikis, application programming interfaces, and open data (Jaeger & Bertot, 2010; McDermott, 2010).

Open government policies in all areas—transparency, participation, and accountability—could not continue as they are without the internet. The fact that open government has made major inroads on the reform agenda is due in large part to the invention and rapid global adoption of the internet. In fact, technology serves as the unifying agent of transparency, participation, and accountability by facilitating the interactive exchange of information. Technology also facilitates open systems and learning for the development of even more technologies and fosters the global spread of such systems.

However, the technological side of open government has also raised some challenging questions about the efficacy of the open government movement. Technology applied to transparency initiatives can have both positive and negative effects on government openness (Murillo, 2015). For example, while crowdsourcing initiatives can sometimes spur better government innovation (Mergel & Desouza, 2013), crowdsourcing has also often been proven to include only a limited number of participants, meaning that policies produced by crowdsourcing have unequal representation of citizen interests (Liu, 2017). Another negative perspective sees open government as a type of cost-saving corporate style of capitalism driven by technology that allows more participation by citizens and reduces financial outlays for the government (Catlaw & Sandberg, 2014). Finally, given that public life inevitably becomes more open following the gradual infiltration of digital technology services into all areas of human life, some worry that open government may lead to mass digital surveillance and automated decision making that diminishes the role of reasoned deliberation about public affairs.

In sum, open government approaches to public sector reform are generally characterized by these four major policy components. But are these reforms likely to be successful? The open government movement is not the first time that policymakers have attempted to fundamentally restructure government functions and relationships with society. To answer this question of what to expect from open government reform, we can turn to previous public sector reform attempts and learn from their successes and failures. While the open government movement has rapidly ascended into scholarly and public policy debate, its future is still hotly debated. By revisiting theories about how past public reforms have waxed and waned over time, we can question the positioning of open government among contemporary reform movements and evaluate its likely future prospects.

COMPETING VISIONS OF PUBLIC MANAGEMENT REFORM

As we have seen above, the open government movement has deep roots in longstanding traditions of democratic government. Further, since the spread of the internet as a popular tool for citizens in everyday life, government reform advocates from information rights, citizen participation, and digital democracy perspectives have all contributed toward a collection of public sector reform ideas, policies, and practices known as the open government movement. But open government is not the first type of public sector reform movement, nor is it the only type of reform that has changed the public sector—far from it. If we take a glance back at government institutions from history, we find many instances of powerful reform movements that sought to redesign and revamp existing institutions.

According to one scholar of the history of public management reform, Paul Light (1998), trends in public sector reform come and go like ocean tides. At one point in time, governments introduce changes to fight perceived inefficiency and waste in government. Then, at another time, they conceive a different purpose for government and instead begin to alter the system around fighting corruption or increasing the scientific rigor of policies. New reform movements arrive and then decline because of changes in dominant political and economic currents (Light, 1998). While there are other theories about public management reforms that do not view reform history as being as cyclical as Light's tidal thesis would have it, most scholars would agree that reforms should be viewed as a cumulative process involving the acts and interests of many actors and organizations. Another influential analysis of reform trends is that they comprise much more unforeseen events that punctuate slow processes of change (Baumgartner & Jones, 1991). But even this view of public sector reforms sees change as long-term and subject to forces that are mostly beyond the conscious control of specific individuals or groups. Government reform is a complex institutional process that is subject to longstanding political, legal, and cultural forces. To a certain extent, these forces constrain what is possible for champions of a new reform vision such as open government.

The structure of public organizations is in a permanent state of flux as government leaders make decisions about what goals and ideals their departments are designed to pursue. Government departments, agencies, and programs change, shifting over periods of routine organizational and political change fostered by electoral processes or, in rarer cases, by nondemocratic means such as violent overthrow. But sometimes when government decision makers change the allocation of resources or personnel in government, it is a result not of everyday turnover or planning but rather of a desire to create more fundamental change by altering the organizational system itself. Such changes can be either internally driven, fostered by external forces, or (more commonly) a combination of both. Such a concerted effort at fundamental change is a key characteristic of public sector reform.

Structural change in public management reform is not just about rearranging the furniture of government departments but also about adopting new tools, laws, processes, and values. It, therefore, involves changes both in structural and normative processes. Structurally, governments are composed of the physical architecture of organizations in things such as the departments, technologies, and people who make the administration of government. While some degree of change in these structural things is continual and normal, system-wide change aimed at redesigning the physical architecture by adopting new policies and responsibilities is unique to reform. However, in addition to the physical components, governments are also composed of normative systems of values: political ideas and institutional norms and processes. Such public values drive the physical characteristics of reform.

Critically, then, we must look to the dynamics and origins of public values when understanding how large-scale and local-scale factors converge in public sector reform. Public values are the ideals in society that permeate beliefs about how the public sector should be run—who should lead, the types of behaviors expected from leaders, what government's role should be, its ultimate goals, and the kinds of returns or outputs that citizens expect from an investment of public resources. Public values are highly changeable over time and can be hard to fathom, but they are still key to understanding the normative and structural decisions of reform (Charles, de Jong, & Ryan, 2011).

In the next section, we review key reform transitions of the last century, with a particular focus on the relevant public values. We can see in the open government reform movement a similar distinctiveness of values, but we can also trace a path of dependency, or at least similarity, with many of the other reform movements that preceded it. Better understanding these similarities can help us develop better-informed expectations of how open government may develop in the future. Should we understand open government reform as yet another tide driven by the political actors of its time—essentially recycling earlier reform ideas and destined to be soon replaced by a different focus—or as something different?

A Brief History of Modern Reforms

Scholars of public management reforms have been actively involved in the study and evaluation of different reform trends. Scholars now characterize the first phase of modern public administration as the orthodox public administration or alternatively *classical* public administration (Dunleavy & Hood, 1994; Denhardt & Denhardt, 2000; Lynn, 2001). It would be more accurate to call the orthodox public administration the first collection of scientific theories in Western public administration at the dawn of the twentieth century rather than a reform movement per se. Subsequent reform scholars and government decision makers used orthodox public administration as a base set of assumptions to build upon in subsequent reforms. Orthodox public administration is a Weberian approach to public administration, so named after the sociologist Max Weber. Orthodox public administration favored a machine-like organization of work units designed to process administrative tasks according to legal precepts and a rational division of tasks according to top-down government. Government reforms during the orthodox public administration period were oriented toward the craft of the skilled government administrator and featured having robust and practical skill sets, including counseling, stewardship, diplomacy, and political wisdom (Rhodes, 2016).

At a later point in the twentieth century, there was a shift in the focus of public administration, which emerged primarily in the United States. From approximately the 1950s to the 1970s, public administration thinkers led by Herbert Simon and Dwight Waldo tried to introduce new principles to challenge the orthodox approaches of public administration. Waldo's book *The Administrative State* (2017), first published in 1948, characterized traditional administrative approaches as aimless, unwieldy, and uninteresting, and he was critical of the rigid separation of the political and administrative spheres. While the focus of how to address these problems was different for Simon and Waldo, their work triggered a long-lasting quest for public officials to tackle administrative incompetence that Lynn (2001) called the "myth of the bureaucratic paradigm" and led to intense debate on the merits and failings of public sector reform in the search for the next big thing—a quest for new management styles that could make public organizations perform to their highest potential.

According to Frederickson (1976), what made the New Public Administration distinctive was a scientific shift to managing a slow process of doing government work more effectively that was more optimistic about the role of the state and public administrators. New Public Administration intellectuals put expert bureaucrats, as agents of public values, at the center of the political-administrative system of democratic government and argued that such experts were essential to delivering not just better government effectiveness but also better outcomes for democratic goals such as equity and fairness.

In the late 1980s and early 1990s, the quest for better government outcomes took on a distinctive new flavor with the rise of the New Public Management. The approach of the New Public Management was to use concepts derived from free-market economics and public choice theory. These theories suggested that self-interested actors in a free market with limited interference, entrepreneurial managers, and customer orientation could liberate the processes of managing public organizations and result in higher quality and efficiency of service delivery. The UK, under Prime Minister Margaret Thatcher, and the United States, under President Ronald Reagan, were the forerunners of the New Public Management reforms, though the cluster of changes associated with this movement would only be called New Public Management by public administration scholars in the 1990s (Hood, 1991).

But New Public Management policies were not restricted to government administrations on the right of the political spectrum, as the case of the management reforms in Sweden led by social democrats shows (Hood, 1995). New Public Management initiatives were prominent in governments with a range of political orientations in the UK, North America, Scandinavia, Australia, and New Zealand (Osborne, 2010b). Indeed, in the 1990s, the New Public Management approach continued in the United States under a center-left Democratic government. Spurred by the ideas outlined in the influential book *Reinventing Government* by David Osborne and Ted Gaebler (1992), Bill Clinton and Al Gore launched a federal-wide system of performance benchmarking in the National Performance Review.

The dominance of the New Public Management model of government reform in many countries around the world gave way to a kind of splintering of public management reforms that continues today. Currently, many new public sector reform movements exist side by side with previous management reforms and are integrated within the overall values and structure of these reforms. Some public management reforms identify with the New Public Management trend, but other efforts do not. Global or regional convergence toward one ideal of management is somewhat of a myth (Lynn, 2006; Pollitt & Bouckaert, 2011). This diversification of New Public Management defines the most recent phase of public management reform. In this phase, starting from about the year 2000, policymakers increasingly integrated New Public Management types of managerial reform with politically and socially oriented reform in the governance tradition. Thus, in the early 2000s, management became rivaled by another reform perspective focused on the concept of *governance* called the New Public Governance. New Public Governance takes a broader, more fundamental notion of government, its ultimate values, and its ability to sustain change by switching attention to government responsibility and capacity through intergovernmental and multisector partnerships (Cheung, 2005).

According to Park and Joaquin (2012), New Public Governance broadens the range of government values beyond a market efficiency perspective. Furthermore, this breadth requires that problem solving is done in a multisectoral, collaborative way; that is, through governance (see Emerson and Nabatchi, 2015). New Public Governance reform movements aim to address the perceived shortcomings of the New Public Management, such as a narrow focus on market principles and managerial control that has led to a thinning of administrative institutions, the hollowing of the state (Terry, 2005), and an obsession with governmental efficiency (Lynn, 2006; Welch & Wong, 2001).

In some respects, the open government approach straddles both the New Public Management and New Public Governance. On the one hand, open government has the New Public Management theorist's faith in private innovation working for a mutual benefit. On the other hand, open government, like the New Public Governance, also views proactive collaboration between governmental and nongovernmental organizations as critical to contemporary public management.

There are many clear distinctions among these different reform approaches in terms of the key values with which they seek to imbue public organizations. However, there is also substantial diversity within each of these categories. Increasingly, scholars note a splintering of approaches rather than the trends merging, dominating, or amalgamating into some sort of synthesis. According to Lodge and Gill (2011), New Public Management, widely perceived by scholars as on the decline, remains a dominant force in reform approaches. Moreover, Lodge and Gill say that the new reform efforts themselves are very fragmented. A number of new public sector reform ideas have been jostling for influence, including new public service (Denhardt & Denhardt, 2015), digital-era governance (Dunleavy et al., 2006), and the open government reform movement itself (De Blasio & Selva, 2016).

This recent period of fragmentation of public sector reform approaches is thus the milieu in which open government emerges. According to Greve (2015), what is unique about the recent scholarly theories of public sector reform is that new movements are now aiming at being the key *post*–New Public Management reform movement. They tend to draw on the major global impacts of information and communication technology and the power of the internet, with its claims to greater effectiveness, increases in network-like organizational structures, and citizen empowerment. La Porte, Demchak, and de Jong (2002) say that these trends are characterized by several shared common approaches to change, including novel uses of information technology, emphases on longer-term outcomes and broader societal challenges, and structures based on networks and collaboration between and within citizens and government.

One perspective that strives to give greater conceptual unity to these divergent later models of governance—of which open government is a part—is Anders Esmark's (2016) concept of *Late Modern Technocracy*. Historically, argues Esmark, we see common themes in each of the reform trends of modern public administration. Scholars have viewed government reforms as a perennial compromise among three basic governance models: bureaucracy, markets, and networks. However, the important new element that Esmark adds to this mix of three elements is *technology*. Late Modern Technocracy is a light-touch form of governance relying on new technologies, data management to assess performance and determine priorities, and engagement with citizens. In such an approach, the government plays more of a role as a platform provider serving to share information, bring together collaborators, and facilitate the transformation of public resources into economic and social value. The affinities between Esmark's concept of Late Modern Technocracy and open government as a reform movement are clear. Both emphasize La Porte, Demchak, and de Jong's (2002) values of digital government transformation, transparency, and a widening out of government obsession with economic efficiencies toward social and democratic values. In the next section, we build on these commonalities in order to apply the lessons from past public sector reform movements to better understand open government itself.

THE FATE OF PUBLIC SECTOR REFORM

Public management reforms can be analyzed and compared on two dimensions: First are the instrumental aspects, designed by decision makers as specific tools or processes to realize organizational changes. We call these the means of reform. Second are the normative aspects, coming from the value perspectives of reformers with attendant sets of ideas about the goals, norms, and ideals that the reforms aim for. We call these the ends of reform. These two elements can be used to better understand the processes of change that usher in a new reform perspective. But they can also help explain the wane or atrophy of reform perspectives. Instrumental processes in the reform's means can go wrong, while reform ends can suffer from internal contradictions, lack of integrity, or competition from other ideas about ends.

These challenges to means and ends can be divided into internal and external organizational foci, as shown in figure 2.1. The internal organizational focus concerns what goes on inside the organization, such as managing

		Reform dimension	
		Means	Ends
Organizational focus	Internal	Implementation problems	Goal ambiguity
	External	Structural barriers	Political conflicts

Figure 2.1
Public management reform and associated risks.
Source: Ingrams, Piotrowski, & Berliner (2020).

employees and decision-making processes. The external organizational focus is about what goes on between the organization and its external environment, such as relationships with other organizations and, especially, the politics that result from these relationships.

Hypothetically, reform movements could suffer problems in any one of the four ways. Each way is applied and elaborated below to the specific case of open government. We apply scholarly research on reform to develop evidence of the full set of risks that characterize each of these four problem areas. In each, we consider the ways that these problems may befall the case of open government with its own set of values, logics of change, and relevant sets of public management and international actors.

Implementation Problems
Design-reality gaps

The success of open government reforms is related to the ability of reformers to design and implement changes that reflect the values of the reform. For smooth implementation, the designs of open government need to be internally communicated among organizational members. However, cracks may begin to appear in the structure of reforms if gaps emerge between the original ideas of the policy design and the reality of their implementation. As these gaps widen, the probability increases that reforms will fail (Baier, March, & Saetren, 1986).

In the Open Government Partnership, a large number of open government programs fail to be completed on time or with all the stipulated proposals included. However, even if there are no clear instances of failure, the outputs and outcomes of such reforms may simply be hard to evaluate because aspects are hard to detect and measure. In open government, the level of openness that has been implemented by a government seems to be a particularly difficult thing to quantify. Ambiguous goals that are subjective or workload-oriented, rather than objective- and results-oriented, may especially increase the risks of such failure (Heinrich, 2012). Given the oft-cited characterization of open government goals, such as participation and transparency being subjective and ambiguous (e.g., Yu & Robinson, 2012), the risk of design-reality gaps appear particularly acute for open government reform.

Insufficient resources

Many countries where open government reforms are being implemented lack organizational and human resources capacities, skills, and adequate public infrastructure even to effectively deliver the necessary public goods such as education, public transportation, and defense. Further, open government initiatives follow on from years of New Public Management reforms involving structural readjustment programs that encourage increasing reliance on global economic markets and privatization. These changes can make it difficult to organize new public sector reforms centrally. According to Pollitt & Dan (2011), it has also led to the "hollowing" of state institutions through private sector partnerships, has made cost control difficult, and resulted in highly complex governance structures. Open government reformers in many countries inherit these hollowed-out governance institutions and must seek to implement new openness policies where there are internal challenges, such as reform shortages, that continue to be experienced in the wake of the global credit crunch in 2008.

Cross-country relevance

The setting of any public sector reform is a reflection of the unique characteristics of the local or regional environment. The setting includes characteristics such as the quality of networks between government and other organizations, styles and attitudes of leadership and service, and cultural norms around the idea of change (Cole & Jones, 2005). For this reason, even globally successful reforms such as New Public Management were implemented in a more fragmented or contextually nuanced way than we might expect given the nominal adoption of many governments (Osborne, 2010b). In fact, if we set New Public Management as a benchmark for successful public management reform, then the expectation for open government is still of weak potential to be replicated in different country contexts.

Political influence

Problems of implementation in the public sector inevitably encounter complications in the political environment where there are multiple actors with competing interests. Politics has a profound influence on reform. Open government is a global movement, but every country has a unique type of balance among politicians, bureaucrats, and civil society that creates politicization (Moon & Ingraham, 1998). Whatever the style or approach of reform that is being adopted, in order to make reforms enduring, reformers require a certain set of skills and strategies. Donald Kettl (2006) says that the "Modernizing Government [movement], like much cutting-edge work in government reform, struggles to deal with the inescapable dilemma: the search for central, driving themes, on the one hand, and the need to recognize the vast variation among nations, on the other" (315).

Long-term effects of politics mean that it is necessary to study the results of reforms over a long period and that determining the degree of success in a reform movement may rely on an analysis of a complex series of long-term consequences (Callander, 2011).

Politics is inevitable in reform, but policymakers also need to control the formal political *process* of reform. A danger of reforms is that they end up serving ideological and political objectives more than the original goal of improved public sector performance (Brewer & Kellough, 2016; Kettl, 2000). Because different political groups in open government may favor one specific side of a values tension over another (for example, efficiency vs. transparency), it makes it highly likely that political influences favoring a particular set of public values will drive the reform agenda (Durant, 2008). Furthermore, if the balance of political groups is strong, reforms may endure a compromise of values that ultimately leads to implementation being unworkable.

Goal Ambiguity
Inherent value ambiguities

The significant characteristics of public sector reforms described earlier conflict on key points. However, research on public management reform has found that a chief determinant of the success or failure of reform is the way it disagrees internally within its own set of values and principles. In other words, reforms can also have internal disagreements or conflicts among reform principles. This tension is inevitable because reforms seek to accomplish multiple things at the same time that may not be able to coexist comfortably or at all. Indeed, governance is an inherently difficult process that involves trying to balance features such as authority and autonomy that are intrinsically in tension and can undermine managerial effectiveness (Rainey & Jung, 2014).

Several different types of values are in tension in reforms. De Graaf, Huberts, and Smulders (2016) say that there are three governance categories where the attempts to address public values tensions are focused: *proper governance* (integrity, equality, and lawfulness), *performing governance* (effectiveness and efficiency), and *responsive governance* (participation, transparency, legitimacy, and accountability). This divide can be seen clearly in the advocacy camps behind the open government movements. There is a camp focusing on open data, with its attachment to concepts of private innovation and efficiency, and, on the other hand, there is a camp focusing on the democratic function of information, with its attachment to concepts such as participation for supporting public debate and protecting freedom of expression. However, scholars go beyond these two to identify groups of the most central public values. According to Jørgensen and Bozeman (2007), there are as many as eight fundamental values of public governance. Choices must frequently be made among them by reformers, as the values cannot all be maintained simultaneously (Hood, 1991). Jørgensen and Bozeman's eight values are (1) *human dignity*, (2) *sustainability*, (3) *citizen involvement*, (4) *openness*, (5) *secrecy*, (6) *compromise*, (7) *integrity*, and (8) *robustness*. Open government emphasizes at least three of these values (citizen involvement, openness, and integrity) and thus may succumb to problems resulting from the way they conflict with one another.

Interorganizational complexity

As discussed above, tensions among different reform values are, to some degree, inevitable. Reformers must decide how to balance such values. But tensions are not only inherent in the kinds of values chosen by reformers; they are also a product complexity that occurs in modern styles of governance that rely on interorganizational collaboration. This complexity also affected the New Public Management, which, by seeking greater efficiency and flexibility in government, introduced conflicting values among the competing interests of market, state, and civil society (Jørgensen, 1999; Yeung, 2005). New Public Management reforms tended to focus this balance on the "soft power" of networks and the "hard edge" of bureaucracy (Pollitt

& Bouckaert, 2011). Each of these values tends to come with different types of interorganizational arrangements.

Like earlier movements, open government reformers are torn between implementing organizational changes that reflect administrative modernization through better technological efficiency and greater participation from citizens (Nalbandian, 2005). For example, public management reform movements that give more priority to informal institutional arrangements, such as the way informal networks are treated in New Public Governance, can struggle to implement reforms and administrative tools, such as regulations, fines, and incentives (de Bruijn & Dicke, 2006). Open government, by aiming to collaborate more with nongovernmental organizations, also introduces the likelihood of tensions resulting from organizational hybrids, like new public governance. Some evidence suggests that despite the flexibility they offer, collaborations with the private sector or civil society are particularly likely to have complex organizational structures that create ambiguity that then can lead to organizational failure (Cobb & Rubin, 2006; Demortain, 2004).

Interdepartmental discrepancies

Value conflicts in a public management reform may exist not just over a period of time or between different types of organizations but also between different governmental departments or policy areas. There are many types of public values involved in different spheres of public governance—from relationships among administrators and the environment and other stakeholders to intra-organizational actions and the transformation of public interests into decisions. Each of these internal spheres of governmental relationships has a particular constellation of associated values (Jørgensen & Bozeman, 2007). Open government has a whole range of different policy areas and is likely to suffer tensions between the different constellations of values demonstrated by each area. For example, information-intense phases of a project shape the value of accountability, while phases involving collaboration with external advisors or legal and financial complexity affect the value of understanding (Reynaers, 2014). Thus, effective implementation of reforms requires decision makers to make choices about how to balance and synthesize competing reform values in instrumental decisions about organizational processes or goals (Moulton, 2009; Nalbandian, 2005; Pandey et al., 2016).

Structural Barriers
Institutional forces

While some reforms may be wavelike in the sense of being unlikely to continue in the same form over the long term, the opposite problem can also affect attempts to reform. That is, despite changes in government rhetoric and attention-grabbing policy initiatives, the old powers and habits of institutions and groups stay in charge as the most significant external drivers of the reforms. Reform possibilities undergo a process of cultural screening by administrative traditions consisting of institutional structures and cultural ideas about how government and administration should look (Christensen & Lægreid, 2007; Bach et al., 2017). According to Borrás and Radaelli (2011), reforms are driven by "strategic and long-term institutional arrangements" of institutions (463). In this perspective, open government reform is driven by deeply entrenched institutional forces in society that keep control over reforms even though the reforms may seem like a current change (i.e., like a new wave).

Jane Gingrich (2015) calls these powerful instrumental forces the *logics of administrative change*. According to Gingrich's theory, history tends to recycle through reform approaches, but they always emphasize the same value perspective or logic. All governments have these logics, and they tend to shape each subsequent phase of reform. In open government reforms, the logics may strongly influence how decisions are made to balance the interests of political leaders, technology innovators, civil society actors, and citizens. While open government poses several new reform ideas on paper, these logics of administrative change are still in place and therefore influence the prospects of the reforms as they unfold. Deeply entrenched institutional logics inevitably shape the new reform and destine the reform to succumb to a similar set of problems.

The influence of global powers

The entrenched institutional processes of reform show that instrumental processes of domestic open government reform trends are in constant tension with international processes, even when the global picture suggests a dominant process of adoption and integration. Country- and local-level processes that reveal unique cultural or institutional characteristics of an administrative system are intertwined with the large-scale processes of change (Bevir, Rhodes, & Weller, 2003; Pollitt & Bouckaert, 2011). Country- and local-level factors influence the particular paths that reforms take but, simultaneously, larger structural economic and political forces exert pressure and shape the scale and depth of the reforms. We can see evidence of this pattern if we look back on other recent public management reforms. For example, *rechsstaat* countries, such as Germany and the Netherlands, have a strong legal concept of administrative decision making, which means that reforms such as New Public Management and New Public Governance, while influential, are controlled by a system of courts and legal hierarchy (Bach et al., 2017).

Open government reforms also are driven by global political powers. Intergovernmental organizations, such as the Organization for Economic Cooperation and Development, and international multilateral organizations, such as the World Bank, have adopted their own views of open government reforms, and they have financial and political instruments that they wield in order to direct country reforms in a certain direction. While such influences ostensibly have the objective of creating better governance systems, they are criticized for being heavy-handed and creating country path dependency, which prevents the emergence of locally grown reforms.

Economic and technological developments

Additionally, large-scale global processes involving technological developments and economic shifts can influence the shape of reform (Charles, de Jong, & Ryan, 2011). Open government reforms depend on the affordances provided for technological innovations. Through mimetic processes of learning, imitation, and technology sharing among countries, reform movements can diffuse across whole regions leading to similar patterns of change (DiMaggio & Powell, 1991), while economic relationships in terms of trading goods and information are a channel for dispersion of ideas and sharing resources that support reforms. So intergovernmental processes between countries, even across entire global regions, can be significantly influenced by economic fortune.

The problem with these processes for open government reformers is that they are very difficult for individual decision makers to control, let alone the country governments of which they are part, and the path of reform under such circumstances is very unpredictable. Will open government reform end up applied as a one-size-fits-all model by global pressures and intergovernmental institutions? All types of reforms evidence a tension between these global forces from major international institutions and those from local forces. In these instances, domestic actors can do little to adapt new reform ideas to national and local needs.

Political Conflicts
Institutional crises

Research by Boin and t'Hart (2003) shows how limitations in public management reforms come fundamentally from the fact that reforms are driven not by rational-instrumental visions of improvement, as we might expect, but rather from crises that no one planned or predicted. Along this line of reasoning, decision makers drive reforms not for the novelty or potential impact of a reform per se but rather for the need to manage systems that no longer function. This also has implications for the longevity of reforms, which are used to tackle particular crises—not to deliver long-term solutions. Thus, when the New Public Management emerged as a novel reform approach, it was primarily rivaling a prior approach viewing bureaucracies as poorly functioning and bureaucratic (Pollitt & Bouckaert, 2011; Randma-Liiv, 2008). The New Public Management was subsequently treated in Western administrative traditions as a panacea for an impossible range of different bureaucratic problems (Hood, 1991).

The same logic could be applied to open government reform, which has been accused of being a technology-inspired reinterpretation of New Public Management ideas of market liberalism (Bates, 2014; Catlaw & Sandberg, 2014). Some of the drivers of the open government movement, such as the decline of public trust in government and the growing awareness among citizens of government (under)performance and the need to monitor, could lead to knee-jerk reaction without consideration of solving underlying problems of public sector malaise (Green, 2010). If this was the case, we should hold little confidence in its capacity for longevity.

Faddism and short-term perspectives

Open government reformers claim to have a bold plan for change that could bring about fundamental improvements in the public sector. But as we have seen in the discussion of public management reform history, the various types of reform always touted their novelty in order to communicate what value they would add to existing governance practices. Critics of reforms have argued that despite the claims of reform champions, upon closer inspection, the originality of new reform ideas is often unclear (Lynn, 2001).

We characterized reform movements earlier as fluctuating, evanescent phenomena, perhaps analogous to ocean tides, as Paul Light suggested. These characterizations expose reforms to criticism that they are really just fads or temporary fashions that exist as an expression of the desire for something new and different rather than what their champions claim, which is that they are rational-instrumental efforts with intrinsic values of greater effectiveness, efficiency, or better governance.

Competing policy actors

Open government reformers join a chorus of other political actors with different visions for public sector reform. In Kingdon's (1984) multiple streams theory, this competition for policy attention is viewed as a normal part of democratic government. The multiple streams approach to policy change involves numerous and shifting actors and technology management challenges that converge to shape new policy goals and preferences. Occasional shifts to new models of reform are called *policy windows* because, at these sporadic moments, the multiple streams have come together in the right combination of unsolved external problems, pressure for change, and the means to achieve change. Open government is exerting strong sway on the public policy marketplace. But the shifting character of policy windows underlines the seeming fate of many public management reforms as short-lived trends rather than rationally conceived plans with long-term potential (Zahariadis, 2008).

CONCLUSIONS

The idea of open government has deep roots in the theory of government. Since at least the time of the Enlightenment, scholars have debated about the kinds of systems that adequately serve the values and needs of governing and citizenship in a democracy, and they have put the value of openness at the center of those debates. But only since the growth of the mass media—and, more recently, the internet—has the governing basis for access to information and participation created a specific approach to governance focused entirely around openness. Open government emphasizes three different policy areas—transparency, participation, and accountability—and is supported by the fourth component of technology.

Can policymakers be serious that this type of reform can have a meaningful and lasting impact on the organization of governments? We argued here that answering this question involves first considering open government reform alongside the other major reform movements in the modern era of public administration. Open government belongs to an emergent group of reforms called Late Modern Technocracy that emphasizes technology and a mixed approach to adapting the benefits of prior movements such as the New Public Management and New Public Governance. It may be hasty to declare the passing away of these earlier reforms entirely, as one of the critical characteristics of the Late Modern Technocracy is the way these earlier reforms are used and integrated in new ways.

Open government adopts some of the ideas of New Public Management reforms, such as private and nonprofit sector collaboration, a focus on service delivery, and performance measurement. But it is also completely new in other ways, such as in its interest in democracy and technology and its attraction to addressing a diverse range of policy and social goals. What can we expect from this new reform movement? Based on the problems suffered by the New Public Management, there are many reasons to be skeptical. We have highlighted four of the weightiest problems and elaborated how these problems could play out in the case of open government. There has been plenty of time now for public administration scholars to look back on New Public Management, and their findings suggest that we should be very cautious indeed when listening to the optimistic claims of open government supporters.

3 THE OPEN GOVERNMENT PARTNERSHIP AS AN INTERNATIONAL INSTITUTION

To better understand the Open Government Partnership, in this chapter, we place it in the context of both other transnational multistakeholder initiatives and international institutions more broadly. International institutions are "sets of rules meant to govern international behavior" (Simmons & Martin, 2002, 328). These include formal intergovernmental organizations with international legal status, such as United Nations bodies, international financial institutions, and treaty organizations in domains such as trade, public health, the environment, human rights, and anticorruption. But even informal governance arrangements without formal legal status can be considered international institutions when they are based on sustained mutual understandings and practices that shape the behaviors of states and other actors and endure over time, such as international regimes (Haggard & Simmons, 1987) or decentralized policy coordination and legal harmonization on the basis of mutual policy changes (Drezner, 2007).

Transnational multistakeholder initiatives are a particular form of international institution, characterized primarily by their more diverse membership but often also with more flexible and/or informal rules. Raymond and DeNardis (2015, 573) define multistakeholderism as "as two or more classes of actors engaged in a common governance enterprise concerning issues they regard as public in nature and characterized by polyarchic authority relations constituted by procedural rules."[1] Brockmyer and Fox (2015, 11) more specifically define transnational multistakeholder initiatives as "voluntary partnerships between governments, civil society, and the private sector."

Multistakeholder initiatives offer important contrasts with more traditional international institutions like intergovernmental organizations. The latter tend to be state-centric, painstakingly negotiated through formal treaties, and grounded in international law. But multistakeholder initiatives, as their name implies, incorporate stakeholders of multiple types—usually including some combination of states, firms, civil society groups, local governments, private foundations, or other international bodies. Multistakeholder initiatives also often emerge more quickly and flexibly than do traditional intergovernmental organizations. As such, the rise of transnational multistakeholder initiatives in global governance is often seen as complementing and filling gaps left by more traditional forms of international institutions (e.g., Mueller, 2010; Duncan, 2015; Andonova, Hale, & Roger, 2017; Kahler, 2018; Reinsberg & Westerwinter, 2021), particularly through their abilities to overcome some of the traditional constraints, limitations, and conflicts of "hard law" institutions (Abbott & Snidal, 2000).

MULTISTAKEHOLDER INITIATIVES AND INTERNATIONAL INSTITUTIONS

Multistakeholder initiatives have thrived across many different domains, reflecting a general trend toward networks and away from a strict market/hierarchy distinction in global governance. Prominent examples seek to set private standards or otherwise govern the practices of firms in contested areas such as labor, human rights, and the environment, including the Fair Labor Association, the Forest Stewardship Council, the Voluntary Principles on Security and Human Rights, the United Nations Global Compact, and the Kimberley Process Certification Scheme. Other multistakeholder initiatives seek to coordinate public and private efforts toward complex global challenges, such as the Global Alliance for Vaccines and Immunization, the Global Partnership for Education, or the Global Fund to Fight AIDS, Tuberculosis and Malaria. Still, others aim to govern policy areas that are fundamentally global and multisectoral, such as the Internet Corporation for Assigned Names and Numbers and the Extractive Industries Transparency Initiative in the domain of natural resources governance.

In many ways, the Open Government Partnership clearly resembles these other transnational multistakeholder initiatives. Its governance structure features states and civil society representatives with formal parity in their representation and authority on the Steering Committee, and other international bodies and donor organizations also play more informal stakeholder roles. Its rules are not legalized in the form of international treaty agreements, pose relatively flexible obligations, and have little direct enforcement. And like most multistakeholder initiatives, the origins of the Open Government Partnership stand in stark contrast to the slow, formalized, treaty-centric formation of most traditional intergovernmental organizations.

However, the Open Government Partnership is also distinct from many other transnational multistakeholder initiatives in that it does *not* count firms among its formal members or governing body participants. Only states (and, more recently, local governments) are direct members of the Open Government Partnership. Further, as Brockmyer and Fox (2015) discuss, the Open Government Partnership is one of several multistakeholder initiatives focusing specifically on public sector reform itself, alongside others such as the Extractive Industries Transparency Initiative and Open Contracting Partnership.

This chapter places the origins and design of the Open Government Partnership in the context of key concepts in the study of these features of international institutions overall—both traditional and multistakeholder. The guiding motivation of this chapter is to assess which set of dynamics the Open Government Partnership most exemplifies—the old politics of traditional intergovernmental organizations or the new flexible and entrepreneurial models of transnational multistakeholder initiatives. After first reviewing the broader literature in brief, this chapter tells the Open Government Partnership's origin story in detail, from its beginnings as an idea among United States White House staff in 2010 to its launch alongside the United Nations General Assembly in September 2011. Finally, this chapter then presents an overview of the structure and functions of the Open Government Partnership as of roughly 2019 to provide the background for the rest of the book's empirical evidence.

The Creation and Design of International Institutions

Why are institutions created in the first place, and what shapes their design? In this section, we summarize three different theoretical approaches to these questions, emphasizing alternately functional explanations, the agency of policy entrepreneurs, or power and conflict. This draws on past research in international relations but with a particular emphasis on the implications for multistakeholder initiatives like the Open Government Partnership. This focus on institutional design is crucial for later understanding of how different design features enable or constrain different pathways of impact on governance reform.

First, functionalist accounts of creation and design emphasize the specific problems to be solved and governance tasks to be accomplished. That is, they explain the creation and design of institutions by their functions. These may be the direct issues to be governed or second-order problems, such as collective action problems, transaction costs, and information asymmetries that otherwise impede effective governance (e.g., Keohane, 1984). Koremenos, Lipson, and Snidal (2001) argue that the design features of international institutions—namely, their membership rules, issue scope, centralization, control rules, and flexibility—are rational responses to the structures of the problems they aim to address, the number of actors involved, and uncertainty about behavior. Reinsberg and Westerwinter (2021) explicitly relate these factors to multistakeholder initiatives, suggesting that particularly complex global issues make their more flexible institutional designs more attractive. Similarly, Abbott and Snidal (2000) emphasize how key institutional design choices are rational responses to different problem structures, issue types, and levels of uncertainty over future changes, as well as to differing preferences, which we discuss subsequently.

More recent research, often applied specifically to multistakeholder initiatives and other less formal international institutions, takes a more meta-level or "ecological" functionalist view emphasizing how existing arrays of institutions relate to one another and the potential resulting overlaps or gaps. Thus Abbott, Green, and Keohane's (2016) organizational ecology approach suggests that new institutional forms will emerge in "niches" of low organizational density. Green (2014) sees forms of private authority by nonstate actors as emerging where powerful states cannot agree on a course of action and thus leave an absence of governance. Similarly, Gehring and Faude (2014) emphasize divisions of labor across institutions; Andonova, Hale, and Roger (2017) emphasize complementarities; and Reinsberg and Westerwinter (2021) argue that new institutions will avoid duplicating tasks of existing ones. These perspectives suggest another functional motivation for multistakeholder initiatives as fulfilling certain governance functions by *filling gaps* in existing global governance regimes.

A second approach instead emphasizes the agency of key governance entrepreneurs, who strategically seek to create and design new institutions in order to achieve their policy goals. Many scholars have emphasized transnational activists and civil society groups as norm entrepreneurs (Finnemore & Sikkink, 1998) or policy entrepreneurs (Stone, 2019). But Andonova (2017) emphasizes the key role played by *existing* intergovernmental organizations—such as the World Bank or United Nations bodies—as entrepreneurs leading the establishment of new institutional forms like multistakeholder initiatives. And similarly, Abbott and Snidal (2010, 317) see transnational governance initiatives as emerging primarily through "orchestration" by intergovernmental organizations themselves.

Third, other perspectives place greater emphasis on the roles of politics, power, and conflict in the creation and design of international institutions. Longstanding realist critiques expect international institutions to accomplish nothing that would not have happened anyway and suggest that they primarily serve the interests of powerful states. Notably, however, the early realist prediction that international institutions cannot outlive the global structural circumstances of their creation already does not seem to apply to the Open Government Partnership, given that it endured and outlasted the waning of US leadership and interest after 2016. Others suggest that powerful states prefer more informal governance forms that place fewer constraints on their behind-the-scenes influence (Stone, 2013; Vabulas & Snidal, 2013).

In terms of the design of institutions, many more conflict-oriented perspectives emphasize the preferences and bargaining power of key actors, with institutional design decisions reflecting necessary compromises among the interests of different stakeholders competing for influence. For Abbott and

Snidal (2000), states tend to resist "hard law" characteristics of precision, obligation, and delegation and, in particular, are concerned about the "sovereignty costs" of institutions—the loss of domestic authority over decision making. Other scholars posit a tradeoff between stringency and membership in the design of institutions (Prakash & Potoski, 2007; Berliner & Prakash, 2012; Bernauer et al., 2013). As the depth of institutions increases—incorporating stronger monitoring and enforcement provisions—fewer members will wish to join, resulting in less breadth.

For multistakeholder initiatives, these conflicts can play out on multiple levels. The first is between civil society actors—whose participation is essential for the legitimacy and expertise that they bring—and the participating states or firms who agree to undertake some new or different action. Civil society generally prefers greater precision, obligation, delegation, and more stringent monitoring and enforcement provisions. Participating states or firms generally prefer weaker such rules so that they can enjoy the benefits of membership while bearing less in the way of adjustment and/or sovereignty costs. But there can also be contention *among* different types of stakeholders. Some states (or, in other contexts, perhaps even some firms) may be genuine reformers for either principled and/or internal reasons and thus prefer more stringent design features than other states. Different stakeholders may vary in their preferences along the depth-breadth frontier. Some, even in civil society, may prefer an institutional design featuring weaker rules in exchange for the potential benefits of larger membership. Berliner and Prakash (2012) document these types of tensions at play in the design and ultimate membership of the United Nations Global Compact, with states and intergovernmental organizations largely championing the multistakeholder initiative for its breadth of membership, while civil society networks were much more critical of its weak monitoring and enforcement rules.

We highlight several different theoretical perspectives—not necessarily mutually exclusive—that are potentially relevant to the creation and design of multistakeholder initiatives. Functionalist approaches see multistakeholder initiatives as responses to complex global problems, gaps in global governance, and limitations of traditional institutional models. Agency-based approaches emphasize entrepreneurship and orchestration by key actors, particularly nonstate actors and intergovernmental organizations. Conflict-based approaches emphasize the institutional design as a matter of bargaining among different sets of actors—often but not always states and civil society—with different preferences over stringency of rules and breadth of membership.

The Membership of International Institutions and Multistakeholder Initiatives

Why do potential members *join* international institutions? In the first place, they balance expected future costs and benefits. As noted already, these costs include both the adjustment costs of any required changes in policy and/or behavior and the sovereignty costs of lost authority over decision making. The benefits most straightforwardly include the expected value of the governance tasks to be accomplished or the international cooperation to be institutionalized. Such benefits are most visible in economic domains such as trade policy or regulatory coordination.

But many international institutions are concerned with not only economic policies but also states' internal practices, particularly in terms of human rights, democracy, and corruption. In these cases, scholars have turned to broader conceptions of the potential benefits that international institutions can offer. Many liberal perspectives, for example, emphasize domestic political goals of membership in international institutions, such as locking in democracy or good governance (e.g., Moravcsik, 2000) or satisfying key interest groups (e.g., Simmons, 2009). Institutionalist perspectives emphasize how membership can make commitments more credible to external audiences (e.g., Simmons, 2000; Simmons & Danner, 2010). More constructivist approaches emphasize less material external dynamics, including the symbolic force of global norms, the pursuit of international legitimacy, or even pure isomorphic pressure to imitate others (e.g., Meyer et al., 1997; Finnemore & Sikkink, 1998; Wotipka & Tsutsui, 2008).

Similar approaches are relevant for membership in transnational multistakeholder initiatives. Some members—whether states or firms—may be sincere reformers who value the explicit goals of the initiative. Others may be responding more to external normative or isomorphic pressures. Still others may be attracted by a range of benefits—such as symbolic legitimacy, a reputation for reform (David-Barrett & Okamura, 2016), or even potential direct material benefits like increased investment or aid. Of course, in some cases, members may calculate that they can enjoy such benefits of membership without actually making any costly adjustments (e.g., Berliner & Prakash, 2012, 2014, 2015). A final possibility, however—and one that emerges as particularly relevant in the evidence that follows—is that at least some members have actually *miscalculated*, anticipating that membership requires less adjustment than is actually the case. This is a similar dynamic to what Schnell (2018) documents in the case of domestic transparency and anticorruption reforms in Romania.

The Impacts of International Institutions and Multistakeholder Initiatives

Turning to the *effects* of international institutions, a long literature in international relations—only briefly summarized here—debates what effects they have and how. Some scholars see the most important roles of institutions in their abilities to provide information, set standards, reduce transaction costs of collective action, and contribute to dispute resolution, while others see their most important roles as spreading and institutionalizing global norms and spurring processes of social learning. For Abbott and Snidal (2010), international institutions can also "orchestrate" by mobilizing and coordinating actions by other public, private, and international actors.

But a more specific question is of utmost importance for the many membership-based institutions that incorporate formal or informal rules and standards with which members ought to comply: How and why do states comply—or not—with these commitments? For those institutions—including many transnational multistakeholder initiatives—whose governance goals require behavioral and/or policy change by members, this compliance question is paramount. Chapter 1 summarized some of the key existing approaches to this question, particularly as applied to traditional international institutions. Importantly, many of these perspectives suggest that only stringent monitoring and enforcement can ensure member compliance, otherwise many members instrumentally seek only window-dressing membership. But other perspectives see broader opportunities for compliance through learning, socialization, or capacity-building.

These questions are clearly relevant to the Open Government Partnership, given its limited monitoring and enforcement provisions. In the case of another transnational multistakeholder initiative—though with firms rather than states as the key members—Berliner and Prakash (2015) reach pessimistic conclusions on compliance with the United Nations Global Compact. They find that while members do undertake more superficial corporate social responsibility efforts than nonmembers, members actually fare *worse* in terms of more costly, meaningful adjustments.

We return to this debate in chapter 4, where we advocate looking beyond compliance alone and instead emphasize the potential for *indirect* rather than *direct* pathways of change.

THE ORIGIN STORY

Motivations and Methodology

In telling the Open Government Partnership's origin story, we sought to go beyond existing public accounts through in-depth reviews of contemporaneous documents and accounts and interviews with several participants. This approach enables us to pay close attention to the questions discussed in the previous section. In particular, we sought to uncover key moments of uncertainty or contention that may have shaped the trajectory of the Open Government Partnership's creation and design and the goals, preferences, and contributions of the different actors involved. Importantly, it is the resulting institutional design that shapes our subsequent discussion of the potential pathways of impact for membership in the Open Government Partnership.

We drew on an array of different sources in the research for this section. First, we conducted an in-depth review of contemporaneous coverage and discussion of events as they unfolded, particularly emphasizing reporting and commentaries by participants and observers. The authors themselves also followed these developments contemporaneously beginning in 2011, both via social media and email lists as well as through many in-person discussions and attendance at some events. Second, we drew on several published retrospectives, including a 2013 special issue of the *Stanford Social Innovation Review*. Third, we drew on official government and Open Government Partnership documents themselves. Fourth, we conducted interviews with several participants across multiple sectors and in multiple countries.

Interviews included multiple current and former government officials, representatives of different Open Government Partnership secretariat functions, and representatives of nongovernmental entities, whether civil society groups—from several different countries—or foundations. Interviews were conducted in 2018 and 2019. All interviewees were assured that they would only be identified by sector and/or country without naming individuals or identifying specific organizations. As such, we attribute quotes below only to the relevant sector and, in some cases, country. We reference these as GO for current or former government officials and NGO for nongovernmental organization representatives, whether civil society or foundation.

Setting the Stage

The idea for what became the Open Government Partnership first emerged in the Obama administration's National Security Council, where Samantha Power—well known for her work and writing on human rights—was senior director for multilateral affairs and human rights, and Jeremy Weinstein—taking leave from his academic position at Stanford University—was director for development and democracy.

Two main background developments set the stage for this idea—the emergence of the open government movement and growing dissatisfaction with existing models of international cooperation and governance promotion.

First was the emergence of the open government movement as a specific priority of the Obama administration, an emerging new model of public sector reform (the focus of chapter 2), and as a frame to potentially link multiple existing reform agendas. The Obama administration had famously issued an Open Government Directive—emphasizing transparency, participation, and collaboration in government—on its first day in office. This established open government as a major priority for the administration and something that could increasingly be linked to global reform efforts.

Further, although many of the constituent themes of open government—such as transparency, participation, and technology in government—had long featured in both domestic and global advocacy, the years leading up to 2010 saw increasing tendencies to link their distinct issue areas, policy proposals, and advocacy networks under the common heading of "open government." Officials saw this, too, as an opportunity and a chance to further catalyze these linkages across issue silos. A former government official said:

> We had a whole emerging kind of intellectual and experimental and experiential movement around transparency and accountability reforms that had not been knitted together in any concrete way. So, you had your FOIA people, you had your participatory budgeting people, you had your technology and citizen engagement people, civic tech. You had traditional human rights and civil liberties kinds of folks. You had your natural resource transparency community. . . . There was a whole set of organizations pushing around ideas related to governance reform . . . that could be potentially knitted together and harnessed. (Interview, GO)

The second background development was a growing fatigue with existing models—of international cooperation, good governance efforts, and democracy promotion—and a search for new possibilities. Traditional international institutions were seen as too slow and bureaucratic. Traditional international treaties were seen as leading to lowest-common-denominator standards in order to gain near-universal ratification and increasingly difficult to gain political support domestically. Traditional aid conditionality and democracy promotion were often seen as top-down Western impositions lacking in domestic buy-in and often leading to only superficial reforms. On the other hand, new ideas about multistakeholder cooperation, learning networks, soft power, and international norms all offered the potential for new approaches.

One past government official said:

> We were totally informed by the experience of all the prior UN kinds of efforts where governmental peer review is meant to drive progress, but that's a process that yields nothing, right? Or relatively little. And so . . . the idea was that change is going to come from inside the country. (Interview, GO)

Another noted:

> A lot of democracy programming tends to be funding for projects. Some of which is quite good. There's less focus sometimes on how do you really get to the governance that gives you the institutional foundation that over time can yield the benefits. So, you can train election observers, but how do you get the style of governance? . . . So, I think a lot of it was, "How are we going to approach democracy in a developmental fashion as opposed to in a project?" (Interview, GO)

In 2013 in *Stanford Social Innovation Review*, Jeremy Weinstein discusses these issues at length and presents them as having been key motivations for the creation of the Open Government Partnership. He notes a tradeoff between the "legitimacy and authority" of international institutions with "broad or near-universal membership" with the fact that "to secure agreement among a diverse set of countries, significant compromise is typically required." He also notes frequent critiques of international institutions as "opaque, highly bureaucratic, and resistant to change" (Weinstein, 2013, 3).

Weinstein also hails the potential of new forms of multilateral cooperation, which he calls "mixed coalitions," drawing on examples like the Global Fund Against AIDS, Tuberculosis, and Malaria and the International Campaign to End Landmines. He praises such models for their successes as "tackling issues that are not being adequately addressed by existing institutions" and for their abilities to "rely on voluntary and collaborative means of generating action, prioritizing meaningful actions over binding commitments that are routinely ignored," and to "incorporate the expertise and active participation of nongovernmental players" (Weinstein, 2013, 5).

"Get That Paragraph"

On the basis of these background developments, officials in the National Security Council began putting together an idea for some form of global, multistakeholder effort focused on open government and gauging potential interest from others. These included many of the foundations involved in supporting advocacy work in open government and related issue areas around the world, several of which had recently joined with government aid agencies to form a donor collaborative called the Transparency and

Accountability Initiative. According to a 2011 retrospective by Nathaniel Heller, then of the US-based NGO Global Integrity, "At this point, no international multilateral initiative as such was envisioned—the idea was to convene a brainstorming discussion between a small group of leading open government practitioners from government and civil society to discuss possibilities for collective action, whether in the form of a declaration, experience sharing, and/or a more formal initiative" (Global Integrity, 2011).

A former government official noted that:

> [We] then began to convene internally, with folks from the White House, both on the domestic side and the international side, around what was a proposal that would include a kind of compact of some form, a set of principles, a process for generating kind of national commitments and then some accountability mechanism. And the idea was that we would . . . participate as well, and make our own commitments. Which, of course, is quite different than most of the things that came before. . . . So, what did we think that Obama could uniquely do? Well, he could get any head of state that he wanted around the table. (Interview, GO)

Officials in the National Security Council sought to use a speech by President Obama at the September 2010 UN General Assembly meeting as a starting point by ensuring that the speech included a specific emphasis on open government and issued a challenge to other governments to return to the topic in a year's time.

A foundation representative stated that:

> [In] the summer of 2010, we heard sort of whispers around something that Jeremy Weinstein and Samantha Power, then at the National Security Council, were up to. And I hadn't realized it, but they were really busy trying to get that paragraph in President Obama's speech at the General Assembly. . . . Jeremy was saying, "Look we're really trying to get this through, I really don't know what shape it will look like." (Interview, NGO)

As stated by a former government official:

> What we did was use the UN General Assembly speech, and that paragraph in the UN General Assembly speech, to give us the political imprimatur that we needed to drive a process and the establishment of this partnership. And so, we carefully constructed that paragraph . . . that said, "Next year I want to gather." And that

was a totally intentional effort, because we knew one of the hardest things to do in government is get the President's time. And so, we knew that if we could build that into the speech, to pre-commit him to a meeting the next year, that that would solve our bureaucratic problems internally, but also enable us to go to any head of state that we wanted with a clear signal of what we were trying to do. So, that paragraph sort of became the structure for engagement. (Interview, GO)

The speech itself offered the first public hint of the idea that would later grow into the Open Government Partnership. In President Obama's speech to the UN General Assembly on September 23, 2010, he challenged other countries to return the next year with specific commitments in hand:

And when we gather back here next year, we should bring specific commitments to promote transparency; to fight corruption; to energize civic engagement; to leverage new technologies so that we strengthen the foundations of freedom in our own countries, while living up to the ideals that can light the world. (White House, 2010b)

Following this speech, the White House issued a fact sheet on "U.S. Support for Open Government," detailing its own efforts to make government more transparent, participatory, and collaborative, reviewing some existing international efforts, and finally returning to emphasize the reference from the speech. The document reiterated that "President Obama challenged those in attendance to build on this progress" and "invited Leaders to join him next year in making specific commitments to promote transparency, fight corruption, energize civic engagement, and leverage new technologies to strengthen the foundations of open government" (White House, 2010a).

For the officials in the National Security Council attempting to create some kind of global initiative on open government, this speech gave them a deadline of one year—until the 2011 UN General Assembly meeting—to craft *something* that might realize this vision.

The Path to the White House

During the fall of 2010, US government representatives, along with members of the Transparency and Accountability Initiative, began approaching key advocates and policymakers around the world to assess interest in moving forward. These efforts would ultimately result in a January 2011 brainstorming meeting held in Washington, DC, the attendees of which largely became the founding members and Steering Committee of the Open Government Partnership.

At a key meeting in October 2010, the US government officials in the National Security Council first recruited the support of the donor collaborative Transparency and Accountability Initiative, who were able to provide staff support, resources, and a global network of civil society organizations. According to one foundation representative:

> Immediately after [Obama's September 2010 UN speech], Jeremy [Weinstein] and Samantha [Power] contacted us, and they were keen to help us help them think it through. . . . In the sense of, "How can we bring together the best of governments . . . with the best of what philanthropy and civil society has to bring?" So, for example, in the early days, Jeremy was very much saying, "Look, we can use the bully pulpit of the White House, we can see if we can get influential people in the United States government to call their counterparts. . . . But we don't know who to reach out to, we don't have the network. And our embassies don't really have that network either, it's a very specialized network." But, for obvious reasons, the philanthropic community does. (Interview, NGO)

According to a past government official:

> [We] said, look, we have this extraordinary opportunity, here's the concept that we have in mind. . . . We need your help if we're actually going to pull this off. And that's when Martin [Tisné, with the Transparency and Accountability Initiative] got pulled in and we went through this exercise of trying to figure out, who were the governmental champions, who were the civil society champions and how could we staff this thing? Because I was just a government official on the inside with no bureaucracy underneath me to deliver this. (Interview, GO)

The effort, spearheaded by Martin Tisné and supported by the Transparency and Accountability Initiative, then sought to produce a spreadsheet of champions from both governments and civil society groups around the world to invite to a January 2011 meeting at the White House. Those involved explicitly sought to invite bureaucrats from outside foreign ministries who would not traditionally be involved in such efforts.

Describing the process, one foundation representative noted:

> It was a fairly mammoth undertaking. And what we needed to know was how are the countries doing on open government on various indices, and just according to hearsay as well. . . . Using everyone in that Transparency International network, Open Society Foundations, the Right to Information network, the budget transparency network, the extractives transparency network; just to get as many names as possible. And then we ended up with I think 41 or 43 countries in that list. And so, on the basis of that, we then whittled it down to . . . 9 countries to invite to the meeting in January. And then . . . I mean they worked the phones, and Samantha Power was working the phones to get the right people from the different governments to attend. . . . We had a lot of pulling power from the White House to help set this up. A huge amount of political commitment on their part, you know, putting sweat equity in it. (Interview, NGO)

Another civil society representative explained that:

> These very famous spreadsheet exercises, literally just trying to ask all our friends, "Who are the greatest reformers that we know of, both in and outside of government, civil society, who work on this thing that we were sort of maybe starting to call open government?" . . . And a lot of work ended up going into those spreadsheets, and versions of those spreadsheets ultimately led to a meeting several months later at the White House conference center. (Interview, NGO)

And one former government official stated:

> Intentionally, the goal was not to find foreign ministry officials. We were trying to find the senior-most officials in government that we could politically access, who were close to the head of state. And we were bypassing foreign ministries very intentionally. Because foreign ministries are excellent at delivering talking points that are produced by other parts of their government, but they're deeply conservative and they're not the substantive leads. (Interview, GO)

Ultimately, this process led to a decision to invite representatives of nine governments—Brazil, India, Indonesia, Mexico, Norway, the Philippines, South Africa, the United States, and the UK—and nine civil society groups from around the world to a meeting to be held at the White House over two days in January 2011.

The "Magical Meeting"

Writing two years later in 2013, Jeremy Weinstein highlighted the importance of this meeting, writing:

> There are days that stand out from the blur of time on the White House staff—when the power of what's possible at the highest levels of government is visible in the kernel of a new idea. I remember one of those days very clearly: January 21, 2011. We were gathered in the Secretary of War Room, seated around an ornate mahogany table. We had cleared our schedules for what seemed like an unprecedented day and a half of time, just to think. And we were joined by an amazing cast of characters from across the developed and developing world—government ministers shorn of their staffers and talking points, leaders of international movements with networks spanning the continents, and grassroots activists carrying their experiences of pressing for social change into the halls of power. (Weinstein, 2013, 3)

Others later echoed the special nature of this meeting. One civil society participant said, "Everybody describes it as a magical meeting." One former US government official said, "This wasn't the kind of thing where governments went in one room and civil society went in another room and then they came together over lunch and then tried to negotiate a way forward. . . . It was governments and civil society, in the same room, saying, 'How do we do this?'" Martin Tisné (2016) later wrote:

> We walked into the meeting thinking we were exchanging ideas, learning about innovations from around the world, and walked out of it having constituted the founding steering committee of a major global initiative. The memory of that meeting will stay with me for a long time. From my perspective, it was the enthusiasm in that room, the deep sense that innovations really do come "from everywhere" that laid the foundations for what would then become OGP.

On the first day, participants shared examples of open government innovations from their own respective countries. One civil society participant said, "It was like kind of a show and tell. Tell us what you have achieved, regarding accountability and transparency, and what countries could learn from the experience." One former US government official recalled the following:

> When one of the countries participating or when one of the civil society leaders would tell their story, you could start to imagine it, and see it, and people started comparing notes.... And the light bulb there, to me, was governments seeing that civil society—it may be, you know, they hold you accountable and they press you and all that, but you can actually enlist citizens in this thing called government. (Interview, GO)

Building on this inspirational beginning, the organizers of the meeting then moved to propose some form of international open government initiative. According to one foundation representative, a concept note circulated to the participants had outlined a possible "notion of some set of national commitments and some accountability mechanism" (Interview, NGO). This note presented the possibility—according to the same foundation representative—that "a diverse coalition of governments could gather on the margins of the UN General Assembly in 2011 to embrace a set of high-level principles around open government, pledge country specific commitments to put them into practice, and invite civil society to assess their individual and collective progress" (Interview, NGO).

To some extent, the organizers already had a vision of the type of outcome that they hoped would emerge, but this remained uncertain and would be shaped by the discussion in the meeting. As one former US government official recalled, "I think it's fair to say that we went in with a pretty developed framework, but it wasn't one of those things where you go in with a developed framework and say 'You all really like this, don't you? You endorse it so I can go out there and say that this was a collective effort?' It was more genuinely the product of collective deliberation" (Interview, GO).

Another elaborated:

> We had put a lot more thought into what we wanted to get out of it than anyone else who was coming to it for the first time.... We had a sense of where we wanted to get, but we didn't know whether it was possible. We didn't know what people would buy into.... It was a collaborative process. The whole thing was not cooked and designed before anyone was brought in. The idea was that we

had some intuitions about what we wanted to do, but there was no declaration that was written, no bureaucratic structure that was fully designed, no envisioning of the IRM process. There were just the principles that might make for an initiative like this that could work. (Interview, GO)

But the discussions would not necessarily be easy or straightforward. Participants were initially unsure, and many raised concerns over the scope of membership and the extent of accountability mechanisms. One foundation representative recalled:

There was a moment where the meeting had got a little tense in the afternoon. . . . It was starting to emerge that we were looking at this more as an initiative. It wasn't clear how long it would last or not, but it wasn't just a one-off. And it was certainly was starting to emerge that there would be some sort of a membership. And so, the question was then, "Well who are we going to ask to do this?" Obviously it's us, and everyone's bonding, but it can't just be us. (Interview, NGO)

They added that different governments disagreed over different models:

There was a real divergence between a group, I'd say more led by the United Kingdom, that wanted this to be a small elite group. . . . Small and sort of a band of brothers and sisters, sort of leading the pack. On the complete opposite end of that you had Brazil. And the Brazilian perspective was, "Everyone should be included. We should be inclusive. We're all part of this together." (Interview, NGO)

Others were cautious, given the novel setting, without traditional diplomatic representation. But a key moment in reaching consensus to move forward with an initiative came with the Brazilian representative, Jorge Hage, head of the country's comptroller general, agreeing to jointly cochair the initiative along with the United States. In particular, this helped reassure the other developing country participants that the resulting initiative would have broader support and leadership beyond just the United States alone.

The attendees agreed to create an initiative on the basis of the key features that remain part of the Open Government Partnership today—a multistakeholder initiative based on a partnership between governments and civil society; membership on the basis of eligibility criteria, endorsement of a declaration, and voluntary commitments; and some form of accountability on the basis of independent monitoring. Yet the details of these remained to be defined. What would the eligibility criteria be, and who would be eligible? What was the precise role of civil society in the initiative's governance structure? Would the ostensible founding members' governments and foreign ministries support the endeavor? Would anybody show up at the September 2011 UN General Assembly, answering President Obama's call the year before to bring new commitments to open government?

"A High-Wire Act"

Moving forward from the January meeting, the organizers faced the substantial task of filling in these details, building a nascent initiative, and attracting members, all in time for a September 2011 launch at the next United Nations General Assembly meeting in New York City. In the words of a former US government official:

> Getting from January to an event in September with heads of state, announcing an initiative, was like a high-wire act. Every week I felt the whole thing was going to collapse because of something. (Interview, GO)

Through a series of events—first in Brazil in March 2011, where Brazilian president Dilma Rousseff publicly agreed to cochair the initiative, and then in Washington, DC, in July 2011—the organizers sought to solidify and formalize support from the existing founding members and work through the difficult process of establishing more precise rules governing membership. These efforts were led by the same officials in the US National Security Council along with Transparency and Accountability Initiative–supported work by Martin Tisné and Julie McCarthy. The State Department then officially joined these efforts and began publicizing the plans for the initiative. On July 12, 2011, an event in Washington, DC, intended to reintroduce the initiative, present it to potential member countries, and make the effort broadly public for the first time, Secretary of State Hillary Clinton gave a speech encouraging countries around the world to consider joining the new initiative, including offering an economic logic for open government:

> And we've also seen the correlation between openness in government and success in the economic sphere. Countries committed to defending transparency

and fighting corruption are often more attractive to entrepreneurs. And if you can create small and medium size businesses, you have a broader base for economic activity. At a time when global competition for trade and investment is fierce, openness is not just good for governance, it is also good for a sustainable growth in GDP. (U.S. Department of State, 2011)

A key concern over the spring of 2011 was establishing the rules for membership and eligibility criteria. This posed two challenges. The first challenge was in obtaining agreement among those involved who preferred a larger, universal initiative with less stringent requirements and those who preferred a smaller initiative with more stringent requirements. The second challenge was that, given that the initiative began with the eight founding member countries already in place, the ultimate eligibility criteria had to be designed to ensure that those founding members would, in fact, be eligible.

As noted by a foundation representative:

> One of the interesting things was that . . . because the eight governments were in some ways handpicked, because they were great leaders and they were doing great things, it wasn't very robust in some ways. There wasn't a quantitative methodology behind it, in some ways you could say it was almost a qualitative methodology, but it became really difficult from a more quantitative perspective, to figure out what they all had in common on paper, in order to develop the membership criteria that even fit the eight founding members. (Interview, NGO)

A past US government official described the challenges and tradeoffs involved in determining eligibility criteria:

> How do you structure a club? How do we think about who's in and who's out, and do it in a way that doesn't make it look like the decision of this exclusive group that was brought together? . . . You needed to establish a set of indicators that were credible, that allowed for room for movement, so that countries could become eligible, if they weren't already eligible. That needed to include the set of countries that were already there, so they all had to meet whatever criteria you came up with. . . . But if you look at the spreadsheets, it's a little bit like the "you know it if you see it" kind of line. There were countries below the threshold that, if our structure included them, people would immediately say, "This is not a serious initiative." (Interview, GO)

A civil society participant described that, for many civil society groups involved, their preference would have been for a smaller size initially, with more stringent requirements:

> There was some disagreement on what would be the threshold conditions, and who was a no-go.... We weren't on the side of "let's let 60 countries in to start off." I think the civil society saw kind of a 20–30-country [size]; you know you'd need a fairly high bar and a fairly high commitment to being a champion. (Interview, NGO)

Even before the Open Government Partnership's launch, some observers also criticized some of the founding members for gaps in their own open government records. One challenge was that Brazil had still not passed a freedom of information law—envisioned as one of the core eligibility criteria for membership—despite years of campaign promises, civil society pressure, and nearly adopted legislation. In response, in April 2011, President Rousseff "stated her support for a FOI bill, and work on the stalled bill in the legislature was resumed to meet a May 3 deadline she set" (FreedomInfo, 2011). However, she shortly thereafter yielded to political pressure from several powerful politicians, delaying passage of the law—leading to further criticism from freedom of information advocates. Two Brazil-based academics asked, "Is Brazil fit to lead the OGP?" and explicitly raised the credibility issue, writing that without freedom of information passage, "Brazil will not only put into question the credibility of its government, but also that of the newly minted Open Government Partnership" (Michener & Pereira, 2011).

Under the ultimately decided eligibility criteria, however, Brazil remained eligible even without an adopted law, given "3 points" for a constitutional provision for access to information (versus "4 points" for a law in place).

Yet another challenge for the nascent initiative was to ensure that the founding members had initial action plans to announce at the September 2011 launch event. This led to rushed processes that in many of the founding countries incorporated much less civil society involvement than in later rounds. This process in Mexico will be discussed in chapter 5. In the United

States, the development process was criticized not only for being insufficiently participatory (Judd, 2011; OpenTheGovernment, 2011) but also for some of the specific commitments being proposed.

One civil society participant called it "basically a grab bag of stuff they had announced two years earlier. It wasn't anything new. 'Now wait a second, this was supposed to be raising your game.'" But they also noted that although "at that encounter, just about the first impulse of the US bureaucracy was not that encouraging; it got better. And especially with some of the decisions they made that really did overcome internal opposition from people like the Interior Department and elsewhere, to join [the] Extractive Industries [Transparency Initiative]."

Finally, the launch day came, with a total of forty-six countries, including both the founding members and those signing letters of intent to join. A launch event was held on September 20, 2011, at Google's New York City offices, following that year's UN General Assembly sessions, featuring high-profile speeches from President Obama, President Benigno Aquino of the Philippines, the Head of the Office of the Comptroller General of Brazil Jorge Hage, eBay founder Pierre Omidyar, World Wide Web creator Tim Berners-Lee, and Celtel founder Mo Ibrahim. The founding members announced their National Action Plans. And a photograph captured the leaders of member governments and the founding civil society members standing together on stage as equals.

"A Leap of Faith"

Yet, for both the governments and the civil society groups considering participation in the nascent initiative, their willingness had been far from a foregone conclusion. Both governments and civil society groups had real concerns about the risks and costs of participating in such a partnership that put them on an equal footing.

First, civil society groups feared cooptation by governments and a loss of credibility from working with them. Many participants spoke to these concerns. A civil society representative said:

> There was some risk involved, right? Because in a way we were putting our reputations and the reputations of our organizations around an idea that we

were going to strike a deal with a set of governments. And at the same time, there were many other governments that we knew that were going to join that weren't as friendly. So, there was some risk involved in it. (Interview, NGO)

A different civil society representative stated:

I had this argument in [domestic civil society coalition]. My cofounder . . . said, "No way, it's a diversion of our real issues here." (Interview, NGO)

And another noted:

Was it really the right thing to do, or the more effective thing to do, to partner with governments in this sort of kumbaya way? As inefficient and frustrating and incomplete as it often was, we knew we could generate change through antagonistic approaches, sometimes. Sometimes you fail, but you also had stories of success, that you knew were somewhat replicable. . . . Is it better to kind of give that up, and walk in lockstep with government counterparts, if I'm still after the same sorts of change in the world? And it's a very different set of tactics, and different set of trade-offs you have to make. . . . It's like, really? You want us to pretend all this bad blood away, and sort of get into bed with these people? And that's a very fair concern or critique. (Interview, NGO)

A former US government official also recalled these concerns:

For them [civil society members], to even participate in this first round, was taking a leap of faith, right? You're going to be a credible non-governmental organization, you're an activist out there in the space of governance, and you're going to walk into a den with eight or nine governments, and start talking about, "Oh let's have a partnership that's about you governing?" It's like, yeah right! So, there's a leap of faith to come into the room. (Interview, GO)

Second, participation required substantial staff time on the part of civil society groups, who were often under-resourced. One civil society representative summarized these concerns:

Civil society put a lot of sweat equity into this, and took some risks. And I think that's worthwhile mentioning. Our time, our organization's time wasn't covered in any of this, right? So, you know, my organization agreed that I would spend substantial amounts of my time on this, and would in a sense take whatever

> credibility or name or whatever we had into this process. And the same should be said for all of the others. (Interview, NGO)

Another agreed and also noted the potential biases in participation that this might yield:

> And part of it was like, who's willing to donate in-kind time, which was nontrivial. It's why it skewed at the time, and probably still skews today, towards larger INGOs [international nongovernmental organizations] or networks, because they have the fundamental operational liquidity to donate time.... I spent *way* too much of my life on OGP, literally, I got paid zero dollars.... So, can a grassroots group in like Oaxaca really do this? No, realistically, and so it's an interesting bias that creeps in pretty quickly, even though it's not the usual bias of "we're paying you to do something, so you do what we want." It's the inverse, like "who's willing to just donate time, and not just a day or two but like years of time." And it's only more resourced, typically INGO types that can do that. With few exceptions here or there, but not many. (Interview, NGO)

Civil society groups thus brought real concerns to the process of designing the Open Government Partnership and exercised a very real threat of departure as debates proceeded about the stringency of membership rules and accountability mechanisms. However, governments had concerns of their own, both traditional and novel. Their traditional concerns reflected a common wariness of governments about any international institution—over the potential loss of authority, intrusive monitoring, or exposure to international criticism. But less traditionally, governments also faced the novelty of a multistakeholder initiative featuring true parity between themselves and civil society, and one where participation focused on bureaucrats outside of foreign ministries.

A former US government official explained that:

> People didn't necessarily know how to incorporate this different type of innovation into whatever their department was. It's very difficult to get bureaucracies to move.... It's very hard to get people to understand and break out of their boxes and embrace this sort of new way of engagement. (Interview, GO)

In an interview, a civil society participant noted:

> I think governments have to mind much more the consequences of their actions ... much more than we in civil society have. For me, if the Russian Government gets pissed off, well, who cares? But for a government official, it's like they could see a line of dominos falling down much more easily than we did. (Interview, NGO)

Another echoed this, saying, "You know the governments are always super sensitive to equities that we care less about." They also emphasized more traditional concerns over international criticism:

> Most of the governments have a huge aversion to anything that could be perceived as public criticism or shaming or grading of them that's not an A-plus. Which is of course why civil society groups do this all the time. (Interview, NGO)

The potential concerns of governments were most fully realized when, on the eve of the July 12, 2011, US State Department event, India announced that it was withdrawing from the planned initiative. Toby McIntosh, who was reporting on the Open Government Partnership's progress for FreedomInfo.org, wrote that:

> The prospect of having its "action plan" commitments reviewed after a year by local and international governance experts was a key factor that caused India to withdraw, sources said. ... India was concerned about the Independent Review Mechanism that would accompany government self-assessment, preferring not to have outsiders pass judgment on Indian affairs, according to those familiar with the situation. ... In addition, the Indian government may be reluctant politically at this point to engage in a public consultation on transparency, observers said. (McIntosh, 2011)

India's minister of state for external affairs in Parliament offered a justification based on the principle of parliamentary supremacy:

> The government had conveyed its concerns to the US and others that new and additional commitments on governance should be made before the national Parliament, and not in an ad hoc international forum, and that the decision-making process for the government as also performance report and evaluation are also the prerogatives of national Parliament. (Bhaumik, 2011)

One past US government official, reflecting on this setback, said:

> That was really painful. . . . There was just real nervousness about the institutionalization of some mechanism that would shed, both internal and external light on what the Indian government was doing. And so, India preferred universality to exclusivity, and they preferred peer review to vertical accountability. And we tried to open them up. I mean, we engaged at very, very high levels to try and get India back in, but we couldn't. (Interview, GO)

This departure left only eight founding countries and raised questions over whether the ambitious initiative would be able to get off the ground and overcome entrenched opposition. On the other hand, the departure also suggested that the initiative might indeed yield more than just superficial promises if the intended processes had proved unacceptably intrusive to a country that, as recently as a few months earlier, had seemed at the core of the endeavor.

This departure also highlights the very real concerns over sovereignty costs held by many governments—even among the founding members. Participants at the time suggested that similar concerns also emerged among other founding members as well but were ultimately ameliorated. Thus, despite membership in the Open Government Partnership not holding the same international legal status as formal membership in an intergovernmental organization, prospective members approached it with many of the same sovereignty cost concerns in mind.

"The Cool Kids' Club"

In light of the departure of one of the founding governments, it may seem surprising that by the time of the Open Government Partnership's launch in September 2011, twenty-eight more countries had submitted letters of intent to join. This brought the total to forty-six, including the eight remaining founding members. Indeed, many participants were surprised by this level of uptake. Under Secretary of State Maria Otero emphasized at the time that this level of participation was "beyond what we had expected" (FreedomInfo, 2011b). Several more countries indicated that they hoped to join, including several noneligible countries such as Botswana, Mauritius, and Tunisia (FreedomInfo, 2011c). This suggested that the prospect of joining might serve as an impetus for countries to improve their performance on the eligibility criteria.

What attracted so many governments, so quickly, to join this new initiative? Most participants suggested variants on three main explanations: First, for reform-minded governments—or individual officials—participation was motivated by a genuine commitment to drive new open government innovations and to learn from peers around the world. Second, for many participants, motivations may have been largely symbolic, drawn particularly by President Obama's star power, or shaped more cynically by a hope for an easy opportunity for window-dressing participation in a low-cost initiative. And third, whether the motivation to join was more substantive or more symbolic, many new participants may have simply not fully understood the requirements of the process they were signing up to and the extent to which they would bind them to a repeated cycle of National Action Plans and civil society interaction. And in all cases, contributions were also made by substantial outreach by US diplomats, officials from the founding countries, and the civil society and foundation networks involved.

According to a former US government official:

> It was a very modern thing to do, so I think there was an appeal to the event. And look, governments are going to look good if they're there for the launch of something called the Open Government Partnership. . . . I think most of them knew what they were getting into. But I think there were a few who did not. It's the kind of thing where you can look at it, and if you don't read the rules carefully, you can think, "Oh I just signed up to say I will do these things, and then I've got to do a National Action Plan, but I can just issue a report." But then when you realize that, no there's an IRM, and you've got to meet with civil society, then it's a bit more laborious than that, and you can't actually fake it. And that's when, you know, there were a number that joined and then after a year, 18 months or so, it was pretty clear that there were some that they were just trying to fake it. (Interview, GO)

And another explained:

> I had no idea how many would sign up. . . . I had no idea whether people were going to go for it. . . . I mean, I was surprised by how many initially signed up, and I really wondered whether they knew what they were signing up for. And I think some did and some didn't. And that's the reality of these things.

> Governments are making strategic choices about what kinds of signals they want to send, and people wanted to signal that they were engaged. . . . What government, what head of state doesn't want to say, "I'm for making my government better," right? That was a very easy sell politically. (Interview, GO)

As explained by a different US government official:

> Definitely the star factor. Cameron, Obama, the pull of the star factor, the mix of countries that was there, the way it was highlighted. Definitely the "cool kids' club" because it was something different. . . . But there was also a significant diplomatic outreach effort. We wanted more countries to join. We specifically wanted to get countries that were on the cusp of some of these reforms, to act as a catalyst to make some of these reforms. They had a list of countries they wanted to push. . . . There was such a coordinated push. . . . Between the UK and the US they have a large diplomatic presence around the world. There were demarches that went to pretty much every embassy. If you trace pretty much any large summit around the world, OGP was mentioned. (Interview, GO)

In the words of one civil society participant:

> That's one of the big mysteries [why so many countries joined by the launch]. You know, so what are the factors. Having Obama champion it, I think everybody agrees that was a big thing. . . . He had big reach and pull. The US, separate from Obama, had big reach and pull. . . . There were a number of presidents around the world that had an open government agenda and that they were reformers, and they saw this as getting some wind in the sails . . . or there were champions in government that could bring their presidents on board. . . . Some, like the founding eight, knew very much what they were taking on. You know there were some that were hoping to do something real, and there were some that . . . thought they could get something good out of this without investing too much, without it being too uncomfortable. (Interview, NGO)

A similar theme was raised by another:

> Well, because President Obama. It's like a rockstar and you want to be around the rockstar and well, if he says it was cool, you want to be in the picture. . . . They knew they were getting . . . an opportunity with the president of the United States. Beyond that, I don't think they were very clear. (Interview, NGO)

When interviewed, a different civil society participant succinctly stated:

> It was a lot of US diplomatic capital that went in to just selling something. And they were selling a pipe dream, like, "Hey trust us, this will be worth it, can you show up so we can take you off the list and count you?" (Interview, NGO)

For President Aquino of founding member the Philippines, the launch event offered an opportunity to signal both business-friendly reform and political closeness with the US president. At a speech the night before the launch, Aquino "said the Philippines' being chosen to be part of the OGP affirmed that it was 'a good place to do business in and a good country to do business with,'" while coverage of the launch event in Philippines media prominently included a photograph of Obama putting his hand on Aquino's back, with the caption heading, "PAT ON THE BACK" (Avendaño, 2011).

Although many participants at the time emphasized the draw of being on stage with President Obama in 2011, it is notable that the Open Government Partnership continued to attract new members for years after. New members continued to join even after the functioning of the National Action Plan process and Independent Reporting Mechanism were much more visible. Thus, even if some of the initial wave of the decision to join was not fully rational, later decisions can be considered much more so. Reflecting on the later, more fully developed attractiveness of membership, a former US government official said, "It's credible enough, and it's a known enough thing, that if you say you're a member of OGP, that gives you some actual credit . . . like, 'I want to be seen to be in that club.'"

Discussion

In many ways, the Open Government Partnership's founding exemplifies the transnational multistakeholder model—particularly in its speed, flexibility, and aim of overcoming limitations of existing diplomatic and governance approaches. But other elements suggest interesting departures—particularly in the key role of state officials themselves as entrepreneurs and in the politics of institutional design focused on contention over depth and breadth of membership.

To summarize some of the key conclusions from the story of the Open Government Partnership's origins, we find the following:

- Like many multistakeholder initiatives, the origins of the Open Government Partnership were shaped by a desire to overcome the limits of more traditional intergovernmental institutions and to *fill gaps* in existing governance arrangements.
- Unlike many multistakeholder initiatives, it was transnational entrepreneurship by *state* officials themselves—rather than nongovernmental organizations or existing international organizations—that played the initial leading role in orchestrating action by funders, civil society groups, and other states' officials.
- The creation and design of the Open Government Partnership were characterized by their extreme speed, with less than nine months elapsing from the January 2011 White House meeting to its formal launch at the UN General Assembly in September 2011.
- Even though the design of the Open Government Partnership was outside the hands of traditional diplomats and foreign ministries, there were clear *politics* of institutional design focused particularly on contention between depth and breadth of membership.

Of course, even after the formal launch of the Open Government Partnership, much still remained to be done even in terms of developing the core elements of its institutional design—in particular, the crucial details of the operation of the independent reporting mechanism and the establishment of sufficient staff and funding to operate the Support Unit. These would be developed largely over 2012 and 2013. Within its fundamental institutional framework, however, the Open Government Partnership continued to exemplify the flexibility of transnational multistakeholder initiatives through continued iterative developments. These included increasing institutionalization over time, new ways of balancing competing demands from different stakeholders, and new patterns of leadership, such as thematic priorities that often rotated with each new cochair.

However, here we depart from the detailed origin story and transition to elaborate the key elements of the Open Government Partnership's functioning. The remainder of this chapter reviews the key elements of the Open Government Partnership's rules and functions as they stood once they were clearly developed and as they played key roles in shaping the direct and indirect pathways of impact that are the main focus of this book.

OVERVIEW OF THE OPEN GOVERNMENT PARTNERSHIP

This section presents an overview of the structure and leadership of the Open Government Partnership, a discussion of both national and subnational memberships, an overview of the organization's finances, and an introduction to the global and regional summits. While the focus of this book and this chapter is largely on the national-level government, it should be noted that since 2015, the Open Government Partnership has also included subnational members through its Open Government Partnership Local initiative to encourage commitments relevant to the values of transparency, participation, and accountability with a focus on technology. This is a growing component of the organization that will likely see further expansion in the future. We present a snapshot of the structure and functions of the Open Government Partnership from 2019 and early 2020.

Open Government Partnership Budget and Expenditures

As an organization, the Open Government Partnership's budget has continued to grow over time. In 2013, the Partnership's total budget was just under $2.5 million.[2] In 2019, the Open Government Partnership's total budget was just under $10 million—nearly a four-fold increase. Funding for the Partnership comes from private foundations, bilateral agencies, and some member governments. Table 3.1 summarizes the Partnership's income from private foundations and bilateral aid agencies. Many of the foundations and bilateral aid agencies gave multiple times over this period, with many awarding multiyear grants, making a year-over-year analysis breakdown impossible.

Since 2014, the Open Government Partnership has placed emphasis on participating countries contributing to the Partnership's income (Frey, 2014). In 2013, the total per country contribution was $1.5 million, and in 2019 it increased to $2.7 million. In 2018, the country contributions were roughly the equivalent of 27 percent of the total expenditures for that year. Thirty-six countries contributed between $10,000 and $200,000 in 2019.

Table 3.1

Open Government Partnership total funding from private foundations and bilateral aid agencies, 2013–2021

Funding from private foundations	
William and Flora Hewlett Foundation	$8,090,000
Ford Foundation	$5,400,000
Luminate Group (formerly Omidyar Network)	$4,800,000
Open Society Foundations	$3,300,000
Hivos	$2,600,000
Institute of International Education	$79,612
Private foundations total	**$24,269,612**
Funding from bilateral aid agencies	
Department for International Development (UK)*	$11,722,598
US Agency for International Development (US)	$2,199,946
Department of State (US)	$493,826
International Development Research Centre (IDRC)**	$485,717
French Embassy to the US	$40,000
Bilateral aid agencies total	**$14,942,086**

*Grants were in GBP and converted to USD using the exchange rate on January 1 of the year the grants were made.
**Grants were in euros and converted to USD using the exchange rate on January 1 of the year the grants were made.
Note: Open Government Partnership funding sources data is current as of March 1, 2020.

The Open Government Partnership's 2018 budget was nearly $10 million. The largest portion of the budget went to the country and local support unit (25.7 percent); followed by the Independent Reporting Mechanism (21.7 percent); operations (19.9 percent); the global campaign, Steering Committee, and events (14.7 percent); communications (8.6 percent); knowledge, learning, innovation, and capacity (7.6 percent); and lastly, development and fundraising (1.8 percent) (Open Government Partnership, 2018d). The budget data is difficult to analyze over time since what goes into the individual budget categories has changed.

Current Structure and Leadership

The structure and leadership mechanisms of the Open Government Partnership have evolved over time, and the below descriptions explain the state of the various organizational units as of April 2020. As explained below, the organization is governed by an international Steering Committee but has a full-time staff that plays a key role in managing and directing the organization.

The Open Government Partnership is led by a twenty-two-member Steering Committee, with an equal number of government and civil society members. While the government seats are held by the governments—not specific individuals—the civil society members are elected as individuals to represent civil society's interests broadly. Open Government Partnership's own leadership changes and is voted on by other Steering Committee members, with both a government and a civil society member leading the Steering Committee at any one time. On October 1, 2019, the government of Argentina and Robin Hodess from The B Team, a global nonprofit focused on business practices centered on climate and humanity, assumed the roles of cochairs of the Steering Committee (Open Government Partnership, 2019e). The committee has responsibility for fundraising and budgeting and has broad authority to decide organization policy and matters concerning member entry, participation, and disciplinary action. The Steering Committee has three subcommittees within which it conducts work: Governance and Leadership, Criteria and Standards, and Thematic Leadership.

The Open Government Partnership is incorporated as a United States not-for-profit organization with a board of directors that provides fiduciary and legal oversight. The board of directors can have anywhere between three and six individuals as members. As of April 2020, the board of directors has five members, with a mix of government and civil society backgrounds.

The Open Government Partnership utilizes ambassadors and envoys to interface with the public and outside organizations. As of April 2020, there are four ambassadors whose job is to raise Open Government Partnership's profile and complement the work of the Steering Committee. The ambassadors are individuals with high-level positions in other organizations who advocate for the Open Government Partnership. The envoys are a larger group of individuals, comprising more than twenty members, who have played significant roles in the development of the Open Government Partnership and continue to represent the organization.

The Open Government Partnership has a significant number of full-time staff, jointly referred to as the Support Unit, distributed over a range of core areas, including leadership, global, analytics and insights, learning and innovation, operations, country support, Open Government Partnership Local, thematic policy areas, and communications.

There is a five-person leadership team, led by Dr. Sanjay Pradhan as chief executive officer since May 2016. As of April 2020, the Global, Learning & Innovation, Analytics & Insights, Operations, and Communications teams have all had between four and five staff members. The Country Support group is the largest and employs twenty staff members, most of who are full-time. These members are based around the world. The Country Support group supports governments' and civil society groups' local efforts to further transparency, accountability, and participation. The Country Support group is led by Paul Maassen, who has been with the Open Government Partnership since 2012. The Open Government Partnership also employs consultants to work on individual projects.

The Independent Reporting Mechanism, discussed further below, is a small group composed of five full-time staff members. The Independent Reporting Mechanism relies heavily on local and national-level researchers contracted to complete the country assessment reports. The International Experts Panel oversees the Independent Reporting Mechanism. However, the International Experts Panel is an independent body guided by the Steering Committee, but it is not directly accountable to them. The number of International Experts Panel members has varied over time. In early 2020 it consisted of five Steering Committee members and a number of quality control advisors but by the end of 2020, the International Experts Panel consisted of only five members. The changing structure of the International Experts Panel is consistent with the constantly evolving nature of the Open Government Partnership generally.

Joining and Maintaining National-Level Membership

As of April 2020, there were seventy-eight Open Government Partnership member countries: thirty-one in Europe, fifteen in Asia-Pacific, eighteen in the Americas, fourteen in Africa. (In chapter 1 of this book, we include a table with all member countries.) Prospective member countries must meet specific requirements to join according to four eligibility criteria: civic engagement, access to information, fiscal transparency, and public asset disclosure. To evaluate its four eligibility criteria, the Open Government Partnership uses a points-based system that relies upon an array of data sources from third-party cross-national indices of transparency, governance, and democratic performance.

- The civic engagement criterion is measured using the *Economist*'s democracy index indicator of civil liberties, such as media freedom, personal and religious freedoms, and freedom of association (maximum 4 points).
- The access to information criterion is measured using a combination of assessments of freedom of information acts by the Open Society Institute Justice Initiative, the Centre for Law and Democracy, and Access Info Europe (maximum 4 points).
- The fiscal transparency criterion is measured using data from the International Budget Partnership's open budget survey tracker on the availability of two specific fiscal documents—a national executive's budget proposal and its audit report (maximum 2 points).
- Finally, the public asset disclosure criterion is measured using the World Bank's financial disclosure law library to determine whether the country has a law requiring officials to disclose their assets and whether the disclosures are made publicly accessible (maximum 4 points).

Beginning in September 2017, new member countries are required to pass an additional test of having adequate democratic values. This criterion is measured according to the Varieties of Democracy project's considerations of civil society organization entry and exit and civil society organization (non) repression. According to the Open Government Partnership's website, this additional requirement was an "effort to ensure that new countries joining the Open Government Partnership adhere to the democratic governance norms and values set forth in the Open Government Declaration" (Open Government Partnership, 2022, para. 1).

If a country achieves at least 75 percent of these eligibility points and passes the democratic value check, it is considered eligible to join. The Open Government Partnership maintains an updated list showing how each country in the world stands in regards to the criteria. However, eligibility itself is not enough to join the Partnership. It is up to the country to go through a formal process of joining, which begins with the process of developing a concrete action plan. Practical details, such as who the country designates as its lead ministry, must also be in place. Often the lead ministry is the central executive—the president or prime minister's office—but other central ministries, such as public administration and management agencies, treasuries, or foreign affairs and development agencies, are also frequently given the formal leadership role. The government point of contact must then submit a letter of intent to the Open Government Partnership cochairs.

There are a number of things members must do to be in good standing. For example, members must agree to have their progress on commitments assessed by an independent researcher as part of the Independent Reporting Mechanism action plan process. As part of the action plan process, countries must also produce yearly self-assessment reports. Countries are supposed to work in consultation with a range of interests, including civil society organizations, relevant businesses, academics, and individuals, to develop their reports. The action plans are due every two years; however, the 2020 *Open Government Partnership Handbook* acknowledges the difficult nature of making this timeframe fit within domestic election cycles. Countries have done a variety of things to accommodate this reality, including delaying the release of action plans for a year or releasing a second, streamlined action plan once the new administration is in place.

As noted in the 2020 *Open Government Partnership Handbook*, countries must also commit to having a government point of contact in a lead ministry to take the lead on the action plan development and assessment process domestically. Governments agree to participate in a multistakeholder forum to develop and implement the action plans. The multistakeholder forums must have members of both government and civil society and are required to meet every three months.

It is possible for a country's membership to be withdrawn for not meeting the Open Government Partnership requirements, and these requirements have increased over time. Currently, some reasons a country's membership may be withdrawn include not producing action plans in a timely manner, not adequately involving civil society, not publishing relevant material, and not making *any* progress toward implementing *any* of their commitments. However, countries found acting contrary to these are given two full action plan cycles before being placed under procedural review, and then they are still given further chances to improve before being deemed inactive or withdrawn. Membership can also be reassessed through a review by the Steering Committee via the response policy, formerly known as the Policy on Upholding the Values and Principles of Open Government Partnership. There have been three countries, to date, that have had their membership fully withdrawn by the Open Government Partnership (noted here is their year of withdrawal): Azerbaijan (2016), Trinidad and Tobago (2019), and Turkey (2016). Additionally, Hungary (2016) and Tanzania (2017) chose to withdraw. In 2020, Pakistan was made inactive, and Bulgaria, Ghana, Ireland, Israel, Malawi, South Africa, and Jamaica were placed on procedural review.

Action Plans

Since the Open Government Partnership initially focused only on national-level governments, all action plans produced were designated as National Action Plans. As the Partnership and Independent Reporting Mechanism has evolved, though, these plans have become known simply as action plans. However, in this book, the term *National Action Plan* is still used when referring to a national government's action plan. The substance of National Action Plans for countries has changed over time. At one point, all countries were encouraged to be guided by the Open Government Partnership grand challenges when developing their National Action Plans. The five grand challenges were improving public services, increasing public integrity, effectively managing public resources, creating safer communities, and increasing corporate accountability (Open Government Partnership, 2019d). The emphasis on the grand challenges has waned over time, though. In 2015, the requirement to organize National Action Plans around grand challenges was removed, and they are no longer a key component (Open Government Partnership, 2015a). Though the requirement was removed, each commitment currently included in a country's National Action Plan should reflect at least one of the four core open government principles: transparency, citizen participation, public accountability, or technology and innovation for transparency and accountability (Open Government Partnership, 2019d). With that said, if a commitment is associated with the value of technology and innovation, it must also reflect one of the other values. Stated another way, a commitment should not focus on technology without also focusing on one of the other substantive values.

Open Government Partnership admits that the quality and presentation of the National Action Plans widely varies (Open Government Partnership, 2014a). After the first round of National Action Plans was developed and assessed, there were a few main takeaways. First, the countries that produced good plans were largely the countries that had been out-front with the open government movement generally—Brazil, Canada, Israel, Croatia, and Moldova. There were some surprises, though, with Jordan and the Dominican Republic also putting out strong first National Action Plans (Global Integrity, 2012). Second, countries had very different approaches to what a commitment was, with some making grand statements and others providing specific, actionable goals. Much of the subsequent revisions to the National Action Plan and Independent Reporting Mechanism process have been aimed at fixing this problem. Third, the term *open government* was not widely understood in 2012 (Global Integrity, 2012). The Open Government Partnership has struggled to find a proper way to assess the National Action Plans. At one point, the Partnership launched a pilot National Action Plan review with a color-coding scheme (Open Government Partnership, 2012b) to better understand the limitations of the process.

There is a wide range of commitments that governments include in their action plans. While hard to nail down the extent of the practice, it is assumed that many countries include commitments for initiatives they are already working on. For example, the commitments in the first South African National Action Plan were largely seen as an extension of work already being done by the South African Department of Public Services and Administration (Open Government Africa, 2012). The Open Government Partnership felt that some governments were including commitments that were either not on topic, too broad in scope, or already completed. To counter this trend, the Open Government Partnership instituted what are called "starred commitments." Commitments receive a star designation if they are exemplary and have the potential for transformative impact. Joe Powell, then deputy director of the Open Government Partnership Support Unit, elaborated, "OGP was always designed to create a race to the top in action plans, so by adding an assessment of ambition it rewards countries who make difficult to implement commitments which may be of transformative impact" (Mckenzie, 2014).

The practice of starring commitments has both supporters and detractors. Martin Tisné, then the director of policy for the Omidyar Network's government transparency initiative, offered an assessment of the role of the Independent Reporting Mechanism in general:

> The Independent Reporting Mechanism—the independent body that monitors progress of OGP national action plans—has "starred" those government commitments that have significant social impact, are substantially or fully completed, and relevant to OGP values. 24.7% of OGP commitments from the most recent 35 OGP countries to have completed their action plans are starred. This means that out of the 783 government commitments that were recently assessed (those 35 countries from OGP's "second cohort"), 194 commitments were ambitious, in line with OGP values and mostly or fully completed. From a funder's perspective, I think this makes OGP one of the best returns on investment we've had. I can't think of any other program I've been involved in that has led to almost 200 instances of change in 35 countries around the world in less than 3 years. (Tisné, 2014a)

Tisné's blog post and glowing conclusion were critiqued in another blog post on Techpresident.com. In the Techpresident.com post, the question of whether starred commitments were a good indicator of Open Government Partnership's success was raised. A Partnership staffer quoted in the post concluded that it was open to interpretation what the appropriate percentage of starred commitments should be. The staffer also responded that "the percentage of its commitments that were starred is a decent proxy for a country having understood the OGP guidelines and accomplished a good deal during its first year of implementation" (Tisné, 2014a). While it is not clear the extent to which the Open Government Partnership contributes to more open government, it does seem to be getting better at guiding countries to produce and complete commitments that meet the criteria they lay out.

The Role of Nongovernmental Actors in the Action Plan Cycle

Just as within the Open Government Partnership as a whole, individuals and organizations from civil society play a key role in the Independent Reporting Mechanism process. Civil society participation begins with the selection of the country researcher. Per the initial Independent Reporting Mechanism proposal, civil society groups in the member countries have the opportunity to provide informal feedback on the local research candidate shortlist. The in-country researchers who do not already have contacts with civil society are given formal introductions through the Independent Reporting Mechanism.

The public, including relevant civil society groups, should have a role in both the development of action plans and during the implementation (Open Government Partnership, 2019d). In practice, this is not always the case. In Uruguay, some civil society members were more active in the process than others, specifically those that were younger and more adept at information and communications technology. A report assessing the state of participation in the Uruguayan open government National Action Plan development process found that for full cocreation to be achieved, strong political endorsements are imperative (Rivoir & Landinelli, 2017).

The Open Government Partnership 2015 National Action Plan Review found that "opportunities for civil society to be involved in creating or implementing action plans also often don't appear to be spilling over into genuine collaboration or empowerment" (Hughes, 2015). In other words, civil society was given some avenues for input, but, in reality, access was very limited, which affected the final National Action Plans in countries.

In addition to governments, community-based groups and international organizations also play roles in the Open Government Partnership more generally and in the Independent Researching Mechanism process—specifically, academics and the private sector. Academics continue to be involved in the Open Government Partnership in several ways. There have been side events to the Open Government Partnership Global Summits focused on this group, including at Carleton University in Ottawa, Canada, in 2019 (Open Government Partnership, 2019c). In Uruguay, academic actors have become involved in the National Action Plan process. This involvement is in the early stages but is seen as a positive development (Rivoir & Landinelli, 2017). Academics have also served as Independent Reporting Mechanism national assessors (e.g., the UK, United States, and Canada) and have served on the international experts panel.

Like academics, the private sector plays a role in the global summits as well. At the 2019 global summit in Ottawa, the exhibitors were overwhelmingly private sector organizations. The 2019 Articles of Governance explicitly mention the private sector as having a role in the Open Government Partnership to develop, monitor, and support action plan development. With that said, actual engagement with the private sector has been limited. A 2017 working paper commissioned by the Open Government Partnership Support Unit and written by the Basel Institute on Governance at the University of Basel in Switzerland found that the Open Government Partnership is not well known in the private sector, and, so far, the Partnership's private sector initiatives have failed to gain traction (Adjami & Wannenwestch, 2017).

Civil society organizations are not the only actors influencing the development of action plans. Representatives of international organizations and funders also play a key role at times, as they did in Azerbaijan's National Action Plan (Trend News Agency, 2012). In Tanzania, the Open Government Partnership National Action Plan was largely drafted by Twaweza (Dufief et al., 2017). Twaweza is an East African initiative funded by Sida, UK Department for International Development (DFID), Hewlett Foundation, SNV, and Hivos (Twaweza Ni Sisi, n.d.). In 2016, the United States Agency for International Development, through their Facilitating Public Investment project, worked with the Philippines Department of Budget and Management to conduct an intensive country-wide consultation for the Philippines' fourth National Action Plan (Verzosa, 2017). Not surprisingly, we find that international organizations and funding organizations are playing a much larger role in the Open Government Partnership than is identified in the articles of governance. These outside organizations are using their influence to impact the development of National Action Plans and possibly the content of these plans as well.

Overview of the Independent Reporting Mechanism

The action plans that governments produce center on a list of commitments that, if done well, focus on improving transparency, accountability, participation, and innovative use of technology. These commitments are notable for their flexibility in terms of scope and focus, including a wide range of potential issue areas related (and sometimes not so related) to open government. The Open Government Partnership Articles of Governance also place various expectations on governments that serve to guide the participation process. Thus, governments must develop their action plans in consultation with civil society, and they must be relevant to one of four principles (transparency, accountability, public participation, and technology and innovation)—that part has always been around and remains in place. The articles convey that the civil society consultation process should be timely, transparent, serious about dialogue, and it should take the form of a regular forum enabling "regular multi-stakeholder consultation on OGP implementation" (Open Government Partnership, 2015a, 19).

In principle, each member produces a new National Action Plan every two years, thus leading to a cycle of policy commitments and, in some cases, policy fulfillment pushing the open government agenda forward. Local country researchers, overseen by the Independent Reporting Mechanism, assess progress made on the commitments in the plans. The Independent Reporting Mechanism selects the local country researchers based on their research expertise and gives the researchers special training on how to carry out their review of their country's National Action Plan. The Independent Reporting Mechanism researchers come from a variety of backgrounds, with some having university affiliations, others affiliating with local civil society organizations, and others having no formal affiliation at all. The review is normally wide-ranging and ideally draws on broad consultation with governmental and civil society actors who are involved in implementing or monitoring the action plan. At the end of this process, the researcher produces a country progress report. The Independent Reporting Mechanism, which initially only evaluated country-level reports, also evaluated subnational initiative plans at one point but no longer does.

In 2019, the Independent Reporting Mechanism produced 110 reports but believed that it would be unsustainable to continue to produce this number of reports given the limited resources available to the independent body. A report commissioned by the International Experts Panel in 2017 on the relevance, effectiveness, and efficiency of the Independent Reporting Mechanism offered a list of possible recommendations for supporting the independent body (Blomeyer & Sanz, 2017). The process of reworking the unit is called the IRM Refresh and was approved by the Open Government Partnership Steering Committee in February 2020. The new processes were beginning to be implemented in 2020 (Miranda, 2019; Open Government Partnership 2020a). The IRM Refresh planned to focus on products and processes that are simpler, more fit for purpose, results-oriented, and prioritized. Some key differences between the new model and the older model are that the new model will provide input during the cocreation phase; the Independent Reporting Mechanism will provide a review of the action plan at the policy or thematic level; instead of having researchers in each country, a smaller pool of Independent Reporting Mechanism researchers will complete all the reports; and the action plan reports will focus on results. The plan was for the first products from the refreshed Independent Reporting Mechanism to come out in 2021 for 2020–2022 Action Plans (Open Government Partnership, 2020a).

Independent Reporting Mechanism program management team

The number of Independent Reporting Mechanism staff and the roles they play has changed over time. As of April 2019, there were five full-time staff members. The staff report to the chief of the Independent Reporting Mechanism (in the past, this role was referred to as the director of the Independent Reporting Mechanism). The chief oversees the hiring and training of local researchers, all that goes into the publication of the progress reports, the subsequent publication of Independent Reporting Mechanism reports, and works with the International Experts Panel to ensure quality in the process. This independent body also employs consultants and copy editors to produce the country assessment reports, when necessary, to meet deadlines (Open Government Partnership, 2014a). The primary takeaway here is that, like the Open Government Partnership generally, the number of Independent Reporting Mechanism staff has grown from two, initially, to five. This number does not take into account the number of consultants, editors, and local government researchers for whom the Independent Reporting Mechanism is responsible.

Criteria and standards subcommittee oversight

The criteria and standards subcommittee of the Open Government Partnership Steering Committee plays an oversight role of the Independent Reporting Mechanism. This sub-committee oversees the selection and vets the International Experts Panel members. It also oversees the hiring of the Independent Reporting Mechanism staff and the drafting of the government self-assessment reports (Open Government Partnership, 2012b). As of November 2017, the criteria and standards subcommittee consisted of eight members—four individuals from civil society and four individuals representing their governments. Similar to the other subcommittees, it is cochaired by one civil society and one government member.

International Experts Panel

The International Experts Panel is the body responsible for overseeing the Independent Reporting Mechanism process. The panel members are intended to broadly represent the Open Government Partnership participating countries, but panel members are not required to be from member countries. The International Experts Panel was initially set up to have ten members—five of who are technical or policy experts and five of who are high-profile senior advisors. The panel members are appointed by the Open Government Partnership Steering Committee (Open Government Partnership, 2012b). The technical advisors play a direct role in the quality control of the reports and are compensated for their time. The senior advisors play a larger role in strategic advice and outreach on the Independent Reporting Mechanism reports.

An early critique of the Independent Reporting Mechanism, which came out of the London summit, was that it needed "more high-level political advisors to provide researchers with 'political cover'" (Vila & Wilson, 2013). The mechanism has struggled to find the right balance of people to serve on the International Experts Panel to provide both the technical feedback and the political cover it needs.

Recognizing the politically sensitive nature of these roles, the Independent Reporting Mechanism has a conflicts of interest policy that applies to both the International Experts Panel members and the individual in-country researchers. With this policy, the mechanism attempts to avoid any actual or perceived conflicts of interest, like working for the government that they are assessing.

Country researchers

Country researchers or local researchers are the individuals responsible for researching and writing the country assessment reports. The local researchers are identified through an open recruitment process and by recommendations from existing networks. Ideally, candidates have ten years of experience publishing research, a background in academia or public policy, and have experience working on relevant policy issues, such as governance, transparency, accountability, or participation (Open Government Partnership, 2012b). However, in practice, the level of experience of the researchers varies greatly. In the past, all Independent Reporting Mechanism researchers were encouraged to go to a multi-day in-person training meeting, but virtual trainings were also an option. Events at the global and regional summits were also developed for Independent Reporting Mechanism researchers to exchange ideas and knowledge. If a researcher does not meet the terms of their contract, they can be removed from the project.

Independent Reporting Mechanism Reports

Within the Independent Reporting Mechanism reports, sometimes referred to as country assessment reports, a country's progress on its National Action Plan is evaluated. The country assessment reports are written by the in-country researcher and incorporate a wide range of input from different stakeholders (Open Government Partnership, 2012b). The Independent Reporting Mechanism does not assess countries comprehensively on their governance but rather focuses only on the National Action Plan development and implementation of commitments in each country's individual context. The initial Independent Reporting Mechanism proposal stated that the reports would be reviewed by the International Experts Panel, and the governments would have a chance to comment and offer feedback (Open Government Partnership, 2012b). The governments cannot veto any part of the report, but they can offer feedback to correct factual errors or provide more information to clear up any confusion if needed. The reports are published in both English and the relevant local language. The International Experts Panel works with the local country researchers to adhere to the guidelines developed. In 2014, the criteria and standards subcommittee endorsed the Independent Reporting Mechanism in developing a procedures manual to include operational definitions (e.g., relevance) to aid in-country researchers in making their assessments (Open Government Partnership, 2015a).

Per the initial approving document, the Independent Reporting Mechanism report would be prepared every year for each of the participating governments. The reports for the founding eight countries were to be done by September 2013, and the remaining fifty country assessment reports were to be completed in rounds after that (Open Government Partnership, 2012b). All reports have an executive summary to allow for easy comprehension and comparison. The number and scope of Independent Reporting Mechanism reports have changed over time. Per the September 2017 mechanism procedures manual, the Independent Reporting Mechanism produces two reports for each country—one at the end of the first year of implementation of a country's National Action Plan (the country assessment progress report) and the second at the end of the two-year implementation cycle. The end-of-term report was required beginning in 2016 (Open Government Partnership, 2015a). Again, this model is likely to change with the IRM Refresh.

At the February 2016 meeting of the criteria and standards subcommittee, the International Experts Panel told the subcommittee about a new assessment in the end-of-term report that evaluates whether a country's commitments measurably opened government. This additional assessment is consistent with the general trend of more reports and assessments required as part of the Independent Reporting Mechanism process. The big picture takeaway is that the Independent Reporting Mechanism began with one required report (midterm assessment) and now has two required reports (midterm assessment and final assessment). Both of these reports are much more extensive than originally conceived. As a result, there has been a rather quick increase in the assessments done for each country in the action plan cycle.

The underlying data from the Independent Reporting Mechanism reports are available to the public either in downloadable form or via an interactive website called the OGP Explorer (https://www.opengovpartnership.org/explorer/all-data.html). After using the OGP Explorer interface, you can export the data into a comma-separated values (CSV) text file.

OGP Local

In 2015, there were discussions on how the Open Government Partnership could continue to evolve to include not only national-level governments but also subnational governments. It was said at the time that "hundreds of governors, mayors and other local officials are knocking down OGP's door to sign up and begin sharing their experiences and accessing new international peers and ideas" (Tisné, 2015). In 2015, speaking at the Open Government Partnership Global Summit in Mexico, Samantha Power, US Permanent Representative to the United Nations, spoke about the integration of subnational actors and urged the Open Government Partnership to think about ways to facilitate this integration outside of a summit environment (Power, 2015). However, at that time, there was also concern that a subnational initiative would distract from the Open Government Partnership's focus and that local governments, particularly cities, already had established networks (Heller, 2016). In the end, it was decided that the initiative would go ahead as a pilot project. The OGP Local program, which began as the subnational government pilot program in 2016 with fifteen participating governments, has been growing. Five of the original local members are based in Europe, four are based in Asia-Pacific, seven in the Americas, and four in Africa.

Initially, the local governments went through a similar action plan development cycle as national-level governments, with a focus on action plans that included commitments centering on transparency, accountability, and participation with the use of technology. However, the program has since evolved. Most notably, changes were made to the required process for local governments when joining the Open Government Partnership. These changes, including the removal of the formal assessment by the Independent Reporting Mechanism, were approved at the Steering Committee meeting held in May 2019, with the goal of allowing the OGP Local program greater flexibility in hopes that more governments can be included.

In May 2020, formal recruitment for the next round of OGP Local members began. Key components of the OGP Local program include an orientation and learning program, a formal mentorship program, learning circles, and office hours with Open Government Partnership staff members (Open Government Partnership, 2020b). While this book is primarily focused on national-level governments, civil society groups, and the corresponding impact the Open Government Partnership has had, we acknowledge that the OGP Local program is growing and has the potential to change the nature of the Open Government Partnership itself. In October 2020, another fifty-six local jurisdictions joined the OGP Local program, bringing the total up to sixty-four-member local governments (Open Government Partnership, 2020d).

In the next chapter, we take our analysis further and look more closely at how not only the structures, rules, governance of the Open Government Partnership but also the related practices, operations, and intended and unintended consequences of these have affected the direct and indirect pathways of change.

4 PATHWAYS OF CHANGE

Thus far, we have considered a range of arguments put forward in scholarly literature by open government advocates. We have also looked at the statements of public officials as to why (and why not) open government might be a success. In chapter 2, we reviewed the recent history of public sector reform and found that it was typical for reformers to experience some early successes but for reforms to later run into various kinds of trouble. In sum, reforms encounter ideological conflicts or insurmountable problems with implementation. Inevitably, these problems lead to alternative ideas being proposed, but the important lessons may be either ignored or too difficult for new reformers to avoid repeating. In chapter 3, we considered various arguments from research in international relations about why national membership in international institutions might—or might not—matter for domestic reforms.

In this chapter, we examine whether the Open Government Partnership, as a transnational multistakeholder initiative, has any chance of bucking this historical trend. We develop our arguments on how the Open Government Partnership could potentially spark new changes that lead to genuine improvements in terms of better governance. In particular, we examine the *direct* and *indirect* pathways through which this change can happen. To do so, this chapter draws on both qualitative and quantitative data to assess the two theories of domestic policy change—a direct pathway and an indirect pathway. We test these further in chapter 5 through a focused, single-country case study.

In this chapter, however, we draw on evidence that is global in scope in order to critically assess the extent to which both direct and indirect pathways may be operating in the case of the Open Government Partnership and to better understand how each works. As well as marshaling evidence of direct and indirect pathways from a multitude of different sources, we embed our arguments in the public administration and political science literature, where a similar stream of ideas has accumulated and grown over time. However, we present a new synthesis of the literature, considering direct and indirect pathways of change not just as two different and complementary sets of change mechanisms but as critical parts of governmental reform that are set into motion by new transnational multistakeholder initiatives, such as the Open Government Partnership.

In the rest of this chapter, we assemble evidence relevant to both the direct and indirect pathways. But first, some conceptual elucidation is needed. We look to a body of multidisciplinary literature on direct and indirect policy effects to show how indirect effects could also play a powerful role in transnational multistakeholder initiatives such as the Open Government Partnership. The building blocks of indirect pathways of policy change already exist in political science, but these building blocks need to be repurposed to explain how they can be applied to a transnational multistakeholder initiative.

EVIDENCE OF THE DIRECT PATHWAY OF CHANGE

In 2013 at the opening of the first Open Government Partnership Global Summit in London, UK Prime Minister David Cameron said:

> I think we'll have more members, more commitments, more enthusiasm, because this is absolutely an idea—not only whose time has come—but has the real transformative potential to help poor countries get richer and to help wealthier countries sustain their advances, and make sure, as I said, that wealth and power in countries is properly shared. (UK Cabinet Office, 2013)

Cameron spoke passionately about the potential that the Open Government Partnership had to foster a process of change, but his speech did not delve into *how* this change could happen. Of course, this was a time to beat the battle drums rather than to reflect and question his own and other leaders' underlying assumptions.

We would not be giving Cameron enough credit if we suggested that his speech and the mood of the first summit were only about beating drums. If we look closer, we can see some assumptions about the main idea of change and how this was reflected in the institutional design of the Open Government Partnership. In the same speech, Cameron stated that "the sustainability of the Open Government Partnership—well, it'll depend on all of us. It'll depend on the politicians making their promises and keeping their promises." When the UK, along with seven other countries, founded the Open Government Partnership, their vision for the organization was informed by an idea of how developing an accountable system of rules and processes for member countries would drive governmental change. These rules and processes—the eligibility criteria, biannual evaluation process, and constitution of the organizational leadership—are all part of the machinery for a pathway of change that we describe as having a *direct* path of causation.

The reasoning of the direct pathway goes something like this: We know from prior experience that if action A occurs, then result B is likely to occur. With this knowledge in mind, a direct pathway of change could be established with an institutional design that—if adhered to—will lead to the desired reform outcome. Thus, for the Open Government Partnership, a system is put in place to institutionalize action, the action is controlled with formal eligibility rules in the Partnership, and this will lead to the intended effect of compliance with commitments. In this direct pathway, the nature of policy impacts are highly intentional on the part of decision makers, and the types of actions needed to bring about the desired effects require a limited number of intervening variables. This direct pathway of change is shown in figure 4.1.

The logic of this pathway is straightforward, but political science scholars have often struggled with its underlying concept of causation, including philosophical disagreements over whether institutional designs and approaches can actually cause real policy changes. Many years ago, the scholars Elkins and Simeon (1979) explained this puzzle when developing their theory of policy influence. Political efficacy makes it possible for policies to have an influence, they argued. Political efficacy is embodied in specific commitments, rules, procedures, and regulations such that individuals who carry them out assume that these commitments have a causal power to

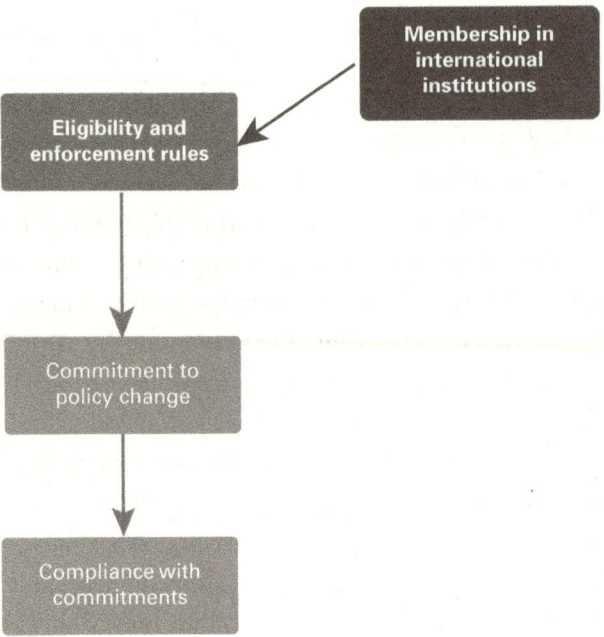

Figure 4.1
Direct pathway of change.

produce the desired effect of the commitments. Elkins and Simeon say that the individuals who carry out these commitments

> do not automatically engage in a particular action; the final action depends as well on the existence of relevant institutions or leadership. The assumption opens the possibility of action, and it disposes the members of the group sharing it to certain actions more than to others. (133)

This shared action, described by Elkins and Simeon, is reflected well in the National Action Plan cycle under the leadership of the Open Government Partnership. The institutional design of the Open Government Partnership is intended to dispose members to produce certain desired actions in the form of open government commitments. As we explained in the preceding chapters, the chief tools used by the Open Government Partnership for driving public sector reforms are the policy commitments—new laws and processes, intergovernmental collaborations, technologies, campaigns, and many other policy ideas—that are developed in a National Action Plan. A carefully developed, formalized system for design, implementation, and evaluation supports these commitments. This system is designed to make the commitments ambitious and relevant to open government with the potential to transform the public sector.

This approach of the National Action Plan cycle has that implicit, direct causal logic. (If A, then B.) In concrete terms, this means that *if* a government implements the right decision-making procedures with a civil society consultation process, appoints a government ministry to oversee the implementation of the commitment, invests resources into its commitments, and endeavors to adhere to the milestones, then it will, to a certain extent, result in more transparency, accountability, citizen participation, and even other public goods, such as legitimacy, satisfaction, and even better democracy.

The direct pathway also represents a causal logic of the kind that epistemologists would call naïve realism. Naïve realism does not mean that the approach is naïve in the sense of facile or uninformed but rather that the idea rests upon a belief that the cause-effect relationships that make up reality are as simple and self-evident as we would expect them to be. In other words, the occurrence of B taking place after A right in front of our eyes is exactly as it appears to be—a causal relationship resulting from the formal membership mechanisms of the Open Government Partnership.

The Independent Reporting Mechanism and the National Action Plan cycle are, therefore, clear cases of the kinds of explicit institutional designs that are intended to produce specific policy outputs with broader governance outcomes. In other words, these mechanisms are part of an intended direct pathway of change.

The challenge is to understand and evaluate how this direct pathway works at a microlevel of actors and policies. These direct mechanisms are, of course, designed to create an impact, and the Open Government Partnership takes the importance of being transparent about its performance seriously. The National Action Plan cycle incentivizes governments to deliver on their commitments, and an open evaluation process helps to leverage external attention and pressure on this process as well as enable learning for the future.

However, as we will see below, this direct pathway of change has shown largely mixed results. We first evaluate the operation of a direct pathway of change before contrasting it with an alternative, indirect pathway of change that we suggest is a more useful analytical approach.

Independent Reporting Mechanism and National Action Plan Cycle

Given that the direct pathway of change is explicitly accounted for in the design of the Open Government Partnership, we can find out how well it performs by zooming in on the formal mechanisms of the Independent Reporting Mechanism and the design and implementation of commitments themselves. We can further analyze the official data on the performance of the commitments through the Open Government Partnership's own data in the Open Government Partnership Explorer. In the examination of the direct pathway, we also illustrate the performance of the National Action Plan by commenting on the opinions expressed by country stakeholders and Reporting Independent Mechanism researchers in the reports. We draw on material from Open Government Partnership progress reports, member self-evaluations, and news articles, as well as conversations with Open Government Partnership staff and civil society organizations that are engaged in the Independent Reporting Mechanism evaluation process.

Commitment compliance and performance

We begin our examination of the direct pathway by looking at reported data from the Open Government Partnership's Independent Reporting Mechanism. We also go further into depth on the types of commitments that have been proposed and their results. Does this consciously designed system of first creating a policy, then implementing, then evaluating it achieve what it is supposed to? Does the Open Government Partnership really benefit from this kind of commitment-based approach? We can address these questions by looking at the outcomes of the commitments through performance statistics created by the official evaluation process undertaken by the Open Government Partnership Independent Reporting Mechanism and the Open Government Partnership country researchers.

We start with some regression analysis to test the significance of predicted relationships of the kind that Open Government Partnership institutional

Table 4.1

Predicted effect of country processes on commitment success

Variables	Model 1 progress		Model 2 impact	
Joint implementation	−0.039	(0.124)	0.229	(0.241)
Accountability	−0.181	(0.304)	−0.235	(0.230)
Measurability	0.528***	(0.114)	0.426**	(0.135)
Goal clarity				
Goal: information	0.141	(0.172)	0.499	(0.415)
Goal: participation	−0.041	(0.144)	1.076**	(0.456)
Goal: accountability	−0.112	(0.136)	0.384	(0.358)
Goal: technology	0.244	(0.161)	0.964**	(0.377)
N	1077		921	
Wald chi2	24.36***		67.37***	
R2	0.026		0.061	

Ordinal logistic regression estimates. The coefficients are log odds representing the change in probability from a unit increase of the independent variable—standard errors in parentheses. Dependent variables are measured as follows: Progress is rated by the Independent Reporting Mechanism researcher on a scale of 0–3 where 0 is not even started, 1 is no or limited completion, 2 is substantial completion, and 3 is full completion. Impact is rated by the Independent Reporting Mechanism researcher on a scale of 0–3, where 0 is no impact, 1 is minor impact, 2 is moderate impact, and 3 is transformative impact. Independent variables are all dichotomous (0 or 1), measured as follows: Joint implementation is a variable indicating whether or not the commitment was developed through a collaborative decision-making process between the government and civil society. Accountability is a variable indicating whether the commitment was given a named, responsible official as the person ultimately in charge. Measurability indicates whether the commitment was designed with explicit and clear milestones against which to measure progress toward completion. Finally, goal clarity is measured as a dichotomous variable for four possible goals on which the Independent Reporting Mechanism researcher can decide if the commitment is clear or not.
Source: Adapted from Ingrams (2017b).
* $p < 0.05$ confidence level.
** $p < 0.01$ confidence level.
***$p < 0.001$ confidence level

designers expected to show positive results. Table 4.1 presents the results of two models of different commitment-level outcomes in terms of implementation and potential impact as assessed by country researchers. Each coefficient shows the direction of change in these outcomes associated with different official policy inputs into the design of these commitments. We used regression analysis with a sample of all (approximately one thousand) commitments from all Open Government Partnership countries between the years 2011 and 2016 to estimate whether the presence of these design characteristics leads to more success. Each of the independent variables shown in the table (joint implementation, accountability, measurability, and goal clarity) are dichotomous (zero or one), taken from the evaluation scores determined by the Independent Reporting Mechanism researcher for each of those countries where the commitments are recorded.

Table 4.1 shows that the processes carefully designed by the Open Government Partnership to procure good results—such as having an official joint implementation process among government ministries, adopting an accountability process with civil society, and designing commitments with measurable and clear goals—do often lead to success. Success, in this case, is measured as whether or not a commitment is substantially or entirely completed within the stipulated timeframe (model 1) or as the potential impact the commitment can have (model 2). But this applies only to the characteristics of *measurability* and *goal clarity*, which are associated with better-performing commitments. This means that ideas, such as using joint implementation and going through the accountability procedures with civil society, do not necessarily lead to better-performing commitments. Despite the hard efforts that national and subnational governments put into using joint implementation and accountability procedures, these things actually appear to make no difference to the performance of the commitments.

The track record of the National Action Plan cycle

We can get a further idea of the performance of the direct pathway by looking at summary statistics from the National Action Plan cycle. Table 4.2 shows frequencies and percentages for the number of completed commitments, number of repeated commitments, patterns or trends in completed commitments, and the distribution of quality characteristics (level of completion and potential impact) across commitments. An impressive 4,094 commitments have been evaluated by the Open Government Partnership Independent Reporting Mechanism as of January 2020. Further, 70 percent of these commitments were found by the Independent Reporting Mechanism researchers to be relevant; that is, they met at least one of the value areas of open government (transparency, participation, technology, and accountability).

Table 4.2
Open Government Partnership commitment statistics (2011–2019)

Commitment characteristics	
Number of country members	78
Withdrawn countries	4
Number of commitments	4,094
Commitment level of completion*	
Not started	14%
Limited	38%
Substantial	29%
Complete	19%
Commitment potential impact**	
Transformative	13%
Moderate	40%
Minor	42%
None	5%
Relevance to open government	
Relevant	70%
Not relevant	30%

* Not including unclear or withdrawn, not determined (ND), etc.
** Not including not available (NA), ND, etc.

However, only a very small percentage (19 percent) of these commitments were ever completed or were intrinsically transformative (13 percent).

The direct pathway as a positive performance trend

In the analysis above, we examined the direct effects using cross-sectional data. This type of data, however, does not allow us to look at another important design in the direct pathways of the Open Government Partnership approach, which is the fostering of positive learning cycles through the commitment design and evaluation process. According to the Independent Reporting Mechanism theory of change, if this positive cycle is working well, there should be an observable improvement in the performance of commitments over time.

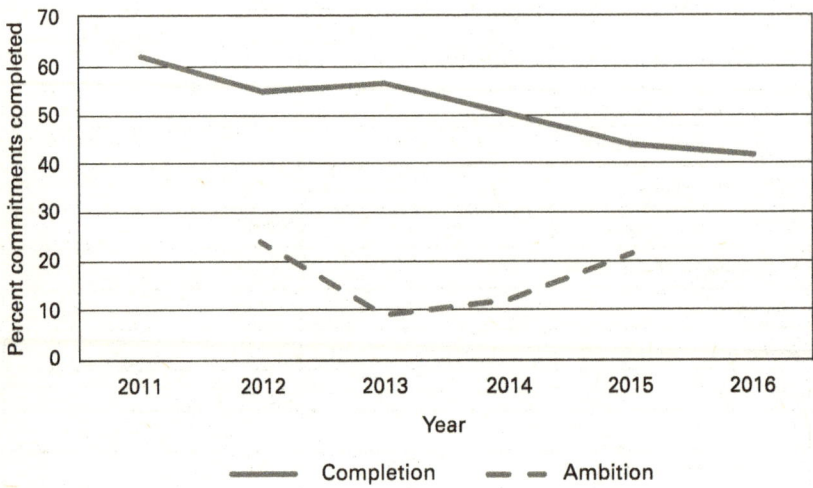

Figure 4.2
Performance of commitments over time.

Figure 4.2 shows trend lines with available data for all commitments between 2011 and 2016 for the commitments' average completion level and ambition rating across all Open Government Partnership members.[1] What would we expect to see if the commitment cycle was improving the open government performance of countries? We should hope to see the virtuous learning cycle that would show a linear progression over the years moving from the left in an upward direction, showing that a greater rate of commitments is being completed over time and/or that the ambition of the commitments is steady or progressing, which would indicate that the countries are learning. In contrast, what we see is that the years seem to be moving downward slightly in terms of the completion level, while ambition levels show no clear sign of improvement.

Stars to Flops and Everything Between

The analyses above suggest that the direct pathway of change has had limited success. Country-level and commitment-level statistical analysis of this kind is insightful because it can give us a broad insight into expected impacts. However, to understand whether and how the National Action Plan commitment process has worked within specific policy fields within countries, we need to pay greater attention to the commitments themselves and the policy contexts in which they are implemented. Thus, we continue the study below by describing how individual commitments perform, and we venture some explanations for why they often fail to have much impact. To get a sense of what the commitments do and how they perform according to the official procedures, we also need to go beyond the numbers to examine what the commitments set out to achieve and how their stipulated objectives did or did not come to fruition.

The main finding of our analysis below is that commitments are a mixed bag of high- and low-performing initiatives. There are some positive stories, but the overall narrative of direct impact created by these commitments is one that reformers with high expectations would find very disillusioning. Although the direct approach appears to work in some cases, it is also frequently unreliable. If we zoom in on specific cases of Open Government Partnership commitments, we see that countries experienced highly varied levels of success—many commitments do extraordinarily well, but some also fail miserably. The most common commitment, for instance, is one that does so-so. It does not completely fall short of what it set out to do, but it also does not make any notable change. In the analysis below, we review both successful and unsuccessful experiences of specific commitments, shedding light on the variability of a direct pathway of change and some of the barriers leading to its occasional failure.

We start our in-depth analysis of commitments by using the Open Government Partnership Explorer data to select a small number of cases to discuss, going beyond numerical indicators. In these selections, we aim to illustrate the diversity of commitment success stories both individually, in terms of how smoothly they were implemented, and organizationally, in terms of their geographical spread and the assortment of policy areas where they are used.

Figure 4.3 shows four broad categories of commitments. Our goal here is not to exhaustively categorize all commitments but rather to identify key archetypes in order to limit the number we analyze according to a range of different success levels. Not every single official-published commitment fits neatly into this matrix, and we only select cases that are distinctly classifiable,

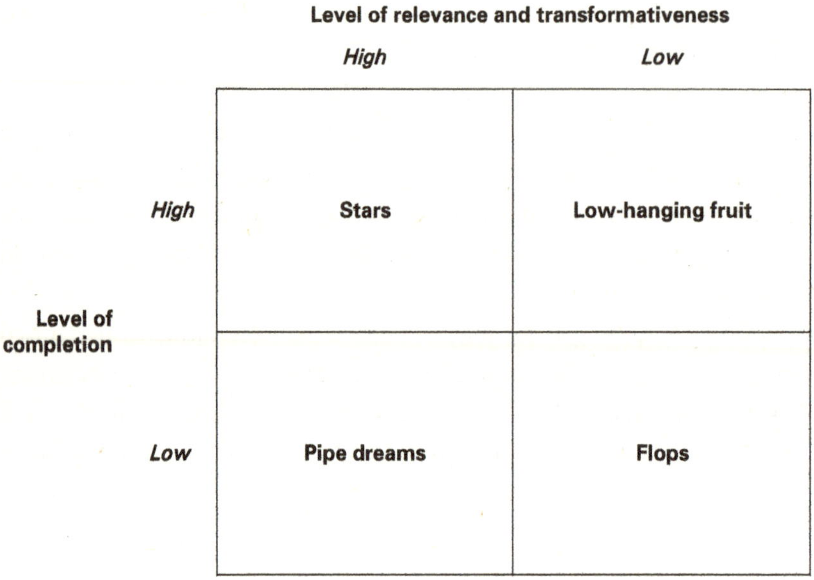

Level of relevance and transformativeness

	High	Low
High	Stars	Low-hanging fruit
Low	Pipe dreams	Flops

Level of completion (vertical axis)

Figure 4.3
Matrix of four types of commitment.

while many others fall somewhere between these four major categories. As all commitments are assessed by the Independent Reporting Mechanism country researcher for their levels of completion (not started, limited, substantial, or complete), relevance, and potential transformativeness, we can categorize commitments as falling within the four cells of the matrix as follows:[2]

- **Stars** are the commitments that do very well. Stars have the hallmarks of prototypical commitments in the way that the Open Government Partnership system is intended. That is, they are designed in such a way that they are relevant to Open Government Partnership values, they are potentially transformative, and at least substantially completed on time.
- **Pipe dreams** are barely completed to any satisfactory degree, but they do impress in terms of their relevance and moderate or major potential for transformativeness.
- **Low-hanging fruit** has a high degree of completion according to their original plan. While they may have minor impacts, they may not be

particularly relevant or likely to lead to substantial public sector transformation. This lopsidedness comes from the fact that their objectives are not ambitious, and their plan is easy to adhere to.

Flops are simply poor performers in every respect. Despite the fact that these commitments show little potential to have a real impact on society (and should thus be comparatively simple to implement), they nevertheless also fail to make progress toward their original stipulated goal.

This schema tells us a lot about how Open Government Partnership commitments might impact the open government quest for transforming government. But we need to know more about what these different kinds of commitments really look like in practice, how they come about, and what this can tell us about the direct effects that the Open Government Partnership aims to put into practice. In this section, we explore these points further.

Stars

Some commitments do genuinely reach an impressive level of ambition and a strong potential to change the public sector for the better. Such commitments can come to fruition with enough wise planning, material resources, and political commitment. In these star commitments, the Open Government Partnership membership formula works precisely as it is intended. In their design and implementation, the commitments may restore the hope of true believers and seem to show that the initiative can indeed deliver direct impacts.

Star commitments often seem to depend on a certain degree of luck (or rather, avoidance of bad luck) along the path of implementation. Random or routine changes in government administration can seriously knock Open Government Partnership commitments out of place because they are typically not legally binding on the new leadership incumbents in government. Star commitments not only rely on a stable environment but also may rely on reaching a certain fortuitous amount of political support and resources. Such policy-window successes normally occur when many actors come together to do something new that is collectively in their self-interest.

One good case of such policy-window successes in open government commitments is the transparency reforms being undertaken by many former Soviet countries as they seek to step out from under the shadow of former regimes and embrace greater public openness about regime secrets.

Ukraine, for example, completed a commitment to open the archives of the USSR internal affairs and secret service from 1917 to 1991. Although in many other post-Soviet countries this process of opening up was accomplished much sooner after independence and was an integral part of democratization reforms (Ninua, 2016), new demands were placed on the Ukrainian government by protesters during the Euromaidan protests in 2014, highlighting the ability of open government commitments to respond to political changes in society. The Law on Access to Archives of Repressive Bodies of the Communist Totalitarian Regime of 1917–1991 requires relevant agencies in possession of sensitive Soviet-era information to send the information to a central repository and sets out the procedures for access and the exemptions. This is a transformative change for Ukrainian citizens, particularly journalists. In addition to important requirements set out in the law, the process of implementation was impressive, too, as the passage of the law was accomplished in a matter of days, exceeding the expectations of the government itself. Further, the process of devising and designing the law was exemplary, too, having been codrafted and sponsored by civil society (Ninua, 2016). The Ukraine Independent Reporting Mechanism researcher found that the law had a major impact on opening government.[3]

Georgia is another good example of a former Soviet country that has used the Open Government Partnership platform to create space for new and sometimes bold political opportunities. Georgia completed a commitment to make government surveillance statistics transparent to the public. The Supreme Court was given the responsibility to ensure that the statistics, going back to 2014, were published in a complete and timely manner. The data, which "includes the number of motions on phone tapping submitted by prosecutors to the courts and the number of motions granted by the courts," provided a basis for civil society to develop a surveillance awareness campaign called This Affects You Too (Gogidze, 2018, 49). The implementation of the commitment was open to amendments during the transition.

The commitment also showed an admirable level of responsiveness to civil society in the way that Open Government Partnership commitments are supposed to. Lobbying from civil society organizations successfully led to the surveillance data adding geographic and crime type levels (Iakobidze, 2017). While the statistics were initially only released by the Supreme Court in response to publicly salient cases, in 2015, all data was released, and annual reports were produced. Independent and professional analyses have taken place as a result of the availability of the data, which has drawn attention to the rise in surveillance by the government over the last few years and the publication of new recommendations for the government (Iakobidze, 2017). The Open Government Partnership reported that Georgia is one of the very few states in the world to publish such statistics and that the commitment is also remarkable for moving outside of the open government focus on the executive to the judicial branch of government (Open Government Partnership, 2016a).

In a different context altogether, the United Kingdom has also taken major steps to address corruption through Open Government Partnership commitments, even though it is often considered among the least corrupt countries in the world. A coalition of ten nongovernmental organizations, called the Bond Group, released a report lamenting the lack of awareness of open government in the UK government and a particular lack of work in fostering participation and collaboration to address the challenge of corruption (Bond Anti-Corruption Group, 2018). The UK launched a commitment to tackle corruption both domestically and through its international development work, led by the Home Office and the Bond Group, by integrating anticorruption work across the government into one strategy. By the end of the action plan time period, the program was complete. The Independent Reporting Mechanism researcher stated that this would have a potentially transformative impact. Subsequently, the impact on openness in the UK was major.

Another type of star commitment is policies that evidence good planning and vision in their design stages, even before implementation. These are often inspired by executive leadership visions that aim high in terms of transformation and that can also be carried out through a clever implementation strategy. In Albania, the government wrote and passed a law on whistleblower protection. To support the reporting of corruption cases, the government also created an online reporting portal. A draft law was already in place by the time of writing the Open Government Partnership action plan, but, in addition to passing the law, a civil society consultation process was used to improve the draft before passage. The Albanian Independent Reporting Mechanism researcher gave this commitment top marks in all respects—it was fully complete within its stipulated timeframe and was relevant and transformative for the public sector. The law was, among other Albanian reforms, credited for positive steps toward better governance (Volintiru & Olivas Osuna, 2018). However, even this impressive achievement did begin to suffer setbacks. The outcome of reported cases of corruption was not reported by the government, and the Independent Reporting Mechanism researcher reported that in its second year of existence, the number of complaints submitted on the portal had halved in number, suggesting that its initial promise had not endured.

On other occasions, star commitments can be driven or supported by the adoption of powerful new technologies that make it possible to transform a particular governmental process. Though it is rare, if not impossible, that a technology can guarantee such a transformation without appropriate reforms to accompany the technology in terms of providing legal, ethical, and political measures. For example, Croatia implemented an online citizen consultation process, including setting up an interactive website, integrating interagency open data of working groups and committees for new laws and regulations, training officials on its use, and publishing annual reports on the performance of the consultation process. The commitment was part of a broader e-government reform that won the Open Government Partnership award for improving services in Europe (Government of the Republic of Croatia, 2015). This commitment was supported by recent legislation on transparency and participation, including the 2009 Public Consultation Code and the 2013 Access to Information Act (Open Government Partnership, 2013a). The Croatian Independent Reporting Mechanism researcher found a lot to be impressed by in terms of concrete outputs, reporting that:

In the two months after the launch of the central portal (through 30 June 2015, the end of the first year of implementation), 1,645 comments on draft laws, other regulations and acts were submitted. In this short period, 84 public consultations were started on the portal, by 17 different government bodies. In the first 60 days over 1,600 users registered, 867 of which are individuals, 419 companies, 126 trades, 80 associations, 33 institutions, 36 cooperatives and another 100 representatives of other legal entities. (Government of the Republic of Croatia, 2015)

Further, over thirty training sessions were carried out for more than 180 officials from all government bodies (Mendeš, 2016). But star commitments may sometimes be less star-like when we look behind the numbers to the more qualitative impacts of the commitments on society. In fact, in the case of the Public Consultation Code and Access to Information Act in Croatia, the Independent Reporting Mechanism researcher still questioned its success. Despite resounding performance in meeting virtually all the milestones within the plan, the researcher stated that "based on the evidence, it does not seem that these milestones, even if fully implemented (as a majority of them are) would really transform the status quo." A Norwegian think tank, Chr. Michelsen Institute, found that the impact of the commitment was dampened by low public awareness and political attention on bigger economic challenges (Montero & Taxell, 2015).

Pipe dreams

Pipe dream commitments had high potential impact but very little actual success in becoming implemented. On the surface, these commitments embody the spirit of the Open Government Partnership view of transformative change in the public sector. They look good on paper, but in practice, they have no real chance of succeeding. Sometimes, as in the case of so-called openwashing, reformers may deliberately create these lofty commitments with the idea that good intentions are sufficient to get public recognition for open government reforms. Ultimately, they may reason, no one will really notice in the end whether the plans are realized or not.

One example is North Macedonia, which launched a commitment that aimed to consolidate its actual participation in the open government commitment design process by creating a permanent government–civil society advisory council composed of central administrative agencies and representatives from civil society. This was a kind of metacommitment that aimed to design processes that would generate useful commitments in the future. The North Macedonian Independent Reporting Mechanism researcher who evaluated this commitment opined that this was a transformative idea. However, the Independent Reporting Mechanism researcher also noted that the said council had actually worsened the quality of open government in the country. The involvement of civil society worsened because there was wide disapproval of the process for selecting civil society representatives for the council. There was also no evidence that any government members had been appointed to the council or that the council had taken shape in any functional way. A major lack of political will was identified by the Independent Reporting Mechanism researcher as a reason for the failure. The democracy-promotion organization, Freedom House, gave North Macedonia its first raise in its civil society score in over ten years. However, the Freedom House description of civil society efforts also notes that reforms have failed to truly transform the quality of dialogue and cooperation between the government and civil society, saying, "Critics stress that the resulting debates are usually brief, and that not all relevant civil society groups are invited to participate" (Freedom House, 2015).

Why does this type of problem occur? There are a variety of possible reasons. The tendency of multilateral organizations to create window-dressing behavior is one reason. In this case, the pipe dream is actually less of a dream and more of a ploy, as the commitment is not designed with any real intention of changing the status quo but rather to look impressive and to win credit and legitimacy from political supporters and the international community. Window-dressing strategies are typically designed to cover up for a lack of action or even act in a fashion contrary to the overt messaging strategy. This window-dressing may be designed to appease civil society or the public for reforms that have no chance of actually happening.

On the other hand, overambitious commitments may not be window-dressing (deceit), but there may be a sincere effort to reform. The shortcomings may be simply a result of a lack of capacity. That is, the commitment shows a poor match between policymaking capacity and the scale of the ambition or unrealistic goals that evidence a lack of planning. Alternatively, the policymaking capacity is potentially sufficient, but unexpected exigencies occur along the implementation path. Some astonishingly bold commitments fall into this category. For example, Mongolia set out to adopt a disclosure system for financial assets of public servants (Zagdragchaa & Tserenjav, 2017), while Trinidad and Tobago set out to "establish a mechanism that allows adequate representation of Civil Society organizations in order to provide feedback to public policy decision making on a regular basis" (Drayton, 2017, 15).

A capacity miscalculation often underlies the ability side of the commitment planning process. The South Korean government committed to proactively publicly disclose all documents that have been signed by officials at a director-general level or higher (Government of South Korea, 2014, 10). This disclosure would amount to an estimated ten million documents in the first year of the commitment's implementation. In addition to this plan, the government wanted to establish a civil society watch group that would monitor implementation, ensuring that all levels of government are disclosing the requisite information in the right forms. The information would be created in a searchable form categorized into ten major policy areas (health, food, safety, child-rearing, finance, education, consumer protection, leisure, job, and housing). The watch group would be selected through an online contest. While the potential impact of the program was said to be moderate, the actual outcome was that the results never fully materialized, and the Independent Reporting Mechanism researcher scored the commitment as only marginal in its effect on open government.

The South Korean case highlights the miscalculation of a future administrative burden. However, because open government places expectations on the role of citizens as information consumers or political participants, the miscalculation of citizen capacity can also bring down a commitment with grand ambitions. For example, Indonesia aimed to draw in the public to help develop conservation efforts in mangrove forests. It also aimed to introduce a waste management system in a traditional market. More broadly, Indonesia also aimed to "enhance public understanding on protecting the environment and also to encourage public participation in environmental policy related decision making" (Open Government Partnership, 2014b, 83). However, virtually nothing happened. The World Bank notes that a major barrier to the conservation of mangrove regions in Indonesia is that the human settlements in those areas are extremely poor (World Bank, 2015). The World Bank framework for financial aid to Indonesia notes that "poor governance and corruption continued to be a major break on the country's prospects from infrastructure development and the delivery of services to environmental degradation" (World Bank, 2015).

It is very difficult to say with certainty whether a pipe dream commitment is a result of a lack of sincerity, a lack of capacity, or, most likely, a result of a political and administrative process where both elements combine in complex ways. Some commitments look too good to be true, and we might suspect a lack of genuine belief among their sponsors that they could ever become a reality. This is especially so if the commitment has strong political appeal to stakeholders, such as citizens, but the chance of holding the government accountable for the commitment is low.

For example, Ghana sought to implement a new system of auditing reports that would be supported by an audit report implementation committee joined by agency representatives, civil society representatives, and independent professionals (Open Government Partnership, 2013b). This choice of committee design was meant to cut off conflicts of interests between agency representatives and the composition of the committee in order to fully comply with the goals of the Financial Administration Act and to ultimately amend the act itself to establish such a committee moving forward. The Independent Reporting Mechanism researcher opined that the plan could have had a real impact on government and stated:

> The government did not begin any of the milestones. In addition, this commitment did not target the appropriate legal documents. It should have targeted the Audit Service Act in order to allow implementation of these changes. The amendments to the Audit Service Act necessary to complete the commitment were not made, hence the commitment was not started. (Adamtey 2016, 24)

Indeed, Ghana's capacity for implementing financial auditing practices may be particularly weak. Historically, the basic auditing procedures, though present in law, have not been used in practice (Development Gateway, Inc., & Opening Contracting Partnership, 2017).

Other commitments seem to falter due to insufficient political or public support for their motivating ideas. This seems to be the case for one Dutch commitment, called Change Attitudes and Procedures Through Smarter Working and Public Servant, designed to change the internal culture of the government. However, it did not have an immediate appeal for citizens or civil society. The idea behind this commitment was that achieving transparency in government relies on a cultural shift and, therefore, public servants should be trained on how to integrate transparency into government in such a way that adds value to government and society. In addition to a program of awareness-raising and training, the initiative aimed to set up a network of "do tanks" that would develop open government models and spread them in society. The initiative was started in 2013, but two years later, the Independent Reporting Mechanism researcher opined that progress had been limited, and the impact on opening government was practically zero. According to the Independent Reporting Mechanism researcher, "Promised research on how to create more public value, did not take place, nor could the IRM researcher find evidence of enhanced social impact through these programmes." The researcher went on to surmise that:

> Though many activities took place that suggest significant progress on this commitment, a closer look on what actually happened, shows that there were no specific efforts to "open up to the outer world." At the end of the implementation period, it became clear that this commitment—while focused on promoting transparency—was not relevant to OGP values because the conferences and networks were mainly being used to address public administration issues such as reorganization and professionalization that did not have any ties to improving public service using open government solutions as their main goal. (Raat, 2016, 31)

Unfortunately, many of the pipe-dream commitments that run into capacity problems are ambitious technology reform commitments that are undermined by flaws in the technology. For example, the UK Independent Reporting Mechanism researcher stated that the UK sought to do the following:

> Work with governments and civil society organizations internationally to create an online space to share experiences of embedding high quality standards into information with a view to building an accreditation scheme to enable citizens and organizations to assess their progress. (Worthy, 2015, 33)

The aim was to help both the UK government and outside states set better healthcare information standards by publishing an index of health resources and inviting collaborations with other countries. However, the commitment never got off the ground. According to the Independent Reporting Mechanism researcher, "Commitment was officially withdrawn due to administrative and legal changes within the NHS and concerns over privacy issues" (Worthy, 2015, 11).

Pipe dreams can sometimes be very well designed, but the ultimate inability they have to move forward can occur in small parts of particular milestones. These commitments can sometimes commit the error of believing that "if you build it, they will come." For example, North Macedonia sought to implement local-level participatory policymaking by using mandatory consultations with citizens on budgeting and planning processes. This was potentially path-breaking as, according to the Independent Reporting Mechanism researcher, "traditionally, local governments in North Macedonia did not cooperate with CSOs and citizens on policy" (Korunovska, 2017, 68). As part of the initiative, civil society organizations would be proactively encouraged to participate in the consultation process. The Independent Reporting Mechanism researcher viewed the commitment as having good potential. It was designed with specific milestones, was relevant to several open government values, and included access to information, civic participation, and public accountability. The researcher also assessed the commitment as potentially having a decent impact. However, the plans were very slow to start. The midterm assessment found that the work had not even started, and at the end of the two years, some discussion had been made among government organizations at the local level, but these steps had not been translated into any concrete action. According to the Independent Reporting Mechanism researcher:

> Some efforts were made in the last year to build the capacity of civil servants to organize and implement Community Forums independently as part of the exit phase of the program. Approximately 100 civil servants from 29 municipalities were trained in 2016. The Community Forums program closed in March 2017, without making the consultations mandatory. They were not included in the new OGP action plan, and the sustainability of this positive initiative is uncertain at the moment. In this sense, no mechanism was established to allow for public accountability in the last two years. (Korunovska, 2017, 69)

Low-hanging fruit

We can understand low-hanging fruit commitments as precisely the opposite of what we have above described as pipe dreams. Low-hanging fruit demonstrates low ambition but is generally completed at much higher rates. These commitments generally involve lower costs—whether in terms of funding, capacity, political opposition, or the extent of administrative changes required. But for this very reason, these are often the most appealing for governments to include in National Action Plans, given their greater likelihoods of implementation success.

In one example, Albania undertook a commitment to "promote and engage local authorities in the Open Government Partnership values" (Government of Albania, 2015, 6). The wording for the commitment specifically states that the commitment was proposed by Albanian civil society organizations. The Independent Reporting Mechanism researcher scored the specificity of this commitment as "zero" and also recorded the relevance to the Open Government Partnership values and the potential impact as negligible. The results of the initiative were a partial success. Several civil society organizations, such as the Institute for Democracy and Mediation (IDM), Mjaft! Movement, and Infocip, worked with local government organizations to raise awareness of open government. However, the Independent Reporting Mechanism researcher also opined that none of these efforts were truly "systematic" in scope or carried out in a coordinated way. A Transparency and Accountability Initiative report found that Albania leverages values, such as transparency and accountability, to win support from the European Union even though that is not a part of their Open Government Partnership commitments (Moses, 2016). The same report notes that civil society in Albania only sees "sporadic" opportunities to promote Open Government Partnership values and that a primary political motivating factor for this commitment was that the government advisor on Open Government Partnership planning was appointed as the Minister of Local Government.

In other cases, low-hanging fruit commitments are easy to implement and require less investment in the design phases because they have already proven success elsewhere or because they follow naturally from other policies or programs that have already been set in motion. For example, Malta launched a commitment to make its beaches cleaner, and Costa Rica had a commitment to "conduct a feasibility study on the modernization of the postal service" (Government of Malta, 2012, 6; Government of Costa Rica, 2013, 13). Both of these may be valuable for citizens and may even be implemented using methods emphasizing transparency, accountability, and public participation, but they do not go beyond what would be considered the normal existing responsibilities of government.

One such commitment that piggy-backed on an initiative that had already started was the Document Management Policy in Brazil. The Brazilian government embarked on a program to train public officials in how to implement its new digitization strategy, the Document Management Policy, in the federal government. Undoubtedly, training is a normal part of adopting any new major program in government, so it is unlikely that Brazil only did this because of its membership in Open Government Partnership. Such a clear reach for low-hanging fruit may seem surprising from an Open Government Partnership founding member, which, one assumes, would be leading with exemplary commitments. In addition to training the officials around the work of the policy, the government planned to increase the frequency of technical meetings between central sectorial and sectional agencies. The Independent Reporting Mechanism researcher believed that this had no relevance to Open Government Partnership values and only minor potential impact. However, it was fully implemented within time. According to comments in the plan submitted by São Paulo for a subnational action plan:

The Training Program "Open Government Agents," which trained more than 14,000 people through workshops and activities that took place in a decentralized way in several districts of São Paulo, aiming to reach the most faraway neighborhoods which concentrates the majority of the city's population and urban problems. Since 2015, this program hired 46 open government agents/educators and received several awards, drawing international attention thanks to its innovative and inclusive training model (Open Government Partnership, 2016b, 2).

Thus, some low-hanging fruit might be old policies that were virtually guaranteed to be completed because they already existed in a previous form of some sort.

Perhaps the hard work of crafting, deliberating, politicking, and voting on a new law has already been completed, and now the next step is simply making a new addendum to the law or merely overseeing the process of *implementing* the law. Some low-hanging fruit commitments are the result of a government's overlapping membership in similar open government initiatives, such as the Extractive Industries Transparency Initiative or projects that governments had committed to through bilateral trade or aid deals with other countries. For example, Denmark provided assistance to Myanmar in the development of "inclusive democratic processes, good governance, and respect for human rights." Ultimately, the Danish government saw this as being a step toward Myanmar potentially becoming a member of the Open Government Partnership. The goals of the commitment were highly specific and targeted at Myanmar Open Government Partnership membership. Further, there were several goals that had already been concretized in a policy paper from the Danish Ministry of Foreign Affairs. The Danish Independent Reporting Mechanism researcher said that, all considered, this had the potential to make minor impacts to open government in Myanmar. Ultimately, the goal of Myanmar becoming a member of the Open Government Partnership was not achieved. According to the Independent Reporting Mechanism researcher, nothing really changed as a result of this commitment, but the work with Myanmar was and continues to be a long-term objective for Denmark (Danida, n.d.).

By virtue of their involvement in other initiatives, governments can pass off such projects as an Open Government Partnership commitment. In other cases, the commitments are not preexisting in the exact form, but the replication of an older policy or program is so similar that the chances of successfully completing the project within a predictable set of costs are very high. The key characteristic of these commitments is that they are relatively easy to complete. For the very same reason, they are unlikely to pose any tough tests or costs of the kind that we would expect from a transformative commitment. Transformative open government commitments must, almost by definition, incur some cost or require considerable action from the government unless—as in very rare cases—they reach pareto optimal outcomes.

Another way that low-hanging fruit commitments come about is not by copying or duplicating existing efforts per se but by doing small things that are genuinely new but that really have little relevance to making government more open. For example, Norway created an electronic mailbox where citizens could offer suggestions on how to simplify the delivery of everyday services. The tool, relying on an open process of sourcing public input, was surely in the spirit of open government. But, according to the Norwegian government, the idea for this commitment had come from the prior administration, and the current administration was merely carrying it out. The mailbox system is part of the default digital communication system for a range of public services (European Union, 2016). However, it may come as no surprise to learn that the Norwegian Independent Reporting Mechanism researcher evaluated the commitment as having no relevance to Open Government Partnership values or potential impact. Furthermore, the commitment was poorly worded in its goals, and as a result, the Independent Reporting Mechanism researcher also opined that it was difficult to tell whether or not the commitment had been fully implemented after two years. The researcher also had "not found evidence of any formal processes through which this document has been considered" (Government of Norway, 2015, n.p).

Similarly, the Ukrainian government launched a national e-government awareness-raising and training for local government. Again, the Independent Reporting Mechanism researcher found this to have unclear relevance to Open Government Partnership values and potential for only minor impact, and by the end of the implementation timeline, the impact on open government had barely been noticed. But the commitment was completed on schedule. In fact, quite a large volume of outputs was generated: 303 trainings of 5,393 local council members. However, the Independent Reporting Mechanism researcher also said that open government was not notably improved as a result. It seemed that such awareness-raising, while tangentially related to the goals of open government, was simply a normal part of rolling out a new government program.

Flops

Flops are those commitments that combine both the weaknesses of pipe dreams and low-hanging fruit but with none of the strengths of the stars. Such commitments have low completion rates coupled with low ambition and open government relevance. Designers of such commitments devised poor ideas that would not have contributed to opening government anyway and, further, were so poorly conceived that they did not even progress past the implementation phase.

For example, Mongolia launched a commitment to developing a web portal to be used for smart services across a wide range of public services. It was unclear exactly what this was or how it would be achieved. How smart services could be rendered on a website or how multiple services could be integrated was never made clear by the designers of the commitment. According to the Mongolia Independent Reporting Mechanism researcher, the commitment was never started. Furthermore, there was no relevance to open government, as the idea was based on a service provision using smart technology, which is normally used to improve the efficiency or effectiveness of public services rather than improve the openness of the government. As the Independent Reporting Mechanism researcher stated, the commitment was simply "not relevant to open government since they did not aim to make more or better information available to the public, improve opportunities for the public to influence decision making, or improve channels for citizens to hold government officials to account" (Open Government Partnership, 2017e).

When Open Government Partnership commitments miss the point of openness in terms of transparency, participation, or accountability, we can be sure that they are not meeting the basic set of goals and expectations in the commitment development and implementation mechanisms of the organization. This is bad enough, but we know that a commitment is a *flop* if the commitment both sets out on the wrong foot and then continues to fail to even make progress toward being realized. Often these two things—relevance and completion—are intimately related in practice. Lack of relevance may produce a sense of purposelessness, which may then translate into a lack of action. How big can such flops really be? And why do flops occur at all?

One possibility is that there is a problem with the leadership behind the commitment. Leaders who are responsible for designing commitments may renege on their responsibilities because they are afraid of creating policies that may expose them to uncomfortable public attention in the future. Examples of such commitments are those that are poorly worded or that, like the emperor's new clothes, spin an idea of something when, in fact, there is nothing there. In other cases, the poor design of commitments may result from a simple lack of understanding rather than any deliberate attempt to sabotage the commitment design and implementation process. *Openness* can be interpreted very broadly, and leaders may miss the point of transparency, participation, and accountability. Such misunderstanding or misconception often occurs because of undue attention paid to technology. New information and communications technology trends may be misinterpreted for openness or for the kind of legitimate openness envisaged by open government advocates. Leadership incompetence can also occur in the implementation phase of a commitment. Like any policymaking process, a series of events can go wrong, leading to miscommunication and to commitments becoming rushed or poorly planned.

Flops reveal just how susceptible to problems the direct model of open government change is. Unfortunately, it can be even worse, as the case of *malicious* flops shows. Of flops, we might say that they were a waste of time, but with malicious flops, we see that the consequences can go completely in the opposite direction, undermining government transparency, participation, and accountability. In one notorious case, the Philippines' commitment to "involve citizens in the war on drugs," the government tried to involve citizens in a program for reporting suspected members of drug cartels, that Amnesty International (2017) said risked enabling vigilante killings. This People's Watch (Masa Masid) was citizen participation for a purpose that would undermine human safety, human rights, and the rule of law. Or, in the words of a researcher at Human Rights Watch, "If the Duterte administration makes good use of MASA MASID . . . a lot more people are going to die" (Williams, 2018).

Our working definition of a flop is one that is irrelevant, lacking in influence, and furthermore shows poor completion progress in practice. Masa Masid is of a more worrying and fortunately rare type of flop—irrelevant, harmful, and so poor in its design and aims that it was legally defunded in the Philippines and the Philippines Open Government Steering Committee had to submit an updated and redacted version of their action plan with the commitment removed.

In some respects, flops can be a puzzle for open government advocates. They tend to lead analysts to look beyond the Open Government Partnership system itself to external explanations for why this happened. Poor quality policies in strong governance countries present puzzling cases because there is a discrepancy between the country's reputation for good governance and the lack of ambition or follow-through shown in the commitment. Possible characteristics of such commitments are that they resulted from a lack of seriousness given to the action plan, suffered opposition from civil society, or were created by governments that were new to the Open Government Partnership and did not fully understand the goals. Alternately, in other countries, they may reflect underlying weak governance structures, resource constraints, and frequently limited policy implementation across the board—rather than being exceptional to open government processes.

Summary of the Direct Pathway of Change

We review our key findings with respect to a potential direct pathway of impact in the case of the Open Government Partnership below:

- Country evidence of the Independent Reporting Mechanism approach to policy design shows mixed results. Regression analysis shows that some policy design approaches work, but others seem to have no impact. However, while individual policy design practices have little impact, it is still likely that having policy design discipline is better than having no policy design discipline at all.
- According to the Independent Reporting Mechanism data, less than half of Open Government Partnership policy commitments since 2011 have

been at least substantially completed, and 82 percent of all commitments have had a moderate or minor potential impact. This is a low rate of success. There is a small proportion of commitments making a difference, but these few are dwarfed by a majority of commitments that fall flat.
- There is no evidence of a linear improvement in policy commitment performance in the Open Government Partnership over time. Over the three stages of the National Action Plan policy cycle in which the majority of Open Government Partnership countries have now participated, performance has remained flat or declined. This is likely due, in part, to the entry of new members with preexisting low levels of open government. There is also evidence that countries are increasingly conforming to an average performance rate.
- On closer inspection, Open Government Partnership policy commitments are a mixed bag. Like any organization, the Open Government Partnership does suffer a small percentage of policy commitments that are flops or failures because they both miss the point of open government and are also poorly designed. A small percentage are stars. Star commitments come about when innovative public officials seize the opportunity of a policy window to match an existing policy problem with an open government solution to transform government. Most commitments could be considered low-hanging fruit or pipe dreams. The former are cases, such as open data initiatives, where new technologies are used to do something slightly different but without any notable change to the actual performance of government or quality of life for citizens. The latter are initiatives that are ambitious but ultimately unfeasible, possibly motivated by the hope of attracting public praise and external funding.

EVIDENCE OF THE INDIRECT PATHWAY OF CHANGE

As we have seen in our assessment of commitments, the results of the direct pathway of change are often disappointingly ambiguous in the case of the Open Government Partnership. It is difficult to see clear patterns of success. For every star, there is also a flop, along with many commitments that fall somewhere in between these archetypal categories.

One possible way of understanding these findings is simply that transnational multistakeholder reform genuinely leads to little in the way of consistent impact. However, another possibility is that such a focus on rational design and direct causation serves to distract attention from less direct effects that remain outside of this immediate and expected range. Direct pathways of change alone may not be the complete picture.

Indeed, scholars of policy change more generally have often made similar arguments in other settings. Beginning in the 1980s, institutional approaches in the social sciences have turned the attention of scholars to increasingly more complex, indirect causal effects relating to policy, political, and institutional forces (Pierson, 1993). This has opened the way for greater acceptance of less visible or directly measurable phenomena, such as human values and norms, as part of the broader interactions of institutions (Hall & Taylor, 1996). For instance, the policy theorist Paul Sabatier (1991, 147) argues that theories of policy change need to go beyond just the immediate concerns of design and planning to also incorporate "knowledge of specific institutions" and "attention to policy communities and substantive policy information." Policy impacts should also be understood as interactions of political actors, their institutional environments, and policy subsystems composed of coalitions, their resources, and strategies.

In the realm of domestic transparency reforms, scholars have also more recently noted the limits of direct approaches to reform impacts. Fox (2015) discusses the limits of narrow "tactical" reforms, often emphasizing what he calls "low-dose" interventions, in contrast with "strategic" approaches emphasizing broader coordinated efforts across larger numbers of actors and over longer periods of time. Michener (2019, 139) similarly emphasizes that the most likely impacts of transparency reforms will be "indirect, diffuse, and gradual."

Another important example of this shift in understanding policy change, and one that extends to transnational settings, is the work on democratization by Levitsky and Way (2006). Their ideas challenge the traditional democratization narrative of conditionality, external pressure, and assistance programs, arguing instead for the less visible institutional consequences and processes brought about by cross-border flows of information, network ties, and other types of linkages. Although their focus is regime-level democratization rather than public sector reforms, we suggest that a similar process of change is at work in the case of the Open Government Partnership, albeit with a different set of mechanisms.

We will elaborate on these mechanisms further in this chapter, but it suffices to say that these mechanisms are the product of the Open Government Partnership's multistakeholder model of institutional design. Prior scholarship has also shown the strength of multistakeholderism as a tool for policy change. International relations scholars in a variety of different institutional settings, such as internet governance (e.g., Mueller, 2010) and global health and sustainability (e.g., Bernstein & Hoffman, 2018; Duncan, 2015; Hale, 2020; Rushton & Williams, 2011), have similarly suggested that new forms of multistakeholder governance, soft law institutions, and civil society collaboration can also introduce new pathways for policy change.

The experience of the Open Government Partnership highlights the importance and relevance of alternatives to a direct pathway of change. The existence and influence of these indirect pathways have not yet been adequately understood or articulated by scholars, particularly in settings relevant to open government reform and multistakeholder governance. We suggest that in such settings emphasizing iterative and participatory institutional design features, indirect pathways of change may be both more dynamic institutionally and also more difficult to measure or control through a strictly top-down form of management. Such effects, in this case, could be brought about *both* by new participatory governance practices and by processes developing because of national membership in an international institution. Crucially, these processes can occur even though they are not intended elements of direct pathways of change emphasizing policy commitment and compliance.

One of the main advantages of the direct pathway and its self-evident causal logic is that it is *highly manageable*, and institutional architectures for producing desired policy effects can be intentionally designed. While the direct pathway relies on a clear institutional design of inputs and outputs, the indirect pathway relies on some of the messier by-products that are created in multistakeholder processes. The indirect approach does not imply a random or chaotic process, but it does certainly introduce the possibility of institutional reforms that move in directions not initially conceived or predicted by policy designers.

It is important to note that just because the indirect pathway to public sector reform can occur through Open Government Partnership participation, it may not necessarily do so without some preconditions in place. Just as a direct pathway requires sound commitments and sound compliance to operate, the indirect pathway requires meaningful participation and iteration, and these strongly depend on the political will and engagement of critical actors in participating countries.

In figure 4.4—an indirect pathway—iterative and participatory processes are not designed as a compliance mechanism that produces the desired change (as they are in the direct pathway) but are still a powerful catalyst for different kinds of byproducts, such as the creation of new norms and policy models, resources and opportunities, and linkages and coalitions.

In the rest of this chapter, we both explain these mechanisms in more detail and explore broader evidence of country-level and global governance

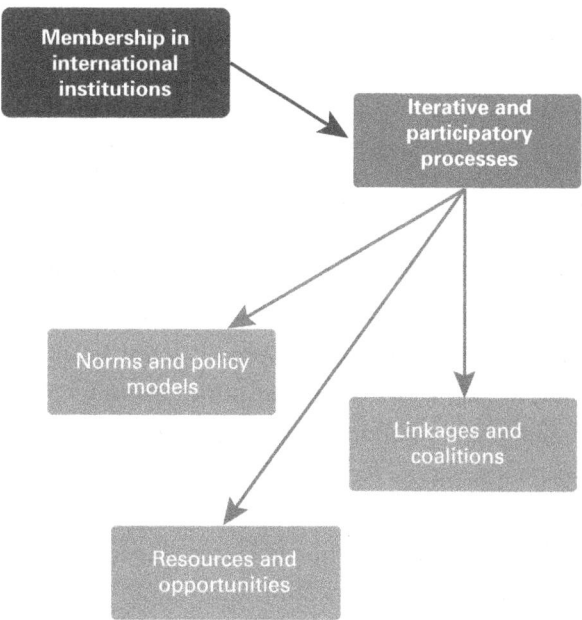

Figure 4.4
The indirect pathway of change.

impacts of Open Government Partnership membership via the indirect pathway. Compared to the analysis of the direct pathway of change, examining the indirect pathway forces us to cast the research net much wider to examine processes that are activated outside of the immediate sphere of National Action Plan commitment planning and Open Government Partnership governance systems.

The analysis looks at three key characteristics of governance impacts: (1) norms and policy models, (2) resources and opportunities, and (3) linkages and coalitions. Changes in these characteristics are extensively examined by drawing on diverse sources of primarily qualitative data, such as the Open Government Partnership country action plans, policy reports by relevant global organizations, country news articles, and civil society blogs.

New Norms and Policy Models

The first type of indirect effect of multistakeholder partnerships that we examine is the emergence of new norms and policy models. In the international context, Finnemore and Sikkink (1998) define a norm as a standard of appropriate behavior. Such norms may not be entirely new in the sense of never having been seen or heard of before but rather may spread from an initially marginal position to complement or even displace earlier norms.

The Open Government Partnership's direct pathway of mechanisms discussed above is consciously designed and planned. While critical for public sector reform success, norms are not easily established this way. Rather, they are complex phenomena and far less controllable. Yet we can still connect the growth and uptake of new norms to the values and models espoused by the Open Government Partnership through an indirect pathway. Although further evidence is necessary to definitely evidence a claim that without the Open Government Partnership these norms necessarily would not have existed and gained in importance, we can still trace the seed of influence from the Open Government Partnership. By tracing key developments over time, we can see how the norms that gathered power and meaning were the same norms that the Open Government Partnership helped set in motion in domestic open government policy reforms and that were catalyzed in their development and spread by key Open Government Partnership processes.

Three Cases: Open Data, Open Contracting, and Beneficial Ownership

Open data

The open data movement has long existed independently of the Open Government Partnership and would likely have made influential inroads into national government technology innovation even in the absence of the Open Government Partnership. However, the role of the Open Government Partnership as a catalyst for the open data norm in governments is important, as the Open Government Partnership and its associated processes helped to raise awareness, motivate actions on open data at national and local levels around the world, and served as a platform that helped launch other associated organizations.

The Open Government Partnership's biannual global summits also shed light on this influence. There were many normative discussions at these summits that set the tone for discussion of the same topics in other high-level policymaking fora. The 2013 Global Summit in London was a key moment in the global open data movement, for example. The United Kingdom—as hosts of the summit—used the opportunity to promote their open data success story and to make domestic as well as international commitments. The country had recently made huge strides forward in its publication of government information and had become the highest-ranked country in the world for open data according to the Global Open Data Index (2014).

The influence of the Open Government Partnership on open data can be seen in table 4.3, showing the Global Open Data Index up to its most recent survey in 2016. Open Government Partnership countries dominate these rankings, while non–Open Government Partnership countries only make the top twenty in a few sporadic cases.[4] This is not to assume clear causal relationships between the Open Government Partnership and the growth of transparency norms in open data initiatives but to recognize that the development of global policy norms is influenced by a complex interplay of actors and organizations in a similar sphere. The Open Government Partnership has been a major, central actor in this sphere articulating the normative power of data transparency, spurring countries to do more with their open data initiatives, and providing a global policy platform to leverage open data initiatives.

Table 4.3
The Global Open Data Index top 20 countries (2013–2016)

Rank	2013	2014	2015	2016
1	United Kingdom	United Kingdom	Taiwan*	Taiwan
2	Denmark	Denmark	United Kingdom	Australia
3	United States	France	Denmark	United Kingdom
4	Norway	Finland	Colombia	France
5	Netherlands	Australia	Finland	Finland
6	Slovenia	New Zealand	Australia	Canada
7	Finland	Norway	Uruguay	Norway
8	Sweden	United States	United States	Brazil
9	Australia	Germany	Netherlands	New Zealand
10	New Zealand	India	Norway	Northern Ireland
11	Germany	Taiwan	France	United States
12	Canada	Columbia	Brazil	Denmark
13	Switzerland	Uruguay	Romania	Mexico
14	France	Czech Republic	Mexico	Colombia
15	Romania	Sweden	Bulgaria	Latvia
16	Portugal	Romania	Canada	Japan
17	Iceland	Netherlands	Spain	Argentina
18	Moldova	Iceland	India	Singapore
19	Bulgaria	Japan	Italy	Uruguay
20	Italy	Chile	Czech Republic	Netherlands

Note: Open Government Partnership member countries shaded gray
* Due to the sovereignty dispute between Taiwan and China, Taiwan has not been permitted to join the Open Government Partnership.

Open contracting

The growth of another global norm can be seen in the case of open contracting. The 2019 *Open Government Partnership Global Report* states that "open contracting continues to gain momentum, and is on the way to becoming a global norm" (2019a, 146). Government contracting with the private sector has always been an important focus on government transparency regulations, but the rise of public-private partnerships in the 1990s and 2000s and the contiguous growth of the so-called hollow state, which is a weakened state infrastructure that is dependent on the private sector for services and vulnerable to capture, has left a vacuum in domestic public policy that the Open Government Partnership has stepped into with notable success.

Analysis by the Open Government Partnership has shown that open contracting has had a greater impact on countries that are members of the Open Government Partnership compared to countries that are not. In 2016, at the Open Government Partnership Global Summit, Colombia, France, Mexico, the UK, and Ukraine together founded a coalition of open contracting countries named the Contracting 5. These five founding member countries pledged to uphold the open contracting data standard and have grown to over forty national and subnational governmental members. The work of the Open Government Partnership and the Contracting 5 has also led to a proliferation of similar transnational multistakeholder initiatives that aim to advance open contracting, such as the Open Contracting Partnership and the Financial Transparency Coalition.

Certainly, open contracting has other supporters beyond the Open Government Partnership, so—like open data—not all of its success can be put down to the Open Government Partnership's influence. In 2015, the year before the launch of the Contracting 5 at the Open Government Partnership Summit, the group of the world's biggest twenty national economies, known as the Group of 20, published "Anti-Corruption Open Data Principles" and "Principles for Promoting Integrity in Public Procurement." This was a key impetus for the work of the Open Government Partnership in this area.

However, the Open Government Partnership was a central catalyst for the spread of the norm, and its national and subnational model of participation was even copied by new organizations that emerged to work on open contracting. What is significant about this cumulation of global attention to the norm of open contracting is the way that the Open Government Partnership efforts spread both policy reforms and a structure of close relationships of its member governments with civil society organizations such as the Financial Transparency Coalition. Of all the country governments that are signed up for the Open Contracting Data Standard, just two—Zambia and Uganda—are not also Open Government Partnership members, suggesting that Open Government Partnership membership is an important factor in leading countries to augment their commitment to new norms such as open contracting. Further, according to the most recent data available from the Open Data Barometer, only one country in the world—Kazakhstan—that publishes open data either on public contracts or on beneficial ownership is a non-Open Government Partnership member (Open Data Barometer, 2017).

Beneficial ownership

Beneficial ownership, which is about understanding who ultimately controls a legal entity, has been a legal concept employed in market trading regulations since the early twentieth century (Feldman & Teberg, 1965). Until recently, however, beneficial ownership was a concept that was rarely discussed in popular news media as an important government reform topic. Several Open Government Partnership countries, including Ukraine and Australia, introduced beneficial ownership registries in 2016—a time when beneficial ownership was beginning to become more prevalent as a priority in public policy. Denmark and Slovakia, both Open Government Partnership member countries, were among the earliest countries to adopt beneficial ownership registers (Open Government Partnership, 2019a). In 2018, the Open Government Partnership, together with the Beneficial Ownership Transparency Network, launched new disclosure principles and "A Guide to Implementing Beneficial Ownership Transparency" (Treisman, 2019). The summit in Ottawa saw the UK government and NGO OpenOwnership launch the Beneficial Ownership Leadership Group, which aims to "drive a global policy shift towards free, open beneficial ownership data and set ambitious best practice" (Treisman, 2019).

A recent report from the Open Government Partnership found that, while beneficial ownership has grown as a global norm, the rise has been comparatively stronger in Open Government Partnership member countries compared to nonmember countries, suggesting that Open Government Partnership membership has had an influence (Open Government Partnership, 2019a). The influence of the Open Government Partnership has also been accelerated by its collaboration with other transnational multistakeholder organizations, such as the Extractive Industries Transparency

Initiative (EITI). A report in 2019 found that member countries were "accelerating or going beyond the EITI standard" in beneficial ownership progress (Open Government Partnership, 2019a, 5).

But perhaps the clearest indication of the beneficial ownership norm taking root is the rates of use of new beneficial ownership country registries and concrete proof that the norm actually leads to consequences for illegal companies. Many Open Government Partnership member countries have made full or partial commitments to OpenOwnership principles even beyond membership, suggesting that the Partnership has acted here as a platform to catalyze the development of other global norms beyond specific country commitments alone. Adoption of formal legal instruments by government—often through commitments—provides a way for complainants, advocates, and other governments to exert more leverage in the adoption and implementation of beneficial ownership. The ability of other issue advocates to use the formal commitment process as a platform then lets them build up their programs/norms in ways that ultimately go beyond the Partnership.

One former Steering Committee member said, "From a campaigners' perspective, OGP offers 'action forcing events' every two years (the country action plans) that can help galvanize political support behind key open government issues. If those issues are replicable, or need in fact to be replicated across countries to succeed (e.g., beneficial ownership), OGP can provide this multiplier effect" (Tisné, 2014b).

Participatory processes

Beyond the spread of the open data, open contracting, and beneficial ownership norms across countries, there is another interesting feature of these new norms—the way that a procedural norm of public participation defines both their conception and implementation.

The norm of participatory government is by no means a new idea, but it is one that has received a notable boost from the Open Government Partnership's model of civil society parity in decision making and implementation. The 2019 *Open Government Partnership Global Report* notes how public participation movements have become part of the growing awareness of country transparency initiatives. According to Fraundorfer (2018), "The

OGP national processes have also created channels of trust and confidence between government and civil society actors" (150). Further, the processes led to a "'virtuous cycle' and contributed to social change promoting new forms of democratic interaction between government and citizens" (151). This account also underlines the need for compliance and commitment from the government in order for the indirect pathway to continue functioning. Previous research on the Open Government Partnership, both across countries (Wilson, 2020) and in Norway (Wilson, 2021), has also emphasized the socialization of norms of participation, even if not always successful.

In Ukraine, separately from its work through the Open Government Partnership, the Ukrainian government and Transparency International brought machine learning tools used to analyze large quantities of data on public contracts to the service of a public participation platform. Ukrainian citizens could not use an open data platform to monitor public contracts, but they could flag concerns and submit their own claims of contracting violations. This was, evidently, a powerful way to build on the Open Government Partnership's values of participation and open contracting, as nearly one million citizen submissions have been recorded so far (Open Government Partnership 2019a, 156).

There is also evidence that these normative changes in the processes of governing collaboratively led to culture shifts in the public sector. In Serbia, one civil society representative said of their eight years of participation in the Open Government Partnership, "Looking back, I can say that the government, or at least some of the public institutions, have drastically changed their position and today recognize the benefits of cooperation with the civil sector" (Selakovic, 2018). The Philippines even saw the spread of the civil society consultation model of the Open Government Partnership to other arenas through its Dagyaw program of virtual town hall meetings. The program was initially launched as part of Executive Order 9 in 2016 and mandated a civic engagement effort in multiple policy areas at the cabinet level.

Open Government Partnership members have also replicated the norm of participation in other contexts beyond specific commitments. According to Inés Pousadela, a research specialist at CIVICUS: World Alliance for Citizen Participation, "Today an unprecedented number of actors in both the government and civil society of Argentina are willing to put open government principles into practice, and the structures are in place to help them do so. There is no going back to a past in which civil society actors had to prove over and over why they should have a say. The ethos of co-creation is here to stay" (Pousadela, 2019, para. 9). Such comments frequently characterize reports from country representatives, referring to the shift to the participatory model of policymaking as a solidification of a "culture of co-creation" (Corrigan & Gruzd, 2018, 6) and a "structure" (Rivoir & Landinelli, 2017, 3) of democratic deliberation.

The subnational open government model

One of the major new policy models promoted by the Open Government Partnership was local level open government. In 2016, the Open Government Partnership launched the Subnational Government Pilot Program with fifteen pioneer subgovernment programs and a larger peer learners network called the Learners' Tier. The idea for local, provincial, or state governments to become members of the Open Government Partnership had been discussed for several years before the first pilots were launched. The pilots were notable for being largely based in the founding countries of the Open Government Partnership, such as Austin in the United States, São Paulo in Brazil, Scotland in the UK, and Bojonegoro in Indonesia. Other subnational pilots, such as Madrid in Spain and Elgeyo Marakwet in Kenya, show that the Open Government Partnership policy model had gained enough trust and evidence of its effectiveness to be introduced to later Open Government Partnership country joiners. The subnational government model evolved into what today is referred to as OGP Local.

Martin Tisné, who at that time was a member of the Open Government Partnership Steering Committee, said in 2015 that the nascent efforts to replicate the Open Government Partnership model at the subnational level were analogous to the TEDx evolution of TED Talks. This may be somewhat of a simplification of a much more complex phenomenon than TED Talks, but the comparison is apt in many respects. It is clear that these pilots were important new iterations of the Open Government Partnership policy model in at least three important respects.

First, they were genuinely experimental in terms of the governance and political design of the pilots. Some subnational members were cities, such as Austin, while others were federal regions or countries within larger states, such as Bojonegoro. Second, the subnational members often emerged in the midst of complicated political situations where the subnational governments were willing to try a new policy model despite the political risks. This is particularly true in the case of Scotland, which had held a referendum on independence from the UK just two years before joining the Open Government Partnership. It is also true in the case of Kigoma-Ujiji, a historically and economically important city in Tanzania that joined in 2016, just a year before the national government of Tanzania decided to controversially withdraw from the Open Government Partnership after several years of failing to deliver on its National Action Plan commitments. Third, the model of subnational open government plans was expected to evolve of its own accord with ties to the original ideas of the Open Government Partnership but able to flourish independently.

What is most interesting in terms of indirect pathways of change is the way that subnational replications of the Open Government Partnership model have also been carried out independent of the official apparatus of the Open Government Partnership—ostensibly through initiatives of national-level decision makers who saw value in taking their experience of open government public sector reform further. Evidence of the nascent, independent growth of urban and regional open government initiatives is indeed starting to emerge in cases where the Open Government Partnership offered a model and an inspiration but was not itself directly involved.

In Argentina, for example, the Open Government Partnership motivated the development of subnational models that were not explicitly part of the Open Government Partnership (or its subnational program), as shown in the "Foro Nacional sobre políticas de Gobierno Abierto: Argentina Abierta" of Argentina. Here, an open government model of participatory governance was developed at a regional level that was explicitly founded on the Open Government Partnership model but scaled down to the municipal level and applied to areas of policymaking that had no formal connection with Open Government Partnership processes. Events so far to bring together policy actors from different sectors to address public policy challenges have been organized jointly with government and civil society organizations, attracted thousands of participants, and taken place in major Argentinian cities, including Cordova, Mendoza, and La Plata, in addition to the capital, Buenos Aires (Borrmann, 2019). As a result, the emergence of local open government initiatives is growing.

In Nigeria and Indonesia, several states and subnational entities have also undertaken similar efforts. In Mexico, by 2017, twenty-seven out of thirty-two states had developed their own open government action plans in an independent program that we detail further in chapter 5 (Open Government Partnership, 2018b).

Resources and Opportunities

In addition to new norms and policy models, multistakeholder partnerships can also create new resources and opportunities for reformers, both inside and outside of government. These resources can include new sources of power, influence, networks, or material support, while opportunities can include new venues or channels of access to decision makers.

Prominent theoretical approaches to social movements emphasize both the importance of material resources (McCarthy & Zald, 1977) and of political opportunities (Kitschelt, 1986)—perspectives that we apply not only to the abilities of civil society groups to effect change but also to reformers inside of government. More internationally focused research has extended these ideas to highlight how transnational decision-making venues (Newman and Posner, 2016; Farrell & Newman, 2018) and transnational networks (Avant & Westerwinter, 2016) can offer reformers opportunities and resources of their own.

More recent observers of the Open Government Partnership (Global Integrity, 2016) have also noted that it can bring new substantive material, such as financial or technical assistance, and immaterial resources, such as networks, political attention, and values that can be used to leverage open government policy positions at national and local levels. In these ways, the Open Government Partnership can make available to reformers new resources and opportunities that were previously scarce. We review several forms of this dynamic here and offer examples.

Domestic network resources

Open Government Partnership member countries bring together government agencies and civil society organizations to design and implement new commitments. These commitments sometimes meet the promises they have made in the outputs they deliver within a specified time period. But what can be forgotten is the indirect way that these collaborations set networks in place that last much longer than their official commitment project plan. The ongoing interaction of the networks also opens up new resources for their members of both material and symbolic kinds. These resources generate very valuable activities from an open government perspective, though the activities can move far beyond the initial scope of the commitment in the National Action Plan. An early Open Government Partnership Steering Committee member, Juan Pardinas, once called this a "social network for reformers."[5]

Alvaro Herrero, then Undersecretary of Strategic Management and Institutional Quality in the Argentinian government, launched the subnational participation of Buenos Aires with the following telling statement about the role of opportunities and resources afforded new public sector actors in open government:

> Agents of change also need a story to tell. They need a framework in which to leverage the different things they want to achieve, bringing them together in a cohesive narrative. I am talking of symbolic resources. And OGP provides that. (Herrero, 2017, para. 5)

An interesting example of these enduring network resources is the President's Task Force for Twenty-First-Century Policing, which the United States launched in its third National Action Plan in 2015. The task force brought together a selection of police departments from across the United States to begin sharing best practices in the use of technologies, such as body cameras and open data, to improve the transparency of police actions. At the end of its term, the commitment failed to reach its goal of finding two hundred police departments to join the open data portal (but it had managed to get to 135) (Government of the United States, 2016). However, among the police departments that did join, the network became a vital resource for sharing ideas and training for the implementation of new open data technologies, such as the data management software IA Pro that was promoted through the network (Ingrams, 2017b). These skills and resources were heavily relied on by police departments facing rising calls to tackle police discrimination in 2018 and 2019. Participation also provided much-needed symbolic value to the police departments that could try to reassure citizens that they were taking concrete steps to address the crisis of secrecy and distrust in the police.

In another example, the nongovernmental organization (NGO), the Access Initiative, used the Open Government Partnership as a platform to advance regional principles on access to environmental information, which it was able to do through advocacy of its ideas across the broad geographical representation of Open Government Partnership countries (Excell, 2012). In an even more remarkable case, in Slovakia, when the Open Government Partnership office responsible for managing and implementing Open Government Partnership commitments fell out of favor with the government, it was able to survive and marshal new open data tools for holding the government accountable by relying on the support of a network of open data NGOs (Schneider, 2015).

Symbolic and political resources

The Open Government Partnership has also brought symbolic and political resources to reformers in many settings. This can be seen in the added prestige, status, and legal support that NGOs, citizens, and other governmental bodies can leverage once their government is a card-carrying member of the Open Government Partnership, pledged to uphold its values. This can give open government advocates a platform to demand that governments better walk the talk.

One important early case in this light is the so-called secrecy bill in South Africa, where civil society groups used Open Government Partnership as "external leverage" in their fight to block the bill and were ultimately successful (Heller, 2011). Political commentators in South Africa were vociferous in their claim that the secrecy bill was inconsistent with Open Government Partnership membership because it introduced penalties for whistleblowers and applied a vague concept of national interest and security to access to information exemptions (Calland, 2011). From that point, the bill went through a politically tumultuous process, being delayed (in part in response to international pressure and the domestic activist campaign against it), eventually approved by Parliament in 2013, and then ultimately rejected by President Zuma (Makinana, 2013). Ultimately, it was never passed, meaning that the campaign that was galvanized in support of what the South African government *should* stand for as an Open Government Partnership member was successful. According to one observer, this was made possible because the Open Government Partnership provides domestic civil society actors with a vehicle "by which to critique government inaction or reward improvements" (Eaves, 2012, para. 6).

A similar case was also reported in Argentina where a domestic Open Government Partnership coalition used their role and their country's membership in Open Government Partnership as leverage on a related but non-Open Government Partnership issue of filling a long-vacant position of the national ombudsman (Bio, 2019).

In other cases, domestic civil society gained structural power through the explicit or implicit threat of exit from Open Government Partnership collaboration. Such exit would threaten the legitimacy of government efforts and their ability to claim symbolic credit internationally. For example, in Peru, some civil society organizations withdrew from the multistakeholder body with the government after an initially agreed commitment about access to information was withdrawn from the final plan (Cameron, 2015). Similarly, civil society organizations in Croatia threatened to withdraw from the collaboration over a government stance toward a new law on how participatory decision making should work (Guillán Montero & Taxell, 2015). In the United States, civil society organizations threatened to scupper the entire action plan development process over their perceived take on the government approach to "participatory theater" (Howard & Wonderlich, 2017). In the next chapter, we also analyze in detail the developments in Mexico whereby civil society groups actually followed through on their threats to withdraw from domestic Open Government Partnership collaboration.

In addition to being a boon to civil society, the symbolic resources of the Open Government Partnership have influenced the capacity of government agencies to implement public sector reforms. In another example from

Argentina, the agency responsible for leading Open Government Partnership participation, the Ministry of Modernization (MoM), received a reputation boost as a result of its impressive work helping the country climb international rankings in the Global Open Data Index and Transparency International's Anti-Corruption Index. From that time on, "responses from interviews conducted during the Organisation for Economic Cooperation and Developments's peer-driven fact-finding missions, and the results of the Organisation for Economic Cooperation and Development Surveys, show that ministries, provinces and institutions from other branches of power clearly recognise the MoM's leadership in the area of open government and reveal a general willingness to co-operate with the Ministry" (Organisation for Economic Cooperation and Development, 2019).

It is worth noting that, while the leveraging of symbolic resources through Open Government Partnership membership has resulted in many positive impacts on public sector reforms, these same resources can also be a tool for harmful kinds of political behaviors. This underlines the politically complex, even messy, nature of indirect pathways of change.

For example, a report from Global Integrity written by Guerzovich and Moses (2016) stated that, in the Philippines, "the Aquino administration has taken advantage of OGP awards and recognition to entice more people, inside and outside the government, to support its political agenda. This includes the administration's strong emphasis on a new good governance framework, for which OGP's investments in enticing high-level political support, including awards, became both a sign of Aquino's reform credentials and a means of sustaining a political agenda over time by bringing more reformers into government" (10) and that the close relationships between civil society and government bureaucrats led to a revolving door of job opportunities between civil society and the government.

New funding sources

Sometimes membership in the Open Government Partnership offers members and participants new ways to access funding, whether for projects involved in specific commitments or even beyond. Participating in the Open Government Partnership is one way that countries can demonstrate their deservedness of foreign aid and international financing and plug into the kinds of political reform agendas that donors are often interested in. The Open Government Partnership has received broad support from the international development ministries of many countries and from major private foundations (Open Government Partnership, 2018a). This has meant that, for many countries, Open Government Partnership participation and political and economic development have been closely related. In 2016, the director of the Institute for Development of Freedom of Information in Georgia, Giorgi Kldiashvili, said of Georgia's efforts to join the Open Government Partnership:

> [We] had support from US Agency for Development. We had a great project with the UNDP to support parliament in being involved [with] the Open Government Partnership. We supported in drafting the action plan, mobilizing civil society, picking up commitments and then consulting and working with the parliament [to have] it adopted. (Open Government Partnership, 2017a)

This kind of collaboration, sparked by actions that originally took place as formal Open Government Partnership commitments, has become a familiar pattern. It has even been further institutionalized with the creation of a World Bank trust fund in collaboration between the World Bank and the Open Government Partnership itself.

Developing new sources of funding for member countries is not an explicit goal of the Open Government Partnership nor something that member countries include in their action plans, and so it is not an intended, direct form of impact. But more indirectly, by participating in a high-profile global partnership, countries may gain greater access to networks of aid organizations, philanthropic organizations, and government development agencies. While in many cases, these funds were already being made available to the same countries, the influence of the open government agenda for major international donors can open up new sources of funding for members, including those that are made available from the Open Government Partnership itself for cross-country technical support (Open Government Partnership, 2014b).

While funding for specific open government projects has grown, so has funding for the assessment of these initiatives and for research addressing their impact and potential. This has been accompanied by an increase in published articles in the broader academic sphere related to open government in areas such as open data (Attard et al., 2015; Zuiderwijk & Janssen, 2014). Articles in the Web of Science library addressing the topic of open government have steadily increased. In 2020 there were 143 articles published compared to 15 in 2010 and just 1 article in 2000.[6] Importantly, investments in research and understanding can pay off over much longer timeframes.

Linkages and Coalitions

Finally, multistakeholder partnerships can also forge new linkages and coalitions both within and across countries that may have their own future effects on public sector reform. We consider three different ways that powerful new linkages and coalitions could come about through the Open Government Partnership: (1) new collaborations among major regional and global institutions, (2) new transnational government-to-government connections, and (3) new linkages among and across other nonstate organizations, including in policy and advocacy communities and ideological coalitions. Each highlights the ways that opportunities for domestic open government policy reform can be shaped by different types of network connections, such as collaboration and coalition building. These connections can, in turn, drive processes of policy learning, enable new political actions and movements, and differentially empower actors with greater network resources (Avant & Westerwinter, 2016). In other settings, such as the joint European Union–OECD Support for Improvement in Governance and Management initiative, studies have also found that transnational networks of experts played key roles in shaping policy transfer (e.g., Stone, 2004; Francesco, 2012).

Collaborations through Major Regional and Global Institutions

The Open Government Partnership is one of many types of intergovernmental institutions working on national policy reform. In helping to form and sustain linkages across countries, it facilitates national and regional actors such as governments and civil society organizations to use open government methods to address new policy challenges (Bellows & Zohdy, 2020). To explore the convergence of open government ideas across intergovernmental institutions, we carried out an analysis of the world's major regional and global intergovernmental institutions, including the United Nations, Organisation for Economic Co-Operation and Development, European Union, Group of 7, Group of 20, African Union, and Asian Development Bank. We searched the official planning and annual strategic documents of the institutions for information about any open government initiatives. We found extensive evidence of open government initiatives across all these organizations. All of the organizations have had some sort of collaboration with the Open Government Partnership. For example, the European Union registered Open Government Partnership as a consulting organization in 2017, and the United Nations has hosted regular side events at the meetings of the United Nations General Assembly. In 2013 and 2016, the African Union hosted an Open Government Partnership Africa regional meeting. But there are also independent open government initiatives being held by the institutions, such as the Organisation for Economic Co-Operation and Development's launch of the open government review literature series in 2014, its Network on Open and Innovative Government in Latin America and the Caribbean in 2015, and the Group of 20's launch of open data principles in 2015.

Open government work is nothing new for the United Nations. It has many practical and legislative projects that stand as potential building points for open government initiatives in important areas such as climate change. In 2015, it adopted the Sustainable Development Goals, which has open government as one of its policy planks. Goal 16.10 is to "ensure public access to information and protect fundamental freedoms, in accordance with national legislation and international agreements" (United Nations, 2015). Furthermore, the United Nations Convention against Corruption aims for better reporting of management of public finances and stronger accounting standards and oversight.

The United Nations has increasingly given attention to the role of open data in tackling climate change. It focuses on "innovation, transparency, accountability, participatory governance and economic growth" (United

Nations, n.d., para. 2). The preamble of the Paris Climate Accord explicitly addresses the importance of "affirming the importance of education, training, public awareness, public participation, public access to information and cooperation at all levels on the matters addressed in this Agreement" (United Nations Framework Convention on Climate Change [UNFCCC], 2015). Several of the articles of the accord also explicitly embrace open government as a tool to address the climate crisis. Article 4(8) requires countries to "provide the information necessary for clarity, transparency and understanding." Article 6(8) envisions collaboration between governments and industry. Most importantly, Article 13 states that its transparency strategies include "national communications, biennial reports and biennial update reports, international assessment and review and international consultation and analysis" (United Nations Framework Convention on Climate Change, n.d.).

We see this growing attention of the United Nations to open government in the Ad Hoc Working Group of the UN that has been tasked with adopting transparency guidelines. It is interesting to see how the policy models the working group has been developing in the six sessions it has held from 2016 to 2018 resemble the models of the Open Government Partnership commitment development. The working group, for example, proposed to track emissions transparently and to help countries meet their targets. It involved a flexible approach, considering the different developmental levels of the countries, the process of semi-independent technical expert review of progress, and a facilitative, multilateral approach to monitoring progress.

Transnational Governmental Linkages

Another form of transnational linkages is between state representatives and other government officials across countries. Many Open Government Partnership events, including not only global summits but also regional networking events, have been important in this respect for fostering linkages that do not necessarily emerge directly from commitments alone.

For example, Croatia has held a series of Open Government Partnership European Outreach and Support meetings. They have been attended by scores of countries and facilitated by global thought leaders and advocates from the civil society sector (Open Government Partnership, 2012a). A counterpart in Africa, the "Africa OGP Convention, organized by Kenya's Elgeyo Marakwet County, took place in 2018" (Bartoo, 2018). Similar events, known as peer exchanges, have been held by the Open Government Partnership Support Unit (Ferčíková, 2018). The United Nations Development Programme has held training sessions for country representatives on how to effectively develop and implement Open Government Partnership commitments (OGP Support Unit, 2017).

In a blog post published by the Open Government Partnership itself, the following quote explains the case for the indirect roles that can be played by such transgovernmental linkages between governmental reformers across countries:

> "Civil servants really do an amazing job, they have difficult tasks to do. This agenda, open government, transparency, often meets a lot of resistance and it is difficult to overcome obstacles within administration. So bringing people together to show that there is a support network, discussing challenges together can be really really beneficial and can really help," says Helen Turek, OGP Program Officer.
>
> One way to deal with lack of motivation or strength to pursue such changes is through regional peer exchange between OGP POCs [Points of Contact] and OGP leaders. Thanks to these exchanges, those state officials who are coordinating the implementation of action plans—sometimes in not such a friendly environment—might not feel as lonely in crisis situations, or demotivated that their huge efforts bring only small changes. (Ferčíková, 2018, paras. 1, 3).

Transnational and Domestic Nongovernmental Linkages

The diversity of the communities involved in the Open Government Partnership can quickly be apprehended through the attendance lists of its global summits—national government ministers, city mayors, business leaders and entrepreneurs, technology developers, human rights lawyers, academics, students, NGO representatives, and citizen advocates. Supporters of open government reforms also span ideological divides and traditional issue silos. By bringing these nonstate actors together in new ways, Open Government Partnership processes—both domestic and transnational—can also create new linkages and coalitions. Although it would be difficult to show all the different potential aspects of this indirect pathway of change, we can highlight some specific examples.

In several national cases, the policy and advocacy communities that had become emboldened and enlarged by the influence of their country's participation in the Open Government Partnership acted as a vital resource of civil society resilience during national leadership transitions that were quite threatening for open government. A notable example of this is the Philippines, where the election of Rodrigo Duterte in 2016 was seen by many as a negative turning point for human rights protections in the country. The president has received heavy criticism for his endorsement of extrajudicial killings of gang drug dealers and his defunding of the Philippines Commission on Human Rights (Dressel & Bonoan, 2019). However, during Duterte's presidency, there has been sufficient momentum among open government supporters for the passage of the Philippines' first freedom of information law, and the country is on to its fifth National Action Plan and an early participant in the subnational membership initiative through the open government region of South Cotabato.

One observer noted that a national civil society coalition in the Philippines, Bantay Kita, "sees OGP as an appropriate vessel to seek allies for reforms within the OGP national and international family (EITI, FOI); a venue to collaborate; an opportunity to push for interlinking advocacies and to build trust among CSOs and between civil society and government" (Pimentel, 2018, para. 25).

In several other cases of national transitions in partisan control over executive power, such as in Argentina, France, and—as will be seen in more detail in the next chapter—Mexico, new political leaders have similarly found reasons to embrace their country's membership in the Open Government Partnership despite it having previously been associated with an ideologically opposed political leader. Here, not only the ideological ambiguity of open government but also the new cross-cutting coalitions that the Open Government Partnership processes themselves, help to forge important roles.

Multistakeholder interactions have also helped to bring together nongovernmental reformers across issue silos. At a global level, Toby McIntosh, writing on tensions between freedom of information advocates and open data advocates, concludes in part that the Open Government Partnership helped to bring them together, thus helping forge a coalition between two previously distinct (and sometimes conflicting) advocacy communities (McIntosh, 2012).

There are also many examples of the Open Government Partnership bringing together broad civil society coalitions within countries that then work together even on other policy areas outside of the remit of specific commitments themselves. For example, the Open Government Network in the United Kingdom was formed at the outset of the Open Government Partnership to gather expert civil society organizations for consultation on National Action Plans. However, the Open Government Network now works far beyond this initial scope, including probing data transparency around COVID-19 pandemic regulations, researching electoral transparency, and pushing the envelope on growing policy issues, such as race and gender equality (McLean, 2020). Similar dynamics played out in Mexico as well, as will be seen in much more detail in chapter 5. Notably, these types of developments often involve not just the quantity of connections but also their quality—including the skills, attitudes, and organizational cultures necessary for effective collaboration and trust between partner organizations and individuals.

Summary of the Indirect Pathway of Change

Below, we review several key takeaways with respect to the indirect pathway of change in the case of the Open Government Partnership:

- The Open Government Partnership has been a catalyst for new norms related to open government. Looking beyond commitments and their compliance, the model of participatory governance has been given new impetus by the Open Government Partnership, and this has spilled over into other arenas, such as regional- and local-level participatory initiatives.
- Other norms that have spread through the mechanism of an indirect pathway of Open Government Partnership activity are open data, open contracting, and beneficial ownership. Although it would be difficult to

demonstrate that the Open Government Partnership was solely responsible for causing this rise, the indirect pathway implies that the development of such norms comes from a complex institutional process in which the Open Government Partnership was a key player and served as a platform for subsequent developments.

- The success of the subnational Open Government Partnership membership pilot has demonstrated how effective the Open Government Partnership policy model can be. Open Government Partnership subnational members are geographically and politically diverse, and they have emerged and persevered in surprising ways, such as the case of Kigoma-Ujiji in Tanzania. Similar models have cropped up even outside of the efforts undertaken directly by the Open Government Partnership itself, such as those in Nigeria, Argentina, and Mexico.
- As a result of the Open Government Partnership's activity (and its engagement with civil society in particular), reformers both inside and outside of government have gained access to new resources and political opportunities, which have, in turn, been successfully used as leverage for further reform. Material resources for open government initiatives from a range of international and national foreign aid agencies, private foundations, and international governance institutions have also grown.
- The interconnectivity of the Open Government Partnership community with other local advocates and major policymaking institutions is shown in the collaboration of previously separate communities, such as democracy and open data reformers. Combining forces has often increased the chances of pressuring governments to adopt reforms. It is also shown in the integration of open government agendas with major global institutions, such as the United Nations, the Organisation for Economic Co-operation and Development, and regional efforts.

CONCLUSION

In this chapter, we developed and illustrated the core theoretical arguments of this book, focusing on the contrast between direct and indirect pathways of change in public sector reform. While similar arguments have been made in past studies in other settings, they have not been used to offer a theoretical lens for understanding the potential for transnational multistakeholder partnerships to effect policy change.

Our main objectives in this chapter were (1) to give more formal conceptual elucidation to these concepts and (2) to offer an empirical picture that distinguishes them and illustrates the different ways that direct and indirect pathways of change can succeed or fail. As presented here, the direct pathway of change comprises the impacts intended by the formal design, implementation, and review model of the Open Government Partnership, while the indirect pathway comprises broader changes in terms of new institutional and political dynamics resulting from Open Government Partnership membership that can be seen both within and across member countries.

Taken together, the evidence on the direct pathway of change suggests that, while it is pursued in a variety of forms (design of commitments, Independent Reporting Mechanism procedures, and institutional capacity building), its successes are mixed and sporadic. In some cases, particularly if we look at rare cases of star commitments, the direct pathway of change shows wonderful results. But, alongside this good news, a great deal of Open Government Partnership membership efforts resulted in very little direct impact. We see this in the slow progress of member countries over time and the gradual concentration of efforts around comfortable commitments that we could describe skeptically as low-hanging fruit or pipe dreams.

In addition to the direct pathway, however, we also see evidence of an indirect pathway of change. This indirect pathway can operate through three main mechanisms: (1) new norms and policy models, (2) new resources and opportunities, and (3) new linkages and coalitions. These mechanisms can also coexist with the main mechanisms of the direct pathway—that is, they are not mutually exclusive. They can also be seen in the ways that policy innovations such as open data, open contracting, and beneficial ownership have spread around the world; how third-party governments at intergovernmental, subnational, or city levels have adopted open government ideas; and how policy communities have gained access to new linkages, resources, and opportunities. To fully understand the impacts of transnational multistakeholder partnerships, it is vital to recognize how this indirect pathway unfolds and to account for it in our attempts to understand and evaluate the Open Government Partnership.

Chapter 5 builds on this by offering more focused evidence assessing both the direct and indirect pathways of impact. It does so by testing specific hypotheses associated with each pathway using qualitative evidence in the context of a detailed single-country case study of the Open Government Partnership experience in Mexico.

5 A CASE STUDY: DIRECT AND INDIRECT PATHWAYS OF CHANGE IN MEXICO

In May 2017, ten Mexican civil society organizations submitted a letter to the Open Government Partnership's Steering Committee formally announcing their withdrawal from the Tripartite Technical Secretariat (STT—Secretariado Técnico Tripartita)—the multistakeholder body coordinating Mexico's Open Government Partnership participation.[1] Their complaints focused on the government's illegal digital surveillance of Mexican civil society groups—including one member of the STT itself—and attempts by the federal government to reduce the scope and ambition of commitments made in Mexico's third National Action Plan.

Concerns by civil society groups over rampant corruption scandals and impunity for human rights abuses were already on the rise, and the digital surveillance scandal proved to be the last straw. This withdrawal of the entire formal civil society coalition left Mexico's Open Government Partnership process at a standstill, despite being one of the initiative's founding member countries, having recently served as chair of the Steering Committee and having been the host of the 2015 global summit.

And yet, just as we have argued for the Open Government Partnership globally, what might appear superficially to be a straightforward case of policy failure actually offers far more insight if one looks beneath the surface. The Mexican case exemplifies the paradoxical character of multistakeholder governance in open government reform where democratic and accountability setbacks still occur, despite attempts to operate in a climate of greater openness and integrity. Beyond the national-level processes of consultation, commitment-making, and implementation, however, broader dynamics had been set in motion—and these continued despite the formal breakdown of official Open Government Partnership mechanisms.

The Open Government Partnership had empowered new actors, serving as "steroids for civil society" (according to one participant [CSO 1]) by giving them a seat at the table and tools for bringing outside pressure.[2] Reformers inside the government were also able to draw on new resources and opportunities to pursue their own agendas within the bureaucracy. New norms of open government and cocreation had taken root, and the Open Government Partnership's model of multisector collaboration was being applied in new policy settings, including a new subnational initiative incorporating both local civil society actors and state governors across political parties. The Open Government Partnership had also established new links with transnational and international actors and helped forge a new coalition of ideologically diverse civil society actors that had little previous experience collaborating with one another. These processes together had also helped to establish a cross-partisan appeal of open government, laying the groundwork for the Open Government Partnership process to be restarted in early 2019, after a new president had taken office. Importantly, these factors combined to contribute to several major legislative achievements, including landmark reforms to Mexico's access to information law and a new national anticorruption system.

While these developments do not necessarily reflect a measurable *quantitative* change in open government policy outcomes, they do reflect the effects of the indirect pathway through the institutionalization of reform dynamics and a *qualitative* change in the nature of interactions between relevant actors in the government and in society. Understanding and taking these developments seriously are essential for both scholars and policymakers of governance reform and international institutions.

This chapter highlights and demonstrates several main themes of our book. We show that in Mexico, the impact of the Open Government Partnership through a direct commitment-and-compliance pathway of change has been limited at best. Commitments were generally narrow or superficial, and some were implemented only partially, not at all, or did not endure following the close of a given National Action Plan cycle. Even star commitments generally reflected policy output without policy outcomes, representing piecemeal reforms that might be useful for specific goals but not for broad-based transformations. However, there were some opportunities for learning and improvement over time through repeated iterations of the National Action Plan–Independent Reporting Mechanism cycle. We thus demonstrate that an indirect pathway of change shows much more potential for more holistic changes and broader processes of institutionalization.

In this chapter, we trace the history of Mexico's membership in the Open Government Partnership through multiple rounds of National Action Plans and three different presidencies through early 2019. We pay close attention to evidence for impact—both of commitments themselves and of the Open Government Partnership's iterative and participatory processes. We proceed chronologically but step back at the end of the chapter to review important legislative and subnational developments that occurred alongside other events and that demonstrate key themes. At the close of the chapter, we assess the overall evidence pertaining to both the direct pathway (compliance-based) and indirect pathway (process-driven mechanisms) of change.

METHODOLOGY AND CASE SELECTION

This case study was carried out through an extensive review of official Open Government Partnership documents, third-party reports, Mexican news media, and in-depth interviews conducted either in Mexico City or remotely. The interviews relevant in this chapter include five representatives of different civil society groups in Mexico, four current or former government officials, and two representatives of the Open Government Partnership globally. The interviews with civil society and government officials were conducted in Mexico City in April 2018 and in August 2018. The authors also attended the 2015 Open Government Partnership Global Summit in Mexico City and several other global summits and other events either individually or collectively. Where referenced in this chapter, interviews conducted by the authors are denoted by organization type (either GO for government official, CSO for civil society organization representative, or OGP for Open

Government Partnership representative) in order to preserve the anonymity of individuals and enable them to speak more freely.

Although our methodological approach in this chapter is generally akin to one of process tracing (Gerring, 2011), it is not strictly focused on testing between rival explanations of an outcome. Rather, our focus is twofold. First, we seek to evaluate the extent to which the Open Government Partnership affected governance reform in Mexico. Second, and more importantly, we seek to test between two rival interpretations of the drivers and salient features of those effects—a direct pathway (emphasizing compliance-based mechanisms) and an indirect pathway (emphasizing process-driven mechanisms) of change. These two rival hypotheses of interest that we seek to test between are thus:

H_1: *To the extent that Open Government Partnership membership had impacts on governance reform in Mexico, this impact was driven by formal commitments and their implementation.*

H_2: *To the extent that Open Government Partnership membership had impacts on governance reform in Mexico, this impact was driven by iterative and participatory processes.*

Of course, much depends on how one defines *impacts* in this setting. Our understanding here is relative, given that reform efforts over short- or medium-term timeframes are so rarely *ever* found to have transformative and measurable impacts on governance (Fox, 2015; Michener, 2019). In the Mexican case, we specifically define the outcome of interest as encompassing both the extent to which public sector governance is transparent, participatory, and accountable, as well as the strategies and tactics by which governmental and nongovernmental actors seek to shape public sector governance. These may thus encompass qualitative as well as quantitative changes, such as shifts in the nature of interactions, the processes of decision making, or the types of policies being pursued.

Our case selection of Mexico is motivated by its status as a highly likely case for direct compliance-based pathways to operate relative to other Open Government Partnership members. Mexico was among the founding countries of the Open Government Partnership and so had played a role in designing the system of rules around National Action Plans and commitments. It was a new democracy, often highlighted as a key factor in shaping compliance. It had a reform reputation to uphold, given its widely hailed 2002 access to information law. It also featured an active civil society in areas of transparency, corruption, and human rights. All these factors suggest a high water mark for compliance mechanisms to be operating relative to other Open Government Partnership members. Yet, instead, we still see limited compliance, making Mexico an important case to assess for evidence of alternative mechanisms at work.

BACKGROUND AND CONTEXT

Mexico was governed for decades by the single-party rule of the Partido Revolucionario Institucional, known as the "perfect dictatorship" for its use of uncompetitive elections as part of a sophisticated strategy to maintain sustained political control (e.g., Magaloni, 2006). However, the 1980s and 1990s saw some gradual increases in democratization and decentralization, particularly with the increasing competitiveness of opposition parties, turnover in party control in some subnational units, and the creation of nascent accountability institutions like the electoral commission (e.g., Eisenstadt, 2004). The crucial transition to democracy took place in 2000 with the presidential election of Vicente Fox Quesada of the opposition Partido Acción Nacional. Although the 2006 election was disputed and marked by widespread protest, the Partido Acción Nacional maintained control under the presidency of Felipe Calderón Hinojosa, with the Partido Revolucionario Institucional then returning to power with the election of Enrique Peña Nieto in 2012.

Although adoption of an access to information law had been a Partido Acción Nacional campaign promise, the initially drafted legislation was relatively weak. In response, a coalition of newspaper editors and academics known as the Grupo Oaxaca raised the profile of the issue, demanded stronger legislation, and were largely successful in shaping the ultimately adopted 2002 law (Michener, 2011a). Coming into effect in 2003, this law was hailed around the world for the strength of its legal design, the independent information commission it created (IFAI—Instituto Federal de Acceso a la Información y Protección de Datos), and the innovative online platform it deployed to manage requests and responses (Bookman & Guerrero Amparán, 2009; Berliner, Bagozzi, & Palmer-Rubin, 2018). Mexico was thus seen as a leading open government champion by many in global reform communities, including those responsible for the founding of the Open Government Partnership.

However, despite the access to information law and an active civil society focusing on issues of transparency, corruption, and human rights, Mexico also faced many challenges for open government reforms to thrive, including high levels of corruption and economic inequality, and ongoing violence and human rights abuses (especially after the launch of President Calderon's drug war after his election in 2006). A civil service reform was initiated in 2003, but it remained highly limited and incomplete, leaving nearly all substantive positions as political appointees (Dussauge Laguna, 2011). Even the widely hailed access to information law was shaped by political considerations, both in its extension to the subnational level (Berliner & Erlich, 2015) and in how officials responded to individual requests (Bagozzi, Berliner, & Almquist, 2019; Berliner et al., 2020).

In 2011, Mexico scored only thirty out of one hundred points on Transparency International's Corruption Perceptions Index (with one hundred being least corrupt)—although this was tied with fellow Open Government Partnership founding country Indonesia and ahead of another founding member, the Philippines. Although Mexico's score then rose over the next few years, reaching thirty-five in 2014 and 2015, it subsequently fell again. However, this drop should be largely attributed to the revelations of corruption scandals associated with President Enrique Peña Nieto and their effect on international perceptions of corruption. A prominent critique of such perception-based measures of corruption is that the publicity of scandals can drive negative shifts in perceptions, even if, in reality, their true effects on corruption are uncertain or even positive (Petersen, 2020).

Thus, although Mexico featured many characteristics that would situate it as a likely case for traditional compliance-based mechanisms with international commitments, these myriad challenges also shaped and limited its potential for open government reform successes.

MEXICO'S OPEN GOVERNMENT PARTNERSHIP MEMBERSHIP: INITIAL PHASES

Mexico was one of the Open Government Partnership's founding members, involved as early as the January 2011 meeting in Washington, DC, where IFAI commissioner María Marván and Juan Pardinas from the civil society group, IMCO (Instituto Mexicano para la Competitividad—Mexican Institute for Competitiveness) were in attendance. Mexico was seen as a global leader in transparency reforms, particularly in terms of its 2002 access to information law, its highly active information commission, and the innovative online information request platform INFOMEX. Interestingly, Mexico's participation in the Open Government Partnership began with IFAI—a formally independent body—and not with a ministry headed by a politically appointed secretary.

As one of the founding members, it was the responsibility of the Mexican government to prepare an action plan of commitments in time for the September 2011 meeting at the United Nations General Assembly when the Open Government Partnership would be formally launched. As with most of the other founding members, this resulted in a process that was widely acknowledged as rushed and generally yielding commitments that were superficial or already underway (Arreola, 2013; Open Government Partnership, 2012c, 15; Gerson & Nieto, 2016, 7–8; GO 2).

One civil society participant wrote that "the initial government approach to OGP was 'business as usual': consultations with CSOs were carried out but at the end of the day the CSO's input was largely ignored" (Arreola, 2013). Meanwhile, a government participant noted that, given the brand-new process and limited timeframe, "it wasn't clear what was the format, what we had to do, what was included" (GO 2).

This process was criticized by civil society groups for its rushed timeframe, limited nature of commitments, and the fact that only one civil society proposal had been incorporated (GO 1). Gerson and Nieto (2016, 8) wrote that "immediately after, CSOs questioned the legitimacy of the plan and threatened to leave and denounce the partnership."

However, unique among the founding members, Mexico's government then embarked on an after-the-fact expansion of its first National Action Plan in a new process initiated in December 2011 (Alianza para el Gobierno Abierto, 2012, 1; Open Government Partnership, 2013c, 34; Arreola, 2013). A new "expanded action plan" was released in May 2012 and "featured a wider set of commitments, each with a unique co-governance structure between civil society and government" (Open Government Partnership, 2013c, 3). Many of these thirty-seven new commitments corresponded directly to specific policy goals of civil society groups in Mexico (Arreola, 2013).

The process of designing the extended action plan was particularly open to civil society groups, who took advantage of the government's initial missteps to ensure that the process yielded concrete steps on specific goals. However, many participants in this process later noted its limitations—the "asks" of the civil society groups were relatively narrow, discrete, and related to their already existing programs of work (GO 2). One civil society participant wrote:

> Ambition of this new set of 37 commitments was low.... Hence, the low hanging fruits of open government were prioritized. Most commitments were built over preexisting work either from CSOs or government (Arreola, 2013).

The Independent Reporting Mechanism report monitoring Mexico's 2011–2013 plan noted:

> The eight organizations consulted for the elaboration of the Action Plan decided to propose proposals that meet their specific information needs to advance their work agenda. This was largely due to the haste with which the process was organized, and the need to move forward on proposals that could be translated into concrete commitments, in the short term and exclusively in reference to the executive branch. But it is also due to a restricted view on the part of some of the organizations about their own work, and to a certain degree of ignorance of the logic of work and the limitations of public management. (Open Government Partnership, 2013c, 115–116, translated by the authors)

Nonetheless, it was noteworthy that a majority of the commitments were ultimately fully or substantially completed, comparing favorably with many other countries where early implementation gaps were much larger. We can assess the implementation of these commitments using the report prepared by the Open Government Partnership's Independent Reporting Mechanism researcher. At this stage, the Independent Reporting Mechanism did not yet conduct end-of-term assessments of commitment completion, so we can only rely on the midterm assessment, bearing in mind that some commitments may have been completed afterward. Nonetheless, even partway through the first (extended) action plan's timeline, sixteen out of thirty-six reviewed commitments were recorded as completed, nine more as substantially completed, seven as limited, and four as not started (Open Government Partnership, 2013c, 4–8).[3]

One example from the extended action plan was a commitment to publicly disclose media advertising spending by government bodies. This had been a major goal of several civil society organizations for many years, particularly Article 19 and FUNDAR, the two groups responsible for the commitment. Such official publicity spending is often criticized in Mexico for being used to shape news coverage and limit the financial independence of media entities. This commitment did not even require the collection of new information, as an internal database already existed and was managed by the Secretaría de Función Pública (Ministry of Public Administration). Yet the commitment was faced with resistance, especially as approval was required from the Interior Ministry, but no approval was forthcoming. One monitoring report reflected that "if there is not any kind of technical or budgetary problem what appears to have been an obstacle is the lack of political will" (Open Government Partnership, 2012d, 9).

Facing this resistance and with a new presidential administration incoming in December 2012, outgoing officials in the Secretaría de Función Pública unilaterally made the existing internal database public, thereby at least partially fulfilling the commitment (Open Government Partnership, 2012c, 9). Interviewees suggested that this incident reflected the importance of reform-minded bureaucrats taking advantage of the Open Government Partnership process to help break through entrenched resistance to transparency (CSO 2;

CSO 5). The resulting official publicity spending database remained publicly available and updated (though with delays and some limitations) even many years later, and it laid a groundwork for continued investigative reporting and analysis by journalists and civil society organizations (Artículo 19, 2015) as well as continued mobilization for increased transparency and regulations of this form of spending.

The Tripartite Technical Secretariat

In the process of developing this expanded action plan, government and civil society groups jointly formed the tripartite STT (Secretariado Técnico Tripartita or Tripartite Technical Secretariat), comprising representatives of civil society organizations, the federal government (represented by the Secretaría de Función Pública), and the independent information commission, IFAI. The goal of this body was to "act as a permanent and institutionalized space for decision-making, consultation, monitoring compliance with the commitments established in OGP, as well as communication between government actors and civil society" (Alianza para el Gobierno Abierto, 2012, 2, translated by authors). Each sector—civil society, the federal government, and the independent information commission—would have one vote on this body.

This multisectoral representation was a response to what was seen as unwieldy initial efforts to coordinate and collaborate among representatives from dozens of different government ministries, IFAI, and multiple civil society groups. One participant noted that these efforts were "not working," "not moving fast enough," and required a smaller group to "streamline coordination" (GO 2). The STT also helped resolve some early tension between IFAI and the Secretaría de Función Pública over who owned the transparency and open government agenda within government by consolidating the latter as the representative of the federal government, with IFAI as the more independent third party between government and civil society.

IFAI's role was interesting, as a government entity yet largely independent (its constitutional autonomy was not guaranteed until a 2014 constitutional reform that also resulted in its name being changed from IFAI to INAI, standing for Instituto Nacional de Acceso a la Información). Traditionally, IFAI had been seen as a champion of transparency reform and an ally to civil society groups, while some in government had tended to see it as a "foreign body" (CSO 1). On the STT, it managed to play a role as a broker, keeping the trust of both civil society and government officials (Gerson & Nieto, 2016, 4; CSO 1).

The civil society members of this body initially included eight organizations, with two more joining a few years later. The coalition formed by these organizations was known as the Núcleo de la Sociedad Civil (Civil Society Core Group). Notably, these eight groups, many that had not previously worked together, included a relatively wide array of ideological and issue focuses.[4]

Some, like CIDAC (Centro de Investigación para el Desarrollo, A.C.), were generally nonpartisan think tanks engaged primarily in research. Artículo 19, the local chapter of the global freedom of expression organization Article 19, focused on human rights issues and was generally more confrontational toward the government. On the other hand, IMCO (Instituto Mexicano para la Competitividad) focused on promoting more business-friendly policy developments.[5] GESOC (Gestión Social y Cooperación) was seen by some as a nonpartisan think tank but by others as right-leaning like IMCO. Cultura Ecológica was an environmental group, while SocialTic (previously called CitiVox) focused primarily on technology and open data. Like Artículo 19, Transparencia Mexicana was also the local chapter of a well-known international nongovernmental organization, Transparency International. FUNDAR engaged in both research and advocacy and focused on a relatively broad range of issues, including human rights and corruption and transparency.

Many stakeholders involved in the Open Government Partnership process in Mexico highlighted the importance of bringing together this relatively diverse array of groups into the same collaborative process, suggesting that they had not previously been used to working in concert on shared goals or processes that crossed the boundaries of their individual issue areas. One civil society participant said that they "used to be in silos" but "now are working together more, across human rights, transparency, digital" (CSO 3). Another said that "civil society organizations in Mexico had been very separated, individualistic" and noted that while transparency organizations in particular had been working together for many years, "the OGP helped create the environment to get together with other organizations" from beyond a narrow transparency agenda (CSO 4).

Even a government official agreed, saying:

> Something that was not very present before is that civil society got conscious that they have to build partnerships and collaboration within themselves. Before, there were some civil society [organizations] with specific expertise in some areas, but they did not dialogue with the organizations with other specialties. So, I think that what has happened with open government is that they have become conscious that if they are partners, they can demand more from the authorities. (GO 1)

Although previous civil society coalitions had operated on issues of transparency, no enduring coalitions had been this broad.[6] In some cases, these organizations had been previously reticent to work directly with the government, preferring more confrontational modes of engagement. These new forms of collaboration were distinct from older patterns of corporatism in Mexico, wherein groups in society were incorporated into ruling party structures or directly controlled (Collier & Collier, 1979).

Several interviewees thus credited the Open Government Partnership with introducing a new culture of collaboration both among civil society groups and between those groups and the government (Gerson & Nieto, 2016; GO 1; CSO 2; CSO 3; CSO 4). One participant even suggested that the most important impact of the Open Government Partnership in Mexico had been in shaping the activities of civil society groups themselves in engaging with government (CSO 2).

On the other hand, despite ideological and issue diversity, this coalition remained quite narrow in other ways. In terms of representation, it incorporated only a small slice of civil society groups operating in Mexico, even of those working on related topics, and was a relatively elite group centered in the capital city. One participant called them "the usual suspects" (GO 2).

Nonetheless, many observers suggested that the STT reflected a new mode of operation for policymaking in Mexico. The announcement of the expanded action plan highlighted that civil society groups and government officials worked together "as peers" on the STT, enabling greater mutual understanding and trust between them (Alianza para el Gobierno Abierto, 2012, 2). The Independent Reporting Mechanism monitoring report of the plan's implementation said, "The establishment of the Tripartite Technical Secretariat (STT) is the most remarkable aspect of the process to promote the Alliance for Open Government in Mexico" (Open Government Partnership, 2013c, 26, translated). In April 2013, Haydeé Pérez of FUNDAR called the STT "a model of co-government" (Pérez, 2013).

In giving civil society groups a seat at the table, the STT also empowered them in both direct and indirect ways. Directly, they were able to contribute to the design of National Action Plan commitments, thereby gaining new ways to achieve their existing policy goals. Civil society's decision-making role at times even went beyond commitments, such as during the planning of the global summit hosted in Mexico City in 2015. One government official involved said that every decision involved in planning still went through the STT, requiring the agreement of both IFAI and civil society representatives (GO 3).[7]

The STT also brought new indirect forms of influence for civil society groups. They were able to forge new links with bureaucrats in relevant ministries, particularly reformers who shared their goals or interests. And participation in the Open Government Partnership could also help bring pressure to bear on more resistant bureaucrats. One government official described how civil society would interact with government officials over the implementation of commitments:

> It was persuasion. It was kind of: Listen, if you don't do that, the cost . . . it will be very high. Because right now civil society is conscious of their rights. They are doing some pressure. But at the same time, it is a priority. You have to play with the power that you have, and speak the name of the president and everything, to try to persuade and eliminate all the resistance that is natural in terms of bureaucracy. (GO 1)

As will be discussed later in this chapter, participation in the Open Government Partnership also brought the ability to leverage international influence, particularly in shaping new legislation and in bringing pressure to bear in preventing rollbacks. Finally, membership in the STT also gave civil society groups a new form of structural power from their implicit threat of exit, which would delegitimize the government's Open Government Partnership participation. One civil society participant said:

> I mean, having and being involved in the process and being recognized by the government as a legitimate partner, it creates liabilities for the government if they decide to behave badly. . . . [Civil society can] leave, and then they're going to suffer from their legitimacy nationally and globally. That's a credible threat for the governments. (CSO 2)

Participants themselves saw these new forms of influence as some of the most important aspects of the Open Government Partnership. One said that "having a policy-building space with government at a high level—this was a change from before" (CSO 3). Another even said that the Open Government Partnership was "like steroids for civil society," noting it enabled them to "pressure government from the inside and the outside" (CSO 1). A government official agreed, saying:

> The first steps that we made with OGP gave a lot of power to civil society, and they gained a lot of legitimacy to put some pressure on the authorities, that they cannot in the subsequent actions take decisions on their own, that they have to be co-constructed, co-created, with the specialization and the knowledge that civil society has. (GO 1)

Notably, at the time the STT was established, no other country had a formal, permanent multistakeholder body to coordinate the domestic Open Government Partnership process (Alianza para el Gobierno Abierto, 2012). Instead, this development reflected the adoption and institutionalization, at the domestic level, of a collaborative and multistakeholder model inspired by the Partnership itself. Mexico's STT would come to be seen as a model to be emulated by many other countries, including those in the Global North. Ultimately, the Open Government Partnership developed new guidelines formally encouraging and ultimately requiring member countries to institute similar formal coordinating bodies (Open Government Partnership, 2018c).

Transition to Peña Nieto Administration

On July 1, 2012, Mexican voters elected Enrique Peña Nieto to the presidency, returning to power the Partido Revolucionario Institucional that had governed for decades until 2000. This was a very fraught period for democracy in Mexico, particularly as the Partido Revolucionario Institucional had been the party of authoritarianism and secrecy—although it now sought to project an image of reform and efficiency.

For the Open Government Partnership, Mexico was the first of the founding members to undergo an executive leadership transition. The new administration could have been hostile towards this initiative of its predecessor and chosen to abandon or neglect it. There was substantial uncertainty, particularly as the Peña Nieto campaign had promised to abolish the Secretaría de Función Pública (Gómez, 2012). Ultimately, this did not take place.

Instead, the transition proceeded smoothly, as the new administration found reasons to embrace the Open Government Partnership, both linking it with its own existing agenda and using it as a way of signaling continuity and commitment to reform (CSO 1; GO 1; GO 2). Gerson and Nieto (2016, 9) note that "Peña's package of institutional reforms ... included explicit commitments to increase transparency, curb corruption, and improve the regulation of financial contributions during electoral campaigns." One government official said that the new administration was "very smart ... they took it as an opportunity to show the world the commitment that the administration will have" (GO 1).

Further, Mexico was selected as the next lead government chair of the Partnership's Steering Committee, a role it would hold for one year, beginning in October 2014 and culminating in its hosting of the global summit in Mexico City at the end of October 2015. This role also brought substantial international attention to Mexico's government, including awards (Notimex, 2014b) and praise from world leaders (Notimex, 2014a).

One important change that was made was the replacement of the Secretaría de Función Pública on the STT. In its place would be the Coordinación de Estrategia Digital Nacional (Digital Strategy National Coordinating Office) in the Office of the President, which was additionally tasked with monitoring the compliance of Open Government Partnership commitments across government. In general, this move was seen as a positive step, helping to signal the stronger commitment to and involvement of the executive in the partnership process. The domestic Open Government Partnership process also received additional resources dedicated specifically toward the implementation of commitments (Ocejo Rojo, 2016, 1–2).

Commitments in Action? Mexico's Second and Third National Action Plans

While Mexico's first National Action Plan had offered civil society groups a novel opportunity to achieve their policy goals, many came to see it as having been too narrowly focused on the disclosure of specific types of information linked with existing civil society advocacy efforts (Arreola, 2013; Open Government Partnership, 2013c, 116; GO 1). The process had also been difficult, with the original iteration criticized as ignoring civil society contributions, but the process led to the revised, extended action plan, which was seen as going too far in the other direction. One government official said that "there had been a bit of trauma about the hundreds of meetings," placing a considerable burden on both officials and civil society organizations (GO 2).

Thus, the STT adopted a new mode of consultation organized around thematic working groups for the design of the second National Action Plan in 2013. Each group would bring together relevant government officials, academic experts, and civil society groups in order to cocreate commitments within that thematic issue area, but without all actors needing to be involved for all commitments, while also promoting commitments broader than the goals of any single civil society organization.

Each working group included roughly fifteen to twenty-five people, with over two hundred individuals involved overall, making the process more broadly consultative than either version of the first National Action Plan had been. The nine themes were: "public purchasing," "digital agenda," "competitiveness and economic growth," "social policy," "environment and climate change," "infrastructure," "budget and fiscal transparency," "justice and security," and "extractive industries" (Alianza para el Gobierno Abierto, 2014).

One official involved said that between the first and second National Action Plans, "there was a ton of learning," because:

> In the first, you could say "this is a commitment of FUNDAR, this is from GESOC [Gestión Social y Cooperación], etc." In the second, you could say "this was from everyone; a meeting of CSOs and government and experts." (GO 2)

In some thematic areas, this collaborative process of developing commitments went relatively smoothly, but in others, it was much more difficult. One participant noted that the "toughest" discussion was for the security-related theme, particularly relating to a database of disappeared persons:

> That one they were fighting for each of the words in the commitment, they were fighting for commas. . . . It was really co-created word for word. (GO 2)

Ultimately, seventeen commitments resulted from this collaborative process. Nine more commitments were selected by the STT out of proposals made by government bodies. Collaboration continued through the implementation process, as each commitment (of those collaboratively produced) was assigned three civil society groups responsible for monitoring progress, with a timeline of follow-up meetings with the relevant ministries (Ocejo Rojo, 2016). The Coordinación de Estrategia Digital Nacional office even produced an online dashboard to enable both participants and the public to track implementation progress, with each commitment color-coded for progress and any status updates made by officials requiring both uploaded evidence and agreement from the involved civil society groups (GO 3).

There were also other tensions in this collaborative process. In particular, not all the civil society groups involved agreed on the best way to manage their interactions with government bodies, particularly when they previously had largely adversarial interactions with them. Some organizations preferred to refrain from outright criticism of government entities that they were officially collaborating with, while others were less comfortable in that position. One civil society participant noted that in this period, "one of the biggest fights" was between Article 19—generally preferring a more confrontational approach—and the other civil society organizations over precisely this tension (CSO 4).

Despite this collaborative process, none of the resulting commitments was ultimately assessed by the Independent Reporting Mechanism researcher as having "transformative" potential impact, and only six were rated as having "moderate" potential impact (Ocejo Rojo, 2016). These six were an "open and participatory entrepreneurship fund," a "detainees register," a "missing persons database," a program to "democratize scholarships for aid and education," an "open data policy," and "participative protection of the environment" (Ocejo Rojo, 2016). Some of these were sector-specific and represented the diffusion and application of open government ideas into new policy areas. Others were more general, particularly the open data policy, which was closely linked to President Peña Nieto's open data agenda.

The Mexican government made implementation a particularly high priority for the second National Action Plan, in large part because of its role in the global spotlight as country chair of the Open Government Partnership Steering Committee and host of the 2015 global summit (CSO 5; GO 3). Ultimately this effort yielded one of the highest completion rates of any National Action Plan. According to the Independent Reporting Mechanism report on the second plan, twenty-four of twenty-six commitments were fully completed, with only two assessed as "limited" completion (Ocejo Rojo, 2016). Interestingly, while some earlier commitments were criticized as one-off disclosures that were never repeated or updated, this was not the case for many commitments from the second plan. A follow-up study several years later found that fourteen of the twenty-six commitments had resulted in websites, platforms, or databases that were still in existence and still being updated (CSO 3).

For Mexico's third National Action Plan, developed over 2015–2016 and planned to be implemented from 2016 to 2018, the STT sought to fine-tune the consultation and design processes. These steps came in response to both the experiences in Mexico of the first two plans and to feedback from the Partnership's global Independent Reporting Mechanism unit based on the experiences of other countries.

First, the process would be more diverse and representative, in part based on concerns that the civil society groups on the STT represented a narrow and elite set of interests. This led to the inclusion of two additional civil society organizations on the STT (Contraloría Ciudadana [Citizen Control] and Observatorio Nacional Ciudadano [National Citizens' Observatory]), the use of an online participatory platform to solicit ideas from the public for commitments, and the involvement of over 350 individuals—government, civil society, experts, and academics—in consultations and workshops (Nava Campos, 2018).

Second, the third National Action Plan would have fewer commitments. In part, this responded to feedback from the Independent Reporting Mechanism, which emphasized a less-is-more approach based on concerns that action plans with too many commitments might ultimately see worse implementation (OGP 1). The third National Action Plan ultimately contained only eleven commitments, aiming for "fewer but stronger and more long-term commitments" (GO 3).

Finally, the third National Action Plan was thematically focused less on access to information, accountability, or anticorruption and instead more on participation and sustainable development. In fact, the action plan was explicitly organized around themes linked to the UN's Sustainable Development Goals. Commitments particularly focused on "information essential for decision-making and monitoring of government actions in areas such as combating poverty, investigation of disappearances, the management of drinking water and the risks associated with climate change," using "inclusive and highly participatory mechanisms or bodies" (Nava Campos, 2018, 19, translated by authors).

Participants praised the plan for both its participatory process (GO 3) and the increased focus on broader social needs (CSO 5). Yet the Independent Reporting Mechanism researcher's midterm report assessed none of the eleven commitments as having a potentially transformative impact—although eight were assessed as moderate potential impact. As of the Independent Reporting Mechanism researcher's midterm report, none of the eleven commitments were assessed as being either substantially or fully complete. Even by the time of the end-of-term report, notably following the turmoil to be detailed below, only five of eleven had reached that status.

Mexico in the Global Spotlight: Steering Committee Chair and Global Summit Host

During the period of these National Action Plans, several other important events were also taking place. We focus on these events to highlight both other, more process-oriented developments that the Open Government Partnership was contributing to, as well as mounting concerns on the part of civil society groups over their participation.

Although Mexico had already been slated to serve as country cochair of the Open Government Partnership Steering Committee, taking over for Indonesia after the 2014–2015 term, this needed to be confirmed with the new presidency taking office in December 2012 (Open Government Partnership, 2012c, 12). The new government's agreement was symbolically important, as it reflected Mexico's continued embrace of the Partnership agenda even after the change in the presidential administration. Mexico would also host the Open Government Partnership's global summit in October 2015, giving the government an important opportunity to showcase its actions on the world stage at an event with a high-level diplomatic presence, including several world leaders. This was particularly important, as the government had made digital government and open data a major part of its agenda.

This spotlight effect proved very important. As already noted, it contributed to the government's focus on achieving a high implementation rate of commitments from its second National Action Plan. One government official noted that the government "made a big effort to do something very important, to bring together all the stakeholders and make this important internationally" (GO 3).

Reformers both inside the government and in civil society made strategic use of Mexico's leadership role and the spotlight it created. They took advantage of these opportunities to pursue reform agendas even beyond the formal scope of the National Action Plan.

In the Coordinación de Estrategia Digital Nacional office's open data team, officials "took a lot of advantage from that moment, for the open government and open data agenda nationally" (GO 3). Although the open data agenda was a priority of the president, it also faced difficulty getting attention, resources, and overcoming resistance from other parts of the bureaucracy. The summit helped give them space on the policy agenda and the opportunity to gain high-level commitments to support their efforts. Officials focused on emphasizing key goals in the draft of Peña Nieto's speech at the summit, hoping that this public commitment would ensure follow-through. One official said:

They made the President commit to them there, in an international forum, so that there was no way back, they had to implement them. . . . Projects that are now very important, and will continue into the next administration, because there's now no way back, they have the support from many stakeholders. (GO 3)

Similarly, another official reflected on the summit's emphasis on open data issues, saying that the open data team "wanted to push something and they found the right tool to do it" (GO 2).

Importantly, many of these commitments were *not* part of the National Action Plan at the time but rather separate initiatives being promoted from inside the government. These included a commitment to publish all contracts involved in the construction of Mexico City's new airport according to the new Open Contracting Data Standard, a pilot program for body cameras by the Federal Police, and the creation of a new online public participation platform by the Interior Ministry (Reforma, 2015b).

The airport commitment deserves particular attention. While this might seem like a limited setting for transparency, it is notable for the size of the project—one of the largest infrastructure projects in the world—and for its ultimate political consequences, as corruption allegations became a major criticism of the Peña Nieto administration and a campaign emphasis of leftist challenger Andrés Manuel López Obrador in 2018, who even called it a "bottomless barrel of corruption" (Montes, 2018). For the Open Contracting Data Standard, this was an important early step in its diffusion both in Mexico and globally. Mexico has gone on to become one of the leading countries around the world in applying this standard to public procurement more broadly (Open Contracting Partnership, 2019).

Civil Society Leverage and the General Law on Transparency

Civil society groups made further strategic use of the opportunities presented by Mexico's leadership role in the Open Government Partnership, again pertaining to matters outside the formal scope of the National Action Plan at the time. A legislative drafting process was underway for a General Law on Transparency, updating Mexico's access to information framework in light of constitutional reforms made in 2014. The drafting process itself was open and collaborative in unprecedented ways, as detailed later in this chapter, and resulted in a draft considered very strong by many civil society groups and experts.

However, in early 2015, the presidency announced eighty-one last-minute changes to the bill (Reforma, 2015a). Advocates saw these provisions as amounting to a weakening of Mexico's access to information regime, particularly in terms of limiting the independence and authority of IFAI, reducing the breadth of proactive disclosure provisions, increasing the scope for secrecy and classification, and even creating the possibility of sanctioning officials for disclosing information (Transparencia Mexicana, 2015b; Montalvo, 2014).

Mexico's transparency advocacy coalition sprang into action to highlight the changes in both domestic and international media and put pressure on the government to reverse them. Importantly, many of these efforts explicitly contrasted the reversals contained in the president's new version of the bill with Mexico's claim of global leadership in the open government agenda. For example, one civil society representative wrote:

> Therefore, I wonder how Mexico can still be the leader of the OGP if there is no willingness from the President's Office to make a change and effectively guarantee RTI [right to information] to all their citizens. (Ruelas, 2015)

Another said, "what worries us, in particular, is that the government that presides over the initiative today is running the risk of not preaching by example" (Mural, 2015, translated by authors).

Civil society groups also sought to leverage Open Government Partnership structures and the global partnership community to apply external pressure. The Mexican Open Government Partnership civil society coalition wrote a formal letter to the STT requesting that the changes be withdrawn (Transparencia Mexicana, 2015a). Transparencia Mexicana distributed a statement calling for support within the global Open Government Partnership community (Transparencia Mexicana, 2015b).

Civil society groups also sought a response from the global level of the Open Government Partnership, although the Steering Committee had, thus far, been highly reticent to become involved in domestic matters falling outside of the formal National Action Plan process elsewhere. In this case, however, the civil society cochairs of the Steering Committee wrote a statement explicitly on their own behalf but published it on the Partnership's website and distributed it through partnership channels. This statement praised the collaborative process that had produced the earlier, stronger draft but highlighted the criticisms of the proposed changes, concluding by drawing a contrast with Mexico's leadership position:

> As Civil Society Co-chairs of the Open Government Partnership, we share these concerns. We encourage the Mexican Government and Congress to seize this opportunity to re-confirm their proven record and commitment towards transparency, access to information and co-creation processes with civil society, as appropriate to their leadership of the OGP. (Kaimal & González Arreola, 2015)

One observer noted how unusual this statement was, given that "the OGP Steering Committee, and its civil society members, has avoiding [*sic*] public criticism of member governments except in a few instances" (FreedomInfo.org, 2015a). However, despite explicitly not being a statement of the Steering Committee as a whole, it was generally covered in domestic media attention at the time as an international rebuke, which further contrasted the reversals to the draft legislation with Mexico's global leadership position (El Norte, 2015; Mural, 2015).

In the end, this campaign was largely successful, as most of the reversals were dropped, and the final bill "does not include 77 of the 81 last-minute amendments urged by the government which had aroused strenuous objections" (FreedomInfo.org, 2015b). The reforms as ultimately passed did indeed reflect most of the gains of the earlier collaborative process. While this was broadly a success of advocacy and activism by civil society groups, the media, and reformers in Mexico, the process highlights important leverage offered by the Partnership, particularly in conjunction with Mexico's role as chair and upcoming host of the global summit. One civil society participant, reflecting on this legislative process, said:

> We used the Open Government Partnership as leverage. . . . They came out with a statement . . . and it was a very soft; the Steering Committee is very soft. But it was still strong for them. And so, the discussions opened up again and we finally got a very good law. But I think it was leverage from the OGP. (CSO 4)

GOVERNMENT SURVEILLANCE AND CIVIL SOCIETY WITHDRAWAL

There was also a darker side to Mexico's year as Open Government Partnership chair. In September 2014, forty-three students disappeared in Ayotzinapa with alleged government involvement, sparking outrage nationally and globally over continued impunity for human rights abuses in Mexico. In November 2014, investigative journalists broke the Casa Blanca scandal—named after the first lady's mansion, purchased from a favored government contractor (Aristegui Noticias, 2014). Peña Nieto was increasingly unpopular, with polls in September 2015 showing only a 35 percent approval rating (Partlow & Martinez, 2015).

Ahead of the October 2015 summit, civil society groups were torn over how best to approach the event. Some felt the obligation to recognize the government for genuine progress in the second National Action Plan, both in its design and high rate of implementation. But others were less comfortable in such a position of praising the government in light of the broader situation outside of the National Action Plan. One participant said:

> For us, it's also complicated because we can't be applauding this kind of government. The problem is that the commitments are not so ambitious . . . it's easy for the government to achieve these commitments. And we are in a very delicate position. So, I think the danger is the image of an organization, and then it's also the political legitimacy we give to a government, but we can't sustain that. (CSO 2)

Ultimately, the civil society coalition released a statement calling for the government to strengthen the rule of law and to focus more of the Open Government Partnership process on human rights and civic space (FUNDAR, 2015). This statement was signed by over 190 organizations across multiple different issue networks (SocialTIC, 2015). At the summit, activists circulated stickers reading "¿Gobierno Abierto & 43 + 26,000 Desaparecidos?" (Open government & 43 + 26,000 missing?), highlighting the forty-three missing students from Ayotzinapa as well as the total number of reported missing persons.[8] Protests were held in streets near the event (Howard, 2015), and at one point, activists even took to the main stage of the summit holding placards bearing pictures of skulls. One participant even noted that this mixed approach of civil society groups to the summit was "a little schizophrenic" (CSO 5). Many international observers were similarly critical, contrasting Mexico's focus on open data with the broader context of deteriorating press freedom and human rights (Howard, 2015).

Following the 2015 Open Government Partnership summit, the situation began to deteriorate further. Many participants suggested that the government "lost interest" in the Partnership, with the exception of its open data agenda (CSO 3; CSO 4). One government official even agreed that after the summit, "it was natural that the boom of open government diminished a bit" (GO 3). The Open Government Partnership coordinating role inside the government was shifted back to the Secretaría de Función Pública, away from the digital strategy unit in the president's office, reflecting a deprioritization of the agenda (CSO 3). The Peña Nieto administration became increasingly unpopular and burdened with proliferating scandals of corruption and impunity. For both the government and civil society groups involved in the Open Government Partnership process, concerns mounted over the possibilities and consequences of continued collaboration.

Civil society groups were becoming increasingly concerned over the disconnect between the discrete open government projects being pursued within the scope of the National Action Plan process and the broader context of declining openness nationally. In this context, some felt that they were being taken advantage of to burnish the international image of the Mexican government, and some participants grew more concerned about their organizations' reputations. One participant reflected on "the president hosting the summit, making statements, building its brand outside Mexico," while at the same time, "nationally, there has been deep incongruency" in terms of "criminal investigations . . . and freedom of expression" (CSO 3). Another noted that the Open Government Partnership had "became more hard to believe" (CSO 1). Another participant said:

> After Ayotzinapa, it was very hard for us to maintain the position sitting with government at the negotiating table. . . . We didn't want to sit at the table for just little commitments or administrative processes (CSO 5).

Yet the government also became increasingly disillusioned, concerned that civil society groups would criticize them no matter what they did. One civil society participant said, "As time passed, they knew civil society was not going to be happy anyway, so they 'threw the towel away,' and political will went away" (CSO 4). It was in this setting that a surveillance scandal led to the ultimate collapse of the national-level collaborative process in Mexico, proving to be, in the words of one participant, "the final drop of water" (CSO 5).

In August 2016, the Toronto-based group Citizen Lab published its first investigation of Pegasus, a "government-exclusive 'lawful intercept' spyware" software sold by the Israeli company NSO Group to governments around the world (Marczak & Scott-Railton, 2016). This initial investigation focused primarily on its use in the United Arab Emirates but noted evidence of sales to other countries, including Mexico. Following this, Citizen Lab was contacted by several Mexican civil society groups, including SocialTIC of the partnership coalition, who "assisted Citizen Lab researchers in collecting suspicious messages from a range of Mexican targets" (Scott-Railton et al., 2017a).

This subsequent investigation, first published on February 11, 2017, by Citizen Lab and the *New York Times*, found evidence of digital surveillance of a range of actors in Mexico, particularly those involved in a campaign for a soda tax (Scott-Railton et al., 2017a; Perlroth, 2017). Subsequent investigations found similar spyware on the phones of a wide range of actors, including journalists, politicians, and human rights and anticorruption activists (Scott-Railton et al., 2017b). Among the targets identified were staff of the partnership coalition member IMCO, including its head (and former global Steering Committee member) Juan Pardinas (Scott-Railton et al., 2017b).

According to Citizen Lab:

> The targets received SMS messages that included links to NSO exploits paired with troubling personal and sexual taunts, messages impersonating official communications by the Embassy of the United States in Mexico, fake AMBER Alerts, warnings of kidnappings, and other threats. . . . To remotely compromise phones, NSO's government customers trick targets to click on a link. When the link is clicked, the phone visits a server that checks the handset model (iPhone, Android, etc.) and then sends the phone a remote exploit for its operating system. (Scott-Railton et al., 2017b)

For example, one of the malicious messages received by Juan Pardinas of IMCO read:

> hey, there is a van outside your house with 2 armed dudes, I took pictures look at them and take care: [malicious link]. (Scott-Railton et al., 2017b)

Civil society groups immediately began debating how to respond. They first worked internally through the STT, sending a letter demanding action. The federal government was represented on the STT at this time by the Secretaría de Función Pública, not the presidency. Yet the matter of surveillance clearly went beyond the scope of public administration alone. One government official said that "in the SFP [Secretaría de Función Pública] they tried to promote it. The Minister of Public Administration sat with them several times and asked what they could do" (GO 3). This official even agreed that the civil society groups "had [a] very valid point on bringing these issues to the table" but protested that the STT was not the right platform for these demands:

> We had a specific level of things we could do, which was not much. We brought it to other authorities, but we ourselves didn't have the tools to investigate what happened. . . . That was all we could do in that space. (GO 3)

Adding to the concern of civil society groups were the government's efforts to water down some of the commitments in the third National Action Plan, reducing their scope or ambition from what had already been agreed (CSO 3; CSO 5).

The civil society coalition debated for three months over what course of action to take and whether or not to withdraw from the STT. One participant suggested that "one side wanted to stay . . . it was very important for them to listen to each other and make agreements first" (CSO 5). But another participant suggested that all members of the coalition "agreed mostly to step away, but disagreed how." Yet all were concerned that—in the words of the same participant—"if we continue, and let them get away with undermining the process, we will be part of a huge simulation" (CSO 3).

Finally, all members agreed on the difficult necessity of leaving and published a letter on May 23, 2017, concluding that "there are no longer conditions for truthful co-creation and honest dialogue within the Secretariat."

They warned the broader Open Government Partnership community that "systematic actions in Mexico should worry all OGP members since illegal and disproportionate digital surveillance is increasingly becoming a characteristic of authoritarian, undemocratic, and opaque governments" (Núcleo de la Sociedad Civil para el Gobierno Abierto en México, 2017a).

The withdrawal was front-page news in Mexico (Reforma, 2017). The Open Government Partnership Support Unit initially published a short statement offering that "we stand ready to offer all our resources, energy and solidarity to Mexican actors to come together and find a way forward" and "sincerely hope that the Mexican government and civil society will be able to re-establish a working relationship in the future built on trust, transparency and accountability" (Open Government Partnership, 2017b). A few weeks later, the global Open Government Partnership Steering Committee cochairs—the governments of France and Georgia and the leaders of two civil society organizations—issued a formal statement promising to discuss the matter at the next Steering Committee meeting and to "reach out to Mexican government officials as well as civil society organizations in advance of the meeting to offer our full support" (Open Government Partnership, 2017c).

At that meeting, the Open Government Partnership Steering Committee "expressed its support for all Mexican stakeholders" and called for two Steering Committee members—one from government and one from civil society—to serve as envoys to visit Mexico on a fact-finding mission (Open Government Partnership, 2017d). These envoys met with stakeholders from the government, the information commission, and civil society groups but issued a largely neutral report that reflected the positions of each side.

Civil society members were generally disappointed by the Partnership's response. One said, "there is no balance between civil society and government. The Open Government Partnership always takes the side of government. They came to Mexico for the mission but the report was terrible" (CSO 4). Another said, "We are playing by the OGP's rules, but from the civil society view, they should take a more political view towards governments. . . . The main ask is to have a sense of the political role beyond procedures . . . it is very slow" (CSO 3).

Reflecting on the civil society coalition's withdrawal, one government official noted the tensions between open government *inside* and *outside* the formal National Action Plan process:

> They made a decision. I respect that, but they unilaterally closed communications channels with the government. . . . The space for the open government agenda was not respected. They brought in a national context. . . . In every country they have these issues that could be brought up by civil society, that could break the dialogue and be a breaking point. You have to balance, as government and as civil society organizations, how much to bring out bigger contextual issues. (GO 3)

In September 2017, the civil society coalition sent a letter to the global Steering Committee requesting that the Mexican government recuse itself and asking for the activation of the Open Government Partnership's response mechanism (Núcleo de la Sociedad Civil para el Gobierno Abierto en México, 2017b). Although the Partnership's response policy entails a lengthy process with many steps, it can ultimately result in a government being declared inactive.

Despite the fact that the July 2018 presidential elections were won by Andrés Manuel López Obrador's new Morena party, handing the incumbent party a resounding defeat, the civil society coalition stuck to their demands for the time being—that the government fully address the problem of surveillance and commit to fulfilling the cocreation process (CSO 3). Many members of the civil society coalition were skeptical that the new administration would seek to renew collaboration, given Obrador's often negative comments about civil society groups as unrepresentative (see, e.g., Proceso, 2018). Although one might see such renewal as low-hanging fruit for the new president, this was not a foregone conclusion given his desire to demonstrate clear breaks from the policies of his predecessors of both parties and ultimate resistance to independent accountability institutions (Webber, 2019).

However, on March 5, 2019, Mexico announced the resumption of collaboration between the Civil Society Core Group, the information commission, and the Secretaría de Función Pública to begin working on both a fourth National Action Plan and to address the surveillance issue, beginning with an agreement "on a roadmap to avoid cases like Pegasus from ever happening" (Open Government Partnership, 2019b).

SUBNATIONAL AND LEGISLATIVE DEVELOPMENTS

The tripartite STT had been widely regarded and often emulated across the global open government community as an exemplar of collaboration between civil society and government officials. The withdrawal of the Mexican civil society coalition and the broader context of corruption and impunity thus could easily have been seen as indicating the failure of this flexible, multistakeholder, transnational approach to governance reform. Indeed, the process had collapsed.

Yet this view would ignore the substantial institutionalization of open government reforms in Mexico, particularly beyond the executive level, and the role of the Open Government Partnership in driving and shaping that institutionalization. This section thus considers two additional, broader effects of the Partnership in Mexico that took place beyond the executive and outside the formal National Action Plan process. First was at the subnational level, in a new mini-partnership modeled after the multistakeholder and iterative structure of the global initiative and focusing on similar values. Second was in the legislative branch, as the Partnership's "culture of collaboration" helped shape the development of important reforms. However, we also carefully consider the causal processes by which these reform efforts proceeded and the extent to which it can be said that the Partnership was at least partially responsible.

Subnational Open Government

First, a new subnational open government initiative was launched in 2015, promoted by the information commission (now renamed INAI). This mini-partnership has its own tripartite structure in every participating state and developed action plans comprising individual commitments. Yet crucially, this structure has nothing to do with the global Open Government Partnership, which has its own distinct subnational pilot program (Jalisco state is the one entity in Mexico that is a member of both).

The initiative began with just twelve states signing on to a Joint Declaration for the Implementation of Actions for an Open Government (Proceso, 2016), and it soon became referred to as "Gobierno Abierto: Cocreación desde lo local," or "Open Government: Co-creation from the local" (Clemente, 2016).

This effort was consistent with Mexico's emphasis on subnational open government as part of its thematic agenda while cochair of the global Open Government Partnership, which led to the Partnership's subnational pilot program. However, that pilot program explicitly pursued a slow-growth strategy, first launching in 2016 with a cohort of fifteen subnational entities.

The INAI-led subnational initiative, however, had grown by 2016 to encompass twenty-three of Mexico's thirty-two states (including the Federal District) and twenty-six by 2018 (Clemente, 2016; Notimex, 2018). Notably, these included states governed by all three traditional major parties across the political left, right, and center. This cross-ideological appeal demonstrates an example of the Open Government Partnership contributing to the building of new coalitions, drawing in political allies that might have previously been more skeptical of this government reform movement.

The core elements of the initiative were the creation of local technical secretariats and the creation and implementation of local action plans. The local technical secretariats were clearly modeled after the national STT, with a tripartite structure comprising the governor's administration, local civil society groups, and the state-level information commission. By the end of 2018, the initiative had expanded to eighteen states with local technical secretariats, which had produced twelve local action plans comprising over seventy commitments (Rodea 2019). Thus, while the follow-through was slower than the rapid wave of states signing on to the initiative, at least some states were indeed taking concrete actions through the designated process.

This structure of collaboration between government and civil society groups was even more novel—and in some ways more challenging—at the subnational level than it had been nationally. Analysts have long noted that reform efforts at the state level in Mexico lag far behind those nationally (e.g., Beer, 2001; Berliner & Erlich, 2015). One civil society representative noted that "in the states, there is much less tradition of sitting at the table with government," and that "it's a completely different way of working, and very hard for civil society to sit at the table with government" (CSO 5). As with the experience of the global Open Government Partnership, the commitments included in these state-level action plans covered a wide variety of issues and levels of ambition.

Initially, the civil society groups participating in the national STT were suspicious of this initiative, particularly concerned about its autonomy from local politics (Alianza para el Gobierno Abierto, 2015; Terrazas, 2015). Some groups were concerned that governors would be able to manipulate the process by selecting which civil society groups could participate (GO 3). However, later on, the national civil society coalition became more involved, particularly in holding workshops to strengthen the capacity of local organizations and offering strategic advice on how to make the best of the multistakeholder structure (CSO 2; CSO 3; CSO 5).

Importantly, this initiative has continued to move forward despite the collapse of national-level collaboration. If anything, national-level civil society groups have even become more invested, working to support local organizations to participate in their own local technical secretariats. One participant even explicitly framed the subnational initiative as an attempt to "institutionalize open government, so as not to depend so much on the presidency" (GO 1).

To what extent can this initiative be considered an impact of the Open Government Partnership via indirect impact? On the one hand, Mexican officials might have pursued some kind of subnational reform initiative even in a counterfactual world with no partnership. Yet, on the other hand, the structure, process, and goals of the subnational initiative are closely and explicitly modeled after those of the Open Government Partnership itself. The timing also closely aligns with the Partnership's own shift to emphasize subnational members.

Indeed, early discussions explicitly saw the initiative as "replicating the national work model" (Terrazas, 2015, translated by the authors). One of the officials involved with the initiative wrote in 2015 that "the starting point of the initiative promoted by INAI is precisely the Mexican experience in the OGP" (Álvarez Córdoba, 2016, 195, translated by the authors). One former government official noted that although the subnational initiative was separate from the Partnership, it was spearheaded by "people who were involved in OGP" and "knew OGP very well," and that the idea had "come from the Mexican experience of the OGP" (GO 2).

Thus, it is relatively straightforward to conclude, in this case, that Mexico's subnational open government initiative would not have existed in anything close to the form or the time in which it took shape if not for the Open Government Partnership itself.

Legislative Collaboration

A second form of institutionalization of the Open Government Partnership is in its "culture of collaboration" taking root in other branches of government and in other policy processes beyond the scope of formal National Action Plan commitments.

Foremost among these was an unprecedented form of multisectoral cocreation in the legislative process that designed the 2015 Ley General de Transparencia that ultimately strengthened Mexico's access to information regime. Earlier in this chapter, we detailed the role of the Open Government Partnership in providing leverage to ensure that the legislation was not weakened at the last minute. Here, we focus on an earlier stage—the process that yielded the original, stronger draft.

In February 2014, Mexico adopted a constitutional reform that greatly strengthened the status and applicability of both the right to information and the information commission itself (Ruelas, 2015). However, this necessitated specific implementing legislation that would update the existing access to information law first adopted in 2002. This new legislation would be known as the Ley General de Transparencia y Acceso a la Información Pública (General Law on Transparency and Access to Public Information).

Initial plans for the drafting of the new law would incorporate consultation with outside experts, but civil society groups instead sought a higher degree of openness and "direct participation in the process" (Ruelas & Mora, 2015). This claim was made particularly in the context of Mexico's leadership role in the global Open Government Partnership and Enrique Peña Nieto's stated commitment to transparency. As one participant put it, "We said if you are going to do this reform . . . you have to do it openly. If you want to actually be an open government, you have to open the parliament during the process of discussion" (CSO 4).

The Mexican Senate was responsive to these demands, creating a collaborative drafting group including representatives of each major political party and civil society members of three different coalitions, several also including members of the Civil Society Core Group working with the STT. Ruelas Serna called this "an unprecedented exercise" that posed new challenges to the participants:

> Those of us who were sitting at the table had no idea of the scope of a drafting group and we did not know if the result would be respected by the other Senators and Deputies, but we were willing to defend our work, what we knew, and what we believed. (2016, 9, translated by the authors)

The drafting group's rules aimed for unanimous agreement on each article of the law but, if necessary, provided for voting with equal representation of each of the three major political parties and each of the three civil society networks—thereby placing the governmental and nongovernmental participants on remarkably even footing, at least in principle. Ostensibly, legislators outside the drafting group would only be able to make unapproved changes where the group members had deadlocked (Ruelas Serna, 2016, 10). The group would also solicit input widely from outside experts and international standards.

This process continued from October to December 2014, involving "200 hours of work and the observations of 20 experts from academia and civil society organizations." The resulting draft was hailed as "groundbreaking," as it strengthened the independence of the information commission, limited the use of exemptions, and expanded the scope of the access to information law to apply across levels of government and even to political parties and unions. However, the draft did contain "two modifications that were not approved by the civil society working group," indicating that the participatory rules of the drafting body were not entirely followed (Ruelas, 2015). Yet it was only later, in February 2015, that the intervention of the president's office resulted in the far weaker draft that sparked civil society mobilization and, ultimately, international condemnation—which, in turn, resulted in a return to the original, stronger draft produced by the drafting group.

The bill that finally passed into law, the Ley General de Transparencia, reflected the success of civil society groups working in the collaborative drafting group. On the global Right to Information Rating assessed by international legal experts, Mexico's score moved up from 120 to 136, making it the strongest such law in the world. The collaborative process was praised by both observers and participants. García (2016, 3) wrote that "Mexico's current General Transparency Law is an example of how international norms together with civil society empowerment can yield significant and tangible improvements in access to information regulations."

Ana Cristina Ruelas Serna (2016) from the civil society group (and STT civil society core group member) Artículo 19 writes that "the process showed how collective work between government and society can mean an important change for the protection of human rights" (12) and that "this unprecedented exercise of co-creation and dialogue allowed us to have a framework that significantly extends the guarantee of the right of access to information" (13).

A similar collaborative legislative process took place regarding Mexico's new Sistema Nacional Anticorrupción (National Anticorruption System), which ultimately created a series of new anticorruption mechanisms spanning all levels of government, introducing new penalties and enforcement mechanisms and incorporating significant elements of transparency and citizen participation. Although its implementation was later criticized, even critics praised the reforms as "a watershed moment in Mexico" (Ahmed, 2017), "a major step forward in terms of increasing accountability for corrupt public officials" (Meyer & Hinojosa, 2018), and "one of the most important breakthroughs for Mexico's civil society since democratization began in the late nineties" (Ríos, 2017).

Newly collaborative legislative procedures were evident both in the drafting of the constitutional reform creating the Sistema Nacional Anticorrupción, approved in February 2015, and in the implementing laws, approved in July 2016.

Responding to civil society demands for greater inclusion in the process and public skepticism of initial proposals, legislators agreed to a substantial role for outside organizations and experts in the process of drafting the constitutional reform. Observers noted that it "includes proposals made by civil society organizations that accompanied the entire legislative process" (Roldán, 2015, translated by the authors).

However, the constitutional reform still required several new laws to be passed for implementation. In an effort to shape these laws, civil society groups (including several members of the STT core group) launched a public campaign for Ley 3 de 3, referring to requirements that politicians disclose three key pieces of information—assets, conflicts of interest, and tax payments. This campaign took advantage of a 2012 constitutional amendment allowing legislative proposals by direct citizen initiative, relying heavily on social media in a petition drive that ultimately collected over six hundred thousand signatures (Ríos, 2016).

The final drafting of the relevant pieces of legislation was done using procedures widely referred to as *parlamento abierto*—open parliament—meaning not just detailed collaboration with civil society organizations and experts (Transparencia Mexicana, 2016) but also the publication of all drafts and live broadcast of all debates both on television and online (Ríos, 2016; D'Artigues, 2016).

Many participants and observers called the process "unprecedented" (D'Artigues, 2016; FUNDAR, 2016) and reflected on the novelty of the experience:

> It was something unprecedented, we could see the discomfort of several actors of the legislative and executive powers to have to interact with civil society, in an open parliamentary scheme. (Enrique Díaz-Infante Chapa, quoted in Universidad Panamericana, 2016, translated by the authors)

Together, these developments reflect an ongoing shift in the *process* of decision making toward increased participation and collaboration, taking place well beyond the formal boundaries of the Open Government Partnership process. Of course, in evaluating the causal role of the Partnership, we must consider that these developments may well have taken place even without it—due to either bottom-up demands of civil society groups themselves or top-down attempts to improve government legitimacy.

On the other hand, many of Mexico's legislative openness efforts have roots in initiatives launched through Open Government Partnership efforts either globally (del Carmen Nava, 2014) or in Mexico (FUNDAR, 2014). More importantly, participants themselves suggested links between their experiences in the collaborative setting of the STT and these later efforts. One civil society representative, reflecting on the overall experience of the Open Government Partnership in Mexico, said:

> I think the biggest accomplishment of OGP in Mexico has happened not within the OGP formal National Action Plans, but with the influence that it has had in the culture of how civil society now engages with government, with congress, with the media; even using terminology that we didn't have in Mexico before. (CSO 2)

And speaking specifically about the involvement of civil society in the new access to information law and the Sistema Nacional Anticorrupción, this representative said:

> That's new: co-creating between civil society and government, using open parliament approaches to develop bills and institutions. I think that's why. And the same organizations that were leading both changes were at the same time having key roles in OGP. . . . Let me put it like this: It didn't start with OGP, but OGP provided us with the framework that we really needed, even the same words—co-creation, open parliament—all these kinds of things were picked from the OGP discourse. . . . We were the same organizations that were pushing in these different areas for those reforms, at the same time as we were working in OGP. We didn't want to bring those kinds of discussions within the OGP sphere in Mexico; they needed to happen in a parallel dimension but using the same model. It was not an accident, we decided to do that. (CSO 2)

SUMMARY AND EVALUATION OF THE DIRECT AND INDIRECT PATHWAYS OF CHANGE

In this section, we look back over Mexico's experience as a member of the Open Government Partnership and evaluate the relative contributions made by both the direct (compliance-based mechanisms) and indirect (process-driven mechanisms) pathways of change.

How much of a contribution to governance reform was made by Mexico's three rounds of National Action Plans? Here we assess the contributions, concluding that commitments themselves have generally been narrow, discrete, and often superficial.

From a global perspective, Mexico's National Action Plan performance appears relatively strong, as shown in table 5.1. Its consultative procedures actually became a model for many other countries, and it implemented (substantially or in full) the majority of its commitments—at least in the first and second action plans. Many of these commitments, however, were not particularly ambitious. In its second action plan, twenty commitments were assessed by the Independent Reporting Mechanism reviewer as having a minor potential impact and six as moderate. In its third action plan, a stronger eight of eleven were scored as having a moderate potential impact. However, no commitment in either plan was evaluated as having a transformative potential impact, compared with 17 percent of all Open Government Partnership's commitments globally. Mexico's first action plan was reviewed before these criteria were in place and thus cannot be compared on this metric. The number of commitments declined over time, although this was partially in response to guidance from the global Independent Reporting Mechanism unit, which began encouraging countries to pursue plans with fewer—but presumably more meaningful—commitments.

More substantively, some of Mexico's Open Government Partnership commitments have indeed played important roles in broader reform

Table 5.1
Summary of Mexico's National Action Plan commitments

Plan no.	Years	Consultation score (global avg.: 3/6)	No. of commitments	Prop. of high ambition commitments (global avg.: 0.542)	Prop. of completed commitments (global avg.: 0.676)
1	2011–13	Not Rated	36[9]	Not Rated	0.694 (midterm only)
2	2013–15	5/6	26	0.231	0.923 (0.731 at midterm)
3	2016–18	4/6	11	0.727	0.455 (0 at midterm)

processes. One example was the commitment to publicly disclose advertising spending by government bodies from the extended version of Mexico's first action plan, discussed earlier in this chapter. But many other commitments were clearly narrow in scope, such as publishing datasets pertaining to higher education or a national catalog of social programs. Others offered relatively loose frameworks for consulting with stakeholders in order to open particular types of data but were lacking in definitive deliverables. Some were clearly flouted, such as the use of consultations in appointment processes or a strategy to prevent conflicts of interest with industry regarding child obesity (CSO 3). Many others, often representing disclosures or data portals in specific sectors or issue areas, were indeed completed but then never updated again after the close of the review process.

Many stakeholders involved in the Open Government Partnership process reflected on their disappointment with the broader impact of commitments or even with the Independent Reporting Mechanism review process. One civil society representative said, "We didn't do well in terms of putting forward commitments that were transformative" (CSO 2). Another said that commitments were "not a good way to go. They are valuable, but often are not updated afterwards . . . they have not changed the culture in institutions" (CSO 4). And another said that "The IRM was useless . . . always six months or a year too late for learning or accountability . . . nobody mentions it" (CSO 3).

Process-Driven Mechanisms of Change

The disappointing nature of most Open Government Partnership commitments in Mexico is precisely as most direct compliance-based approaches to international institutions would predict. Given the Partnership's relatively weak enforcement provisions regarding commitments and their completion, an opportunistic government could easily propose only window-dressing commitments and devote little effort to implementation. Many governments worldwide also faced greater difficulty than expected in devoting the necessary resources, capacity, and intergovernmental coordination towards implementing their partnership commitments (Falla, 2017).

And yet, the direct pathway does not include the full breadth of the Open Government Partnership's potential impacts. Turning to the indirect pathway, emphasizing process-driven mechanisms of change, we do see important impacts of the iterative and participatory processes associated with Open Government Partnership membership in Mexico.

The participatory nature of Mexico's multistakeholder process gave reformers, inside and outside of government, a seat at the table and created new opportunities for them to influence the policy process. It created new forms of formal, informal, and structural power for civil society groups. It brought different organizations together in new coalitions while also demonstrating new models of collaborative policymaking between governmental and nongovernmental actors. While Mexico's formalized multistakeholder forum was, at first, unique among Open Government Partnership member countries, it was quickly emulated by others and was ultimately promoted by new standards and guidelines developed by the Partnership's Support Unit. Globally, the participatory nature of the Open Government Partnership Steering Committee also created new opportunities for leverage, allowing Mexican civil society groups to gain outside support at key moments.

The Open Government Partnership process in Mexico was not only participatory but also iterative. The requirement to develop a new National Action Plan every two years ensured that the political opportunities and resources brought by the cocreation process would be repeated again and again, even across political transitions, and created opportunities for learning from experience both domestically and internationally. The government's need to present new policy commitments in each action plan spurred the demand for new policy ideas and thus furthered opportunities for domestic and international policy entrepreneurs. Notably, although the Partnership rules carry little potential for sanction over poor design or implementation of commitments, they *do* contain sanctions for violation of process requirements. Members must develop new National Action Plans that at least meet basic standards for consultation and cocreation or else can be referred to the Steering Committee.

Together, these Open Government Partnership processes drove several different mechanisms of change that do not fall neatly into a framework of the commitment-and-compliance approach of the direct pathway. These are norms and policy models, resources and opportunities for reformers,

Table 5.2

Summary of evidence from Mexican case for process-driven mechanisms

Mechanism	Evidence
Norms and policy models	• Generic spread of idea and value of open government • Use of models of cocreation in settings beyond National Action Plans: access to information law and anticorruption law • Model of multistakeholder open government promotion: applied in subnational program • Transmission vector for transnational policy models like open data and open contracting standards
Resources and opportunities	• New forms of power for civil society: formal seat at the table, informal influence, structural threat of exit • Space on agenda for open government reforms, ability to get bureaucrats' and politicians' attention (for reformers both in and outside of government) • Outside pressure from international level (as was applied during access to information law)
Linkages and coalitions	• Brought together civil society organization coalition across ideological divides and issue silos • Civil society organizations more willing to collaborate with government • Cross-partisan appeal of open government at both national and subnational levels • International and regional links for reformers in and outside government

and linkages and coalitions. Table 5.2 reviews the key evidence for these mechanisms drawn from the preceding case study.

These mechanisms are also exemplified by the 2019 reemergence of Mexico's national-level collaborative Open Government Partnership process early in the presidency of Andrés Manuel López Obrador, with the government reaffirming its membership commitments and agreeing to develop new policies to prevent surveillance abuses. This development reflected the empowerment of the transnationally linked civil society coalition, the continued cross-ideological appeal of the open government agenda, and the ability of the Partnership to offer useful policy ideas and expertise to support the new government in following through on its own anticorruption platform.

Potential Alternative Explanations

We do not argue that all of these developments—new forms of influence and collaboration among civil society groups, new opportunities for reformers in government, specific legislative developments, and a subnational multistakeholder reform initiative—are solely attributable to the Open Government Partnership. Each was also shaped by other ongoing domestic and transnational dimensions of the politics and ideas of good governance reform. However, our evidence has highlighted key moments, actions, and outcomes that would not have happened without the new resources, opportunities, models, and linkages created by the Open Government Partnership. While some of the developments reviewed above might have occurred in a world with no partnership, the centrality of Open Government Partnership structures and models evidenced suggest that many would not—at least not in the same form and with the same results. This is highlighted, for instance, in the coalitions of civil society groups that had not previously worked together until their collaboration on the tripartite STT, in the procedural and institutional lineage apparent in Mexico's subnational open government program, and in key actors' own explicit understanding of the Open Government Partnership as a political and symbolic resource for reform efforts both inside and outside of government.

Evidence from the case of Mexico is also inconsistent with several possible alternative explanations for these same developments, emphasizing other international or domestic factors. None of these developments were commitments to or requirements of either the Partnership or any other international body. No other international or transnational entities offered Mexican civil society groups the same opportunities for participation and influence. Nor can changes in government partisanship account for the timelines of these developments, given their continuity from Partido Acción Nacional to Partido Revolucionario Institucional governments in 2012 and the renewed Open Government Partnership process under the new left-wing government after 2018. Importantly, processes of transnational policy learning and norm diffusion played out over this period alongside the Open Government Partnership as well as within and through it, so one possibility is that partnership processes simply rode the wave of developments that would have happened anyway. However, we have demonstrated key process evidence of developments that were inseparable from the Open Government Partnership as a transmission belt (for norms of collaborative policymaking), institutional model (the subnational initiative), specific policymaking venue (the STT), focusing event (National Action Plan rounds and global summits), or source of external leverage (first action plan and transparency law reforms).

CONCLUSION

Mexico's experience as a member of the Open Government Partnership thus demonstrates serious limits to the direct pathway of impact but highlights the utility of an indirect approach in shedding light on broader mechanisms of impact that might otherwise be obscured. In Mexico, formal Open Government Partnership commitments were mixed in their ambition and implementation, often relatively narrow and sometimes without any subsequent updating. Yet a focus on commitments alone would both qualitatively and quantitatively understate the impacts of Mexico's partnership membership. The Open Government Partnership played a role in spreading new ideas and policy models and engendering a culture of collaboration that took root beyond the formal National Action Plan process. It offered new resources and political opportunities to reformers both inside and outside of government. Finally, it established new linkages and coalitions both between different factions of civil society and across ideological divides in ways that made it easier for reform agendas to survive political transitions.

Overall, the evidence from this case study offers much greater support for hypothesis 2 than for hypothesis 1. That is, we see evidence of broader mechanisms of impact consistent with an indirect pathway of change but inconsistent with a world in which the effects of membership in international organizations flow only through a direct pathway. This evidence, from a specific case of one country but addressed in substantial detail, complements the broader cross-country evidence in the preceding chapters.

Of course, there are limitations to proving a causal role of the Open Government Partnership with full certitude. Some of the developments reviewed in this case study might have taken place even in a world with no partnership or in a world with an Open Government Partnership but without Mexico as a member. However, the centrality of the partnership structures and models to these processes suggest that many of them could not have occurred otherwise—at least not in the same form nor with the same outcomes.

Although the Obrador presidency has presented new challenges for open government advocates in Mexico—as each new presidency has done, in turn—the Open Government Partnership continues to present opportunities for reformers and linkages both among civil society groups, between civil society groups and government officials, and with transnational actors and ideas. Whoever the next president of Mexico is following the 2024 election—as presidents are constitutionally limited to a single term—the evidence presented in this chapter suggests that the Open Government Partnership will continue to offer valuable linkages, resources, and ideas regardless of political party and ideology. It will continue to shape reform efforts not only through formal commitments but through indirect mechanisms as well.

6 EPILOGUE: LOOKING FORWARD

Can a transnational multistakeholder partnership, like the Open Government Partnership, positively impact domestic public sector reform focused on transparency, accountability, participation, and technology? Our contribution to this debate highlights an overlooked, process-based mechanism of organizational membership—what we call an indirect pathway of change. This theoretical approach highlights alternatives to more commonly-studied direct pathways of change—emphasizing the motions of membership and compliance—to instead emphasize how flexible, stakeholder-driven forms of participation can spawn wider virtuous effects.

In addition to contributing this new theoretical framework, we have also offered evidence supporting the relevance and importance of these indirect pathways in the case of the Open Government Partnership. In chapter 4, we reviewed evidence from settings around the world to illustrate multiple indirect mechanisms, including through norms and policy models, opportunities and resources for reformers, and linkages and coalitions both within and across countries. In chapter 5, we focused in more detail on an in-depth case study of Mexico's membership in the Open Government Partnership. Here, we used qualitative case study evidence to test between two alternative hypotheses concerning the nature of potential impacts and found substantially greater evidence consistent with an indirect pathway than a direct pathway.

For the Open Government Partnership itself, several closely related features are its remarkable staying power and its ability to evolve after seeming to suffer major setbacks. After the dramatic events of its founding, which we detailed in chapter 3, many observers doubted that the Open Government Partnership would endure, particularly after a decline in attention and investment from the United States government. And yet, the Partnership endured and evolved through a rapidly changing global environment and major shifts in the priorities of key member countries. Our theoretical approach in this book suggests that sustainability itself has been driven by the *processes* of membership and the indirect pathway of change, which have endowed the Partnership with the flexibility, dynamism, and breadth of appeal to weather these changes. In this final section of the book, we take time to look at the larger forces that affect the open government movement going forward and the implications of our findings in a range of academic fields and areas of practice.

THE FUTURE OF OPEN GOVERNMENT

In a globalized world where the contest of ideas on how to govern societies spans the globe and the seeds of new ideas spread and develop in complex ways, there is more need than ever for social scientists to understand how transnational multistakeholder organizations contribute. Scholars working within different disciplinary perspectives, such as international relations (e.g., Andonova, 2017; Bäckstrand, 2006; Tallberg et al., 2013), public administration (e.g., Bryson, Crosby, & Bloomberg, 2014; van Zyl, 2014), and sociology (e.g., Castells, 2008), have growing understanding of the advantages of empowered third-party organizations, such as civil society organizations and companies in facilitating positive policy outcomes. These relationships play a key role in the transmission and realization of open government. We need to take these third parties and their roles in public sector reform seriously rather than seeing their role as merely incidental. The future of open government may depend on how well governments can tie nongovernmental organizations and businesses into networks that support transparency, accountability, and participation, and deliver political justice in reforms.

In addition to there being good scientific reasons for broadening our views of reform, our reader may reasonably wonder how the narratives of global political and economic crisis and pandemics fit in with the indirect pathways of change and the Open Government Partnership. Writing in early 2021, it would be difficult to conclude a book about open government without at least briefly referring to some of the most high-profile global political issues of the 2020s thus far regarding the rise of national populism and the coronavirus pandemic.

At the time of writing, populist leadership—elected premiers who came to power on the back of a popular reaction against the global political elite—has a foothold in three of the founding eight Open Government Partnership countries: Jair Bolsonaro in Brazil, Rodrigo Duterte in the Philippines, and Andrés Manuel López Obrador in Mexico. In another founding country, the United States, the four-year presidency of Donald Trump has concluded with a transition back to a mainstream leader in Joe Biden. None of these populist leaders are outright supporters of open government by any stretch of the imagination, but they have often embraced alternative appeals to transparency in terms of personal openness and integrity while snubbing traditional document- or data-oriented kinds of transparency (Roelofs, 2019). Their curious mixture of whimsical censorship and bombastic claims to be honest men with nothing to hide who publish their populist views widely on social media sets difficult precedents for the open government movement. While open government values like transparency and accountability have suffered gross harm on their watches, such as the withdrawal of public information from government websites (Ellington, 2019) and intimidation of citizens and the press (Timberman, 2016), there have also been some successes, such as the passage of the Philippines' first freedom of information policy.

It is also of note that none of those leaders have publicly tried to undermine their countries' participation in the Open Government Partnership. It is likely that strong civil society organization in countries such as Brazil and the Philippines has played a major role in checking greater extension of autocratic powers that the likes of Bolsonaro and Duterte would likely prefer to wield in order to advance their own political agendas. We suspect that the indirect pathway of the Open Government Partnership membership in these countries has generated norms and networking mechanisms that have galvanized public sector changes despite the extreme rhetoric of their leaders and are shifting the political playing field in ways that generate opportunity and space for more pro-open government actors to move into and exploit—similar to the ways that we found in Mexico. These indirect pathways may be influential enough to lead to a dramatic revitalization of politics if prodemocracy leaders are elected to replace them. If the same leaders are reelected, and civic space continues to be squeezed, then it is possible that the indirect pathways themselves will become less effective at resisting repression, and alternative futures will become narrowed. We did not study the maintenance and longevity of indirect pathways for this book, but we would certainly agree that more research here will be key in the future to seeing how effectively the pathways work.

The year 2020 saw the crisis of the dangerous COVID-19 pandemic that spread rapidly around the world, leading to 2.7 million deaths in the first year. The pandemic, carrying such a dangerous epidemiological threat, became a contentious area of government public health policy. Open government was challenged on many fronts: Citizen movement became tightly controlled, experts and citizens questioned the information origins and scientific basis of policy decisions, governments defended their prerogative to intervene in people's private behavior, and new tracking technologies were developed with short shrift given to important discussions about data privacy and ownership. We will be dealing with the consequences of policy reforms that took place in the shadow of the coronavirus crisis for years to come.

In general, the increased reliance on centralized government leadership to improve the response at a whole-society level of collective responsibility pushed the envelope in terms of what kinds of public sector reform are up for debate and the kinds of democratic decision-making processes that are necessary to achieve them. In the future, this could be used as leverage for new reforms, whether of the open government sort or via other approaches. Certainly, however, the trend is toward reforms that promote the value of resilience, whereby societies seek to strengthen their long-term political ability to navigate major challenges, such as pandemics, migration, and climate change. Indirect pathways, emphasizing the diversity of stakeholders and interconnectivity, should play a vital role in strengthening societal resilience.

At the center of the concerns about the pandemic was a debate on how to protect open government as governments tried to strike a balance between closing down as a necessary public health measure and remaining open to criticism and accountability for their decisions. The scale of the cost to human life caused by the pandemic has been catastrophic, and, in some ways, there is very little that open government can do to help the situation, directly at least. The way that the pandemic has influenced open government is perhaps an easier topic to explore and one that fits well within our model of direct and indirect pathways of change. It is clear in the way that the governmental response to the pandemic highlights inherent tensions in the open government view of public sector reform that evaluations of open government performance qua official government compliance with rules of commitment production, cross-sectoral collaboration, and good membership behavior would be poor or mixed in success. We covered these reasons in depth in chapter 2. How, for example, should governments ensure the protection of human rights, such as the right to health, education, equal treatment before the law, and privacy, while also supporting transparency and accountability? It is certainly possible to find sensible balances in pandemic-tackling policies, such as tracking people with symptoms and managing a testing or vaccination program, but this needs to be done carefully to ensure open government values.

In August 2020, the Open Government Partnership published "A Guide to Open Government and the Coronavirus: Open Response, Open Recovery" (Open Government Partnership, 2020c). It emphasizes the need for governments to move quickly and to use the collective power of government and civil society to find solutions in the midst of uncertainty. There was no time for pandemic measures to be implemented within the two-year cycle of the National Action Plans. But many of the reports' suggestions were actionable because of the new norms, resources, and expert and policy communities that had experience collaborating on prior commitments. As a result, there was "a strong set of OGP members who can demonstrate leadership" on pandemic policies carried out according to the principles of open government (Open Government Partnership, 2020c, 8). According to the report, countries such as Argentina and Brazil were able to use existing transparency and open budgeting websites to add coronavirus-related content tracking, spending, and policies. In many Open Government Partnership member countries, there were robust multistakeholder advisory councils and trustworthy civil society organizations that could be resourced to help deliver medical care. The issues have evolved as the pandemic has progressed, with the focus broadening to include the intersection of open government and vaccine procurement and distribution (Falla, 2021; Robinson, 2021).

While social equity was already an issue deserving more attention in the field broadly (see Blessett et al., 2019), the pandemic further highlighted the relationships between open government and equity that were already present (Porumbescu, Piotrowski, & Mabillard, 2020). In the United States, freedom of information acts were used to access previously unavailable data on COVID-19 infections, which then helped reveal racial inequalities (Sedacca, 2021).

More generally, the Coronavirus pandemic has underlined the important connection between transparency and the effective implementation of reforms—even emergency reforms instigated by a major crisis. Coming at a time when government policies—as well as the data and processes on which the government policies themselves are based—are implemented with open government technologies, such as social media and open data, it is especially clear that open government remains both important and valued by the public (OECD & GovLab, 2021; Pyo, Reggi, & Martin, 2020). The words *transparency* and *accountability* are used everywhere to characterize the kinds of government decision making necessary for public trust and the willingness to comply, as well as to constantly warn of the risks of corruption or failure resulting from public procurement decisions that have been made through nontransparent procedures (Transparency International, 2021).

Yet, global tensions and the economic and political fallout from the pandemic present an unpredictable future for the Open Government Partnership. It may face existential obstacles as funders switch their priorities to protecting national economies and health research. To some, open government may appear to be a luxury, and the Open Government Partnership will need to argue that open government is relevant. Indirect pathways will need to be part of this argument to the extent they foster shared norms, discussion, and network collaboration. There will also need to be renewed efforts by researchers to harness the benefits of the indirect pathway and examine the complex ways it is interdependent with the direct pathway. The indirect pathway, mediated by different actors, is difficult to manage in terms of traditional ends-means forms of rational planning.

While more evidence is needed for what works best, a clear principle for indirect pathway building is to take advantage of the elements that make it work as a political dynamic—linkages among organizations, norms and values, long-term planning, and horizontal forms of decision making. If the Open Government Partnership—and by extension, other transnational multistakeholder initiatives—can take up the language of the direct and indirect pathways, then this kind of linked, process-driven approach to public sector reform is likely to become more institutionalized in practice.

BUILDING ON PRIOR WORK

Earlier academic writers also noticed the potential for process-based dynamics to compete and interact with ends-oriented behavior change in institutions. In a variety of fields, scholars have highlighted changes as political institutions become more horizontally organized and open to participation from a greater array of stakeholders (e.g., Ansell & Gash, 2008; Mueller, 2010; Raymond & DeNardis, 2015; Tallberg et al., 2013; Bryson, Crosby, & Bloomberg, 2014).

In this book, we have sought to build on these views to highlight how process-based dynamics can indirectly lead to outcomes that create surprising benefits for organizations and even society as a whole. This indirect pathway seems to be at work in the multistakeholder and participatory character of the Open Government Partnership, and it persists even if the direct pathway of change is sometimes failing, as was the case for Mexico. In chapters 2 and 3, we covered the existing scholarship in the fields of international relations and public administration to explain the mechanics of public sector reform via an international multistakeholder initiative. It is worth restating what the key literature is and how we contribute to a new discussion and line of investigation.

Our elucidation of the indirect pathway applies a theoretical approach to understanding public sector reform and the influence of transnational multistakeholder forms of governance. The indirect pathway of change represents a different, concurrent pathway for reform impacts, separate from a direct pathway operating through individual commitments and their implementation. The implications of this are significant for many fields that intersect with information policy—from public management and technology studies to international relations and the study of the multistakeholder governance in global and domestic policy reform. This approach adds a new, interdisciplinary thread of inquiry to an already burgeoning field.[1]

In the public administration and management arenas, we depart from the current predominant focuses on organizational and individual factors that determine the success of domestic public sector reform to instead develop a more transnational perspective by bringing in insights from international relations literature. The theories of policy reform in public management, particularly looking at the roles of actors and policy communities (e.g., Baumgartner & Jones, 2010), the institutional dynamics of policy systems, and Sabatier's (1991) argument for the need to study specific institutions and their policy communities, were important areas of inspiration for our theory of the indirect pathway of change and how it triggers broader dynamics. But our approach offers an opportunity for public management theory to go much further by fusing a traditional focus on internal organizational behaviors that can be managed with an appreciation for institutional processes resulting from national and subnational participation in international and transnational institutions. This requires a shift in conceptual thinking about the origins of policy influence, and it poses a challenge for public management scholars to link local institutional change with transnational and global policymaking.

In the field of international relations, not all scholars have shared the dominant emphasis on the direct impacts of international institutions through commitments and compliance. Many have long emphasized the potential for soft law institutions to drive processes of learning, normative change, or nonstate-actor mobilization and interaction (e.g., Abbott & Snidal, 2000; Dai, 2005; Trubek and Trubek, 2005; Ruggie, 2007; Slaughter, 2009; Bach & Newman, 2010; Newman & Posner, 2016).

More recently, research has demonstrated positive effects of transnational multistakeholder governance in a variety of arenas (e.g., Bäckstrand, 2006; Mueller, 2010; Brockmyer & Fox, 2015; Reinsberg & Westerwinter, 2021). Many of these effects critically rely on the process of participation rather than adhere to legally stipulated promises and goals of the participation. Scholars such as Duncan (2015) and Rushton and Williams (2011) reveal how global health and sustainability compacts generate positive rewards because of the costs of participation rather than in spite of them. Recent ideas of global experimentalist governance (e.g., De Búrca, Keohane, & Sabel, 2014) suggest how processes of iterated policy experimentation, implementation, and learning can drive improved outcomes over time.

We draw these approaches together by suggesting that they should inform understanding of transnational policy reform by shifting the attention of researchers to the processes themselves rather than seeing those processes as simply a means to an end. In our approach, the actions most relevant to the indirect pathway are the participation, deliberation, and collaboration among diverse stakeholders; the relationships that these create; and the repetition of these processes over time, which together can establish dynamics with long-lasting and powerful effects. Although the nature of international institutions has indeed transformed, these changes also feed back into the nature of domestic policy reform efforts themselves. This indirect pathway is a missing ingredient in existing understandings of how public sector reform occurs and, therefore, how such reform should be evaluated in its level of success. The Open Government Partnership, despite its flaws, illustrates this pathway of change based on partnership.

Our argument also has implications for any other developing transnational efforts employing multistakeholder, participatory, and/or iterative institutional design principles. These include multistakeholder initiatives in other fields, such as public health, corporate responsibility, and internet governance. Many more traditional international institutions also increasingly incorporate participatory and iterative elements, such as the United Nations'

Universal Periodic Review of human rights, the Sustainable Development Goals, and the Paris Agreement treaty on climate change. Similarly iterative and participatory approaches to policy change have also been pursued within the framework of the European Union's Open Method of Coordination (Zeitlin, 2009)—including in related areas of e-government (Criado, 2012).

Our approach offers the potential for a more optimistic assessment of the extent to which such transnational efforts might lead to meaningful domestic changes in their respective issue areas through indirect pathways of changing norms and policy models, empowering reforms, and building new linkages and coalitions—all, in turn, driven by repeated cycles of participatory interaction, collaboration, and assessment. A key implication of this book is that observers should aim to assess such efforts not only on the basis of direct accomplishment of the specific goals undertaken but also on the potential for broader indirect effects.

For example, our approach has clear implications for the Paris Climate Agreement, which also emphasizes repeated voluntary pledges matched with transnational stakeholder participation and iterative review—albeit on a slower five-year timescale. Many observers might focus their primary attention on governments' pledges themselves, the extent to which they constitute meaningful contributions to climate change mitigation and adaptation, and the extent to which they are ultimately implemented in practice. Although we would absolutely agree as to the importance of these factors, our approach additionally highlights the importance of indirect pathways of change that might operate alongside these direct pathways. The processes of iterative and participatory pledge-making, implementation, and review may themselves have indirect effects in terms of spreading norms and policy models, empowering reformers, and creating new linkages and coalitions. Of course, these mechanisms may not, in fact, be in operation in all settings, but our approach sets them up as new and important empirical questions.

The indirect pathway also adds to debates around transparency in information policy. Scholars have long argued that open government is not just about having laws for freedom of information and open data (e.g., Roberts, 2006) based on the simplistic formula of more information equaling more transparency. More management and rules per se do not necessarily lead to more open government. Like freedom of information laws, rules of behavior and promises about those rules do not necessarily mean governments will be more open in practice. On the contrary, bold promises are often made (the kind of commitment we named a pipe dream) with no realistic intention of delivering. Transparency scholars argue that to be transparent, there must be an element of monitoring and institutional compulsion toward actors in power to be honest and open (Meijer, 2009). Indirect pathways do not compel authorities to be more open, but they can set better conditions for openness by spreading new norms to different actors and incentivizing behavioral change through the availability of new resources.

Similarly, the digital technologies that the Open Government Partnership harnesses to the service of transparency and participation are important to study within broader institutional analyses. Jane Fountain (2004) predicted that information and communication technologies would gradually transform the entire quality and effectiveness of government, with multiple layers of transparent government interaction with businesses and citizens. What the experience of the Open Government Partnership shows is that the direct integration of technologies often has only a limited effect on public sector reform unless indirect pathways are also operating in a way that involves broad communities of collaborators to harness technology's effects. The idea that technology has a social aspect is familiar, but we offer an alternative theory for how the social side of the sociotechnical can be understood—as a process, practice-based set of human and organizational relationships that are based on agreed rules and procedures for how to adopt and use technologies but whose full potential can only be understood through the indirect pathway of normative, political, and institutional changes that take place as a result.

While the indirect pathway is, in many ways, the most interesting part of our theory, we should not forget its critical counterpart, the direct pathway. Our key point is that, in contrast to the surprising influence of the indirect pathway, the direct pathway of change is often constrained by inherent limitations and vulnerabilities in the way it works. We set the direct pathway alongside the complementary, more fruitful indirect pathway to contrast the successes and failures of the Open Government Partnership. In chapter 2, we showed how the direct pathway continues to underwhelm the optimistic hopes of public sector reformers, and in chapter 4, we looked at the evidence of the direct pathway in the Open Government Partnership. As public management and political science scholars familiar with the history of cyclical attempts at reform, we approached the Open Government Partnership with skepticism, based on the data put forward over decades showing how bold new reform ideas driven by a top-down approach in the public sector struggle to deliver on their promises. Once all the evidence has been assessed, it is unsurprising why this happens, especially because a multitude of things can go wrong—and often many at once. Rules introduce perverse incentives that undercut the original rules, the goals of the reforms are ambiguous or hard to measure in terms of their impacts on government and society, implementation or resource barriers surface, different values underpinning the reforms conflict, and central leadership and political supporters of the reforms disagree.

Public management, particularly the New Public Management theory, is familiar with the shortcomings of direct pathways of change—the idea that policy change is produced by commitments and rules focusing on performance management, incentives, and results (Piotrowski & Rosenbloom, 2002; Piotrowski et al., 2018). That view has been displaced by post–New Public Management approaches, recognizing the dependency of government policies on other policy actors and networks. A particular strength of open government is that it has a strong normative vision with substantial international support, not least in the Open Government Partnership. As the participatory, multistakeholder model of the Open Government Partnership offers something novel in its potential to drive indirect pathways of change, it will be interesting for public management scholars to monitor open government reforms around the world and compare how successful their efforts will be to the New Public Management and post–New Public Management movements that do not have an international membership organization to represent them.

We also wanted to give the direct pathway of the Open Government Partnership a fair assessment. A simple fail-or-succeed approach to categorizing public sector reforms—including the impact of the Open Government

Partnership—would fall into a facile, thumbs-up/thumbs-down appraisal and would overlook positive lessons. Thus, when evaluating the claims of open government scholarship and the ambitions of the Open Government Partnership, we approached different claims with an open mind. Indeed, when we looked at the Open Government Partnership commitments, from the grimmest flops to the shiniest stars, there are aspects of the direct pathway that sometimes work. In fact, one can always depend on at least a narrow set of programs and commitments conceived through the direct pathway to come to fruition. Rather, it is the evaluation of a narrow focus on commitments as a whole that shows their limitations. The most accurate description, given that the majority of the commitments are lacking in either relevancy, ambition, and/or implementation, is that the direct pathway has an underwhelming impact and frequently disappoints.

WRAPPING UP

Are we being unduly negative about the potential for direct impacts of participation in multistakeholder partnerships like the Open Government Partnership? Such evaluations inevitably depend on one's prior expectations. In the case of the Open Government Partnership, our expectations were not set unusually high. Rather, we examined the explicit goals of its early leaders and architects when they designed and launched it. We also examined the philosophy and the intellectual roots of the open government movement and the lofty expectations of the open government approach to public sector reform.

However, we remain positive about the potential impact of well-conceived, politically supported, and expertly implemented open government commitments. We are enthusiastic about the positive efforts being made by open government researchers and practitioners to learn how open government initiatives can be designed with more transformational impact (e.g., Piotrowski et al., 2019; Porumbescu, Cucciniello, & Gil-Garcia, 2020; Berliner & Wehner, 2022).

However, the purpose of this book is to uncover and elucidate another dimension of this discussion—the counterpart to the direct pathway—the underestimated and frequently overlooked indirect pathway and its attendant mechanisms and impacts on public sector reforms. More work needs to be done to explore the potential downsides and limitations of open government policies in practice, the equity implications of open government reforms on different groups, the part administration plays in implementing these programs, the long-term impacts of the indirect pathway of change in multiple contexts, the potential of openness in legislative and other collective decision-making bodies, and the potential contributions of new technological tools. In future work, additional country and subnational case studies applying our conceptual framework would add depth to our understanding of how these pathways work in practice. We expect the field of open government and its component practices of transparency, accountability, and participation to continue to grow in the near to mid term.

Notes

CHAPTER 1

1. The information in the book is accurate up to January 2021, with a few references added after that date. Because of that, the Russian-Ukraine war is not addressed in this book. The Open Government Partnership did issue a statement, "The Open Gov Community Stands with Ukraine," on February 28, 2022 (https://www.opengovpartnership.org/news/statement-from-the-chairs-of-the-ogp-steering-committee-on-ukraine/).
2. Civil society organization representative, interview with author, Mexico City, April 2018.

CHAPTER 2

1. The material in the chapter further develops arguments we previously made in: Ingrams, Piotrowski, & Berliner (2020).
2. The success of Obama's transparency policies has been seriously questioned. Scholars have made some probing critiques (e.g., Coglianese, 2009).

CHAPTER 3

1. Multistakeholder partnerships are thus distinct from the country-to-country partnerships written about by Abrahamsen (2004).
2. All monetary amounts in this section are US dollars, unless otherwise noted.

CHAPTER 4

1. Due to the length of the action plan cycle and the commitment review process, at the time of writing, only data for fully evaluated commitments up to 2016 are available. Data are missing for "ambition" in 2011 and 2016.
2. We included 1,935 commitments for National Action Plans between 2014 and 2018 that have been evaluated and published in the Open Government Partnership Explorer up to

December 2020. Item measurement is as follows: (1) Stars are relevant, completed or substantially completed, and have transformative potential impact. (2) Low-hanging fruit are relevant, completed or substantially completed, and have minor or no potential impact. (3) Pipe dreams are relevant, withdrawn, not started, or have limited completion, and have moderate or transformative potential impact. (4) Flops are not relevant, have minor or no potential impact, and are withdrawn, not started or have limited completion.

3. At the time of the invasion by Russia in 2022, Ukraine was midway through implementation of a Third Action Plan that would see increased efforts to modernize its digital records systems. Given the extreme disruption and violence of the Russian invasion, open government reforms in Ukraine are not likely to be top priorities for the near future.

4. While there is not space to replicate the full Global Open Data Index here, comparison of the index with Open Government Partnership member lists also shows that fewer countries further down the index are Open Government Partnership members. Data on the index is available at https://index.okfn.org/place/, and Open Government Partnership members at https://www.opengovpartnership.org/our-members/.

5. Slaughter, Anne Marie (@SlaughterAM), "Open Government Partnership is 'a social network for reformers' Juan Pardinas at #pdf12 @OpenGovPart," Twitter, June 11, 2021, 12:21 p.m.

6. The Web of Science keyword search included all peer review articles across all scientific fields with the words *open government* in the title or abstract.

CHAPTER 5

1. This chapter draws on analysis and evidence that also appears in more abbreviated and thematic form in our previously published work, Berliner, Ingrams, & Piotrowski (2021).

2. As explained later in this chapter, we indicate for each interview quotation the organization type of the interviewee. We use CSO to reflect civil society organization representatives.

3. The Independent Reporting Mechanism only reviewed thirty-six of the thirty-seven commitments, as the final one—a "Transparency Innovation Prize"—was not part of the Open Government Partnership consultative process but added separately by the government (Open Government Partnership, 2013c, p. 8).

4. Even the *Economist* (2015) commented on ideological divides among Mexican civil society in 2015, noting that "grassroots organisations can be dismissive of their more technocratic brethren, labelling them neoliberal and government stooges."

5. In 2017, IMCO received the Templeton Freedom Award for "exceptional and innovative contributions to the understanding of free enterprise, and the public policies that encourage prosperity, innovation, and human fulfillment via free competition" (Atlas Network, 2017).

6. Notably, the well-known Grupo Oaxaca that was closely involved in the original 2002 passage of Mexico's access to information law (Michener, 2011a) was largely a coalition of journalists

and academics rather than civil society groups from different ideological and sectoral backgrounds. It also did not persist as an organized coalition engaged in sustained activities.

7. However, this may be exaggerated, as civil society groups decried their exclusion from the opening ceremony of the summit, which was held at a different location than the rest of the event (Garduño, 2015).

8. Two authors were present at the summit.

9. The Independent Reporting Mechanism only reviewed thirty-six of the thirty-seven commitments. See note 3.

CHAPTER 6

1. To demonstrate, we performed a keyword search in the Web of Science digital library across all social science journals for words that capture the central open government norms: *transparency* and *participation*. Since 2011, large upward growth is shown in all areas, with a 196 percent growth in articles with a *transparency* keyword and 136 percent with a *participation* keyword.

References

Abbott, K. W., Green, J. F., & Keohane, R. O. (2016). Organizational ecology and institutional change in global governance. *International Organization*, *70*(2), 247–277. https://doi.org/10.1017/S0020818315000338

Abbott, K. W., & Snidal, D. (2000). Hard and soft law in international governance. *International Organization*, *54*(3), 421–456. https://doi.org/10.1162/002081800551280

Abbott, K. W., & Snidal, D. (2010). International regulation without international government: Improving IO performance through orchestration. *Review of International Organizations*, *5*(3), 315–344. https://doi.org/10.1007/s11558-010-9092-3

Abella, A., Ortiz-de-Urbina-Criado, M., & De Pablos-Heredero, C. (2017). A model for the analysis of data-driven innovation and value generation in smart cities' ecosystems. *Cities*, *64*, 47–53.

Abrahamsen, R. (2004). The power of partnerships in global governance. *Third World Quarterly*, *25*(8), 1453–1467. https://doi.org/10.1080/0143659042000308465

Abu-Shanab, E. A. (2015). Reengineering the open government concept: An empirical support for a proposed model. *Government Information Quarterly*, *32*(4), 453–463.

Adamtey, N. (2016). *Ghana end of term report 2013–2014*. Washington, DC: Open Government Partnership.

Adjami, M., & Wannenwestch, S. (2017). Promoting private sector engagement in the Open Government Partnership: A discussion paper. International Centre for Collective Action, June 2017. https://baselgovernance.org/sites/default/files/2019-02/promoting_private_sector_engagement_in_the_open_government_partnership_-_basel_institute_-_june_2017-2.pdf

Adler, S. (2015). OGP needs a reboot. LinkedIn, December 2, 2015. https://www.linkedin.com/pulse/ogp-needs-reboot-steven-adler/

Ahmed, A. (2017). Mexico's government is blocking its own anti-corruption drive, commissioners say. *New York Times*, December 2, 2017. https://www.nytimes.com/2017/12/02/world/americas/mexico-corruption-commission.html

Aitamurto, T., & Landemore, H. (2016). Crowdsourced deliberation: The case of the law on off-road traffic in Finland. *Policy & Internet, 8*(2), 174–196.

Alianza para el Gobierno Abierto. (2012). Alianza para el Gobierno Abierto: Plan de Acción Ampliado. May 31, 2012. http://gobabiertomx.org/wp-content/uploads/2014/08/Plande-Acci%C3%B3n-Ampliado.docx

Alianza para el Gobierno Abierto. (2014). *Plan de Acción 2013–2015 Mexico: Una nueva relación entre sociedad y gobierno*. January 29, 2014. https://www.opengovpartnership.org/wp-content/uploads/2019/06/pa_aga_2015-1.pdf

Alianza para el Gobierno Abierto. (2015). Señalamientos del núcleo de sociedad civil de la Alianza para el Gobierno Abierto (AGA) sobre los ejercicios locales de gobierno abierto impulsados por el IFAI. May 5, 2015.

Alonso, J. (2011). *Open data: Seeing well beyond the portals*. WebFoundation, September 21, 2011. https://webfoundation.org/2011/09/open-data-seeing-well-beyond-the-portals/

Álvarez Córdoba, Francisco Raúl. (2016). Las alianzas de gobiernos subnacionales en México: La Iniciativa de gobiernos abiertos subnacionales en México. In I. Luna Pla, J. A. Bojórquez Pereznieto, and A. Hofmann (Eds.), *Gobierno Abierto: El valor social de la información pública*, 195–203. Mexico City: Universidad Nacional Autónoma de México.

Amnesty International. (2017). *"If you are poor, you are killed:" Extrajudicial executions in the Philippines' "War on Drugs."* London: Amnesty International.

Andonova, L. B. (2017). *Governance entrepreneurs: International organizations and the rise of global public-private partnerships*. Cambridge: Cambridge University Press.

Andonova, L. B., Hale, T. N., & Roger, C. B. (2017). National policy and transnational governance of climate change: Substitutes or complements? *International Studies Quarterly, 61*(2), 253–268. https://doi.org/10.1093/isq/sqx014

Andrews, M., Pritchett, L., & Woolcock, M. (2013). Escaping capability traps through problem driven iterative adaptation (PDIA). *World Development, 51*, 234–244. https://doi.org/10.1016/j.worlddev.2013.05.011

Ansell, C., & Gash, A. (2008). Collaborative governance in theory and practice. *Journal of Public Administration Research and Theory, 18*(4), 543–571. https://doi.org/10.1093/jopart/mum032

Aristegui Noticias. (2014). La casa blanca de Enrique Peña Nieto. November 9, 2014. https://aristeguinoticias.com/0911/mexico/la-casa-blanca-de-enrique-pena-nieto

Arreola, A. G. (2013). Comments on the IRM Mexico report. Open Government Partnership Blog, October 22, 2013. https://www.opengovpartnership.org/stories/comments-on-the-irm-mexico-report/

Artículo 19. (2015). Libertad de expresión en venta. Article 19. https://www.scribd.com/doc/276117398/Libertad-de-expresion-en-venta

Atlas Network. (2017). 2017 Templeton Freedom Award winner. https://web.archive.org/web/20210308180542/https://www.atlasnetwork.org/grants-awards/awards/the-2017-templeton-freedom-award

Attard, J., Orlandi, F., Scerri, S., & Auer, S. (2015). A systematic review of open government data initiatives, *Government Information Quarterly*, *32*(4), 399–418. https://doi.org/10.1016/j.giq.2015.07.006

Avant, D., and Westerwinter, O. (Eds.). (2016). *The new power politics: Networks and transnational security governance*. Cambridge: Oxford University Press.

Avendaño, C. O. (2011). Aquino stars in New York. *Inquirer*. https://globalnation.inquirer.net/13179/aquino-stars-in-new-york

Bach, D., & Newman, A. L. (2010). Transgovernmental networks and domestic policy convergence: Evidence from insider trading regulation. *International Organization*, *64*(3), 505–528. https://doi.org/10.1017/S0020818310000135

Bach, T., van Thiel, S., Hammerschmid, G., & Steiner, R. (2017). Administrative tradition and management reforms: A comparison of agency chief executive accountability in four Continental Rechtsstaat countries. *Public Management Review*, *19*(6), 765–784.

Bäckstrand, K. (2006). Democratizing global environmental governance? Stakeholder democracy after the World Summit on Sustainable Development. *European Journal of International Relations*, *12*(4), 467–498. https://doi.org/10.1177/1354066106069321

Bagozzi, B. E., Berliner, D., & Almquist, Z. W. (2019). When does open government shut? Predicting government responses to citizen information requests. *Regulation & Governance*, *15*(2), 280–297. https://doi.org/10.1111/rego.12282

Baier, V. E., March, J. G., & Saetren, H. (1986). Implementation and ambiguity. *Scandinavian Journal of Management Studies*, *2*(3–4), 197–212.

Banisar, D. (2006). The right to information in the age of information: Human rights in the global information society. In W. J. Drake & E. J. Wilson III (Eds.), *Human rights in the global information society* (pp. 73–89). Cambridge, MA: MIT Press.

Bartoo, V. (2018). Kenya's Elgeyo Marakwet County hosts Africa OGP convention. Open Government Partnership, May 29, 2018. https://www.opengovpartnership.org/stories/kenyas-elgeyo-marakwet-county-hosts-africa-ogp-convention/

Bates, J. (2014). The strategic importance of information policy for the contemporary neoliberal state: The case of Open Government Data in the United Kingdom. *Government Information Quarterly*, *31*(3), 388–395. https://doi.org/10.1016/j.giq.2014.02.009

Baumgartner, F. R., & Jones, B. D. (1991). Agenda dynamics and policy subsystems. *Journal of Politics*, *53*(4), 1044–1074.

Baumgartner, F. R., & Jones, B. D. (2010). *Agendas and instability in American politics*. Chicago: University of Chicago Press.

Bearce, D. H., & Bondanella, S. (2007). Intergovernmental organizations, socialization, and member-state interest convergence. *International Organization*, *61*(4), 703–733. https://doi.org/10.1017/S0020818307070245

Beer, C. (2001). Assessing the consequences of electoral democracy: Subnational legislative change in Mexico. *Comparative Politics*, *33*(4), 421–440. https://doi.org/10.2307/422442

Bellows, A. & Zohdy, N. (2020). *Is the coronavirus catalyzing new civic collaborations for open government?* Washington, DC: Carnegie Foundation.

Benito, B., & Bastida, F. (2009). Budget transparency, fiscal performance, and political turnout: An international approach. *Public Administration Review, 69*(3), 403–417.

Berliner, D., Bagozzi, B. E., & Palmer-Rubin, B. (2018). What information do citizens want? Evidence from one million information requests in Mexico. *World Development, 109*, 222–235. https://doi.org/10.1016/j.worlddev.2018.04.016

Berliner, D., Bagozzi, B., Palmer-Rubin, B., & Erlich, A. (2020). The political logic of government disclosure: Evidence from information requests in Mexico. *Journal of Politics, 83*(1), 229–245. https://doi.org/10.1086/709148

Berliner, D., & Erlich, A. (2015). Competing for transparency: Political competition and institutional reform in Mexican states. *American Political Science Review, 109*(1), 110–128. https://doi.org/10.1017/S0003055414000616

Berliner, D., Ingrams, A., & Piotrowski, S. J. (2018). The future of FOIA in an open government agenda for freedom of information policy and implementation. *Villanova Law Review, 63*(5), 867–894.

Berliner, D., Ingrams, A., & Piotrowski, S. J. (2021). Process effects of multistakeholder institutions: Theory and evidence from the Open Government Partnership. *Regulation & Governance*. https://doi.org/10.1111/rego.12430

Berliner, D., & Prakash, A. (2012). From norms to programs: The United Nations Global Compact and global governance. *Regulation & Governance, 6*(2), 149–166. https://doi.org/10.1111/j.1748-5991.2012.01130.x

Berliner, D. & Prakash, A. (2014). The United Nations global compact: An institutionalist perspective. *Journal of Business Ethics, 122*(2), 217–223.

Berliner, D., & Prakash, A. (2015). "Bluewashing" the firm? Voluntary regulations, program design, and member compliance with the United Nations Global Compact. *Policy Studies Journal, 43*(1), 115–138. https://doi.org/10.1111/psj.12085

Berliner, D., & Wehner, J. (2022). Audits for accountability: Evidence from municipal by-elections in South Africa. *The Journal of Politics*. https://doi.org/10.1086/716951

Bernauer, T., Kalbhenn, A., Koubi, V., & Spilker, G. (2013). Is there a "depth versus participation" dilemma in international cooperation? *Review of International Organizations, 8*(4), 477–497. https://doi.org/10.1007/s11558-013-9165-1

Bernstein, S., & Hoffmann, M. (2018). The politics of decarbonization and the catalytic impact of subnational climate experiments. *Policy Sciences, 51*(2), 189–211. https://doi.org/10.1007/s11077-018-9314-8

Bevir, M., Rhodes, R. A., & Weller, P. (2003). Traditions of governance: Interpreting the changing role of the public sector. *Public Administration, 81*(1), 1–17.

Bhaumik, A. (2011). India chooses supremacy of Parliament over open govt. *Deccan Herald*, August 30, 2011. https://web.archive.org/web/20161228061231/https://www.deccanherald.com/content/187234/india-chooses-supremacy-parliament-over.html

Bingham, L. B., Nabatchi, T., & O'Leary, R. (2005). The new governance: Practices and processes for stakeholder and citizen participation in the work of government. *Public Administration Review*, 65, 547–558. https://doi.org/10.1111/j.1540-6210.2005.00482.x

Bio, D. (2019). La Argentina sigue sin Defensor del Pueblo: cuál era su función y por qué el puesto está vacante desde 2009. Infobae. https://www.infobae.com/sociedad/2019/09/28/la-argentina-sigue-sin-defensor-del-pueblo-cual-era-su-funcion-y-por-que-el-puesto estavacante-desde-2009/

Birchall, C. (2011). Introduction to "secrecy and transparency": The politics of opacity and openness. *Theory, Culture & Society, 28*(7–8), 7–25.

Birkinshaw, P. (1997). Freedom of information and open government: The European community/union dimension. *Government Information Quarterly, 14*(1), 27–49. https://doi.org/10.1016/S0740-624X(97)90050-2

Blessett, B., Dodge, J., Edmond, B., Goerdel, H. T., Gooden, S. T., Headley, A. M., Riccucci, N. M., & Williams, B. N. (2019). Social equity in public administration: A call to action. *Perspectives on Public Management and Governance, 2*(4), 283–299. https://doi.org/10.1093/ppmgov/gvz016

Blomeyer & Sanz. (2017). 2017 final report: Review of OGP's independent reporting mechanism. Open Government Partnership, December 12, 2017. https://www.opengovpartnership.org/wp-content/uploads/2018/03/IRM-Review-Final-Report_Blomeyer-Sanz_20171212.pdf

Boin, A., & t'Hart, P. T. (2003). Public leadership in times of crisis: Mission impossible? *Public Administration Review, 63*(5), 544–553.

Bond Anti-Corruption Group. (2018). *Bond Anti-Corruption Group report on UK compliance with the UN Convention against Corruption (UNAC) Second Cycle Review, Chapters II (Prevention) and V (Asset Recovery)*. London: Bond. https://www.bond.org.uk/resources/bond-anti-corruption-group-report-on-uk-compliance-with-the-un-convention-against

Bookman, Z., & Guerrero Amparán, J. P. (2009). Two steps forward, one step back: Assessing the implementation of Mexico's Freedom of Information Act. *Mexican Law Review, 1*(2), 4–51.

Boone, A. L., & White, J. T. (2015). The effect of institutional ownership on firm transparency and information production. *Journal of Financial Economics, 117*(3), 508–533.

Borge Bravo, R., & Esteve del Valle, M. (2017). Opinion leadership in parliamentary Twitter networks: A matter of layers of interaction? *Journal of Information Technology & Politics, 14*(3), 263–276.

Borrás, S., & Radaelli, C. M. (2011). The politics of governance architectures: creation, change and effects of the EU Lisbon Strategy. *Journal of European Public Policy, 18*(4), 463–484.

Borrmann, R. W. (2019). Post data #2. Gobierno Abierto en Argentina (2015–2019). https://www.linkedin.com/pulse/post-data-2-rudi-werner-borrmann/?originalSubdomain=es

Bovens, M. (2007). Analysing and assessing accountability: A conceptual framework 1. *European Law Journal, 13*(4), 447–468.

Bovens, M., Goodin, R. E., & Schillemans, T. (Eds.). (2014). *The Oxford handbook of public accountability*. Oxford: Oxford University Press.

Bowman, J. S., & Stevens, K. A. (2013). Public pay disclosure in state government: An ethical analysis. *American Review of Public Administration, 43*(4), 476–492.

Brandeis, L. (1971). *Other people's money*. New York: A. M. Kelly.

Brewer, G. A., & Kellough, J. E. (2016). Administrative values and public personnel management: Reflections on civil service reform. *Public Personnel Management, 45*(2), 171–189.

Brockmyer, B., & Fox, J. A. (2015). Assessing the evidence: The effectiveness and impact of governance-oriented multi-stakeholder initiatives. *Transparency & Accountability Initiative*, September 2015.

Bryson, J. M., Crosby, B. C., & Bloomberg, L. (2014). Public value governance: Moving beyond traditional public administration and the new public management. *Public Administration Review, 74*(4), 445–456. https://doi.org/10.1111/puar.12238

Calland, R. (2011). Blow the whistle at your peril. *Mail & Guardian*. https://mg.co.za/article/2011-10-17-blow-the-whistle-at-your-peril/

Callander, S. (2011). Searching and learning by trial and error. *American Economic Review, 101*(6), 2277–2308.

Cameron, B. (2015). *Battling a cancer: Tackling corruption in Peru, 2011–2014*. Innovations for Successful Societies, Princeton University. https://successfulsocieties.princeton.edu/publications/battling-cancer-tackling-corruption-peru

Castells, M. (2008). The new public sphere: Global civil society, communication networks, and global governance. *ANNALS of the American Academy of Political and Social Science, 616*(1), 78–93. https://doi.org/10.1177/0002716207311877

Catlaw, T. J., & Sandberg, B. (2014). "Dangerous government": Info-liberalism, active citizenship, and the open government directive. *Administration and Society, 46*(3), 223–254. https://doi.org/10.1177/0095399712461912

Charles, M. B., de Jong, W., & Ryan, N. (2011). Public values in Western Europe: A temporal perspective. *American Review of Public Administration, 41*(1), 75–91.

Chayes, A., & Chayes, A. H. (1993). On compliance. *International Organization, 47*(2), 175–205. https://doi.org/10.1017/S0020818300027910

Cheung, A. B. (2005). The politics of administrative reforms in Asia: Paradigms and legacies, paths and diversities. *Governance, 18*(2), 257–282.

Christensen, T., & Lægreid, P. (2007). The whole-of-government approach to public sector reform. *Public Administration Review, 67*(6), 1059–1066.

Civicus. (2016). *Open Government Partnership undermined by threats to civil society.* December 2, 2016 [press release]. https://www.civicus.org/index.php/media-resources/media-releases/2664-open-government-partnership-undermined-by-threats-to-civil-society

Clark, D. (1996). Open government in Britain: Discourse and practice. *Public Money & Management, 16*(1), 23–30.

Clemente, A. (2016). 23 entidades se suman a la iniciativa Gobierno Abierto del INAI. *El Financiero,* December 22, 2016. http://www.elfinanciero.com.mx/nacional/23-entidades-se-suman-a-la-iniciativa-gobierno-abierto-del-inai

Cobb, P. D., & Rubin, B. A. (2006). Contradictory interests, tangled power, and disorganized organization. *Administration & Society, 38*(1), 79–112.

Coglianese, C. (2009). The transparency president? The Obama administration and open government. *Governance, 22*(4), 529–544. https://doi.org/10.1111/j.1468-0491.2009.01451.x

Cole, A., & Jones, G. (2005). Reshaping the state: Administrative reform and new public management in France. *Governance, 18*(4), 567–588.

Collier, R. B., & Collier, D. (1979). Inducements versus constraints: Disaggregating "corporatism." *American Political Science Review, 73*(4), 967–986. https://doi.org/10.2307/1953982

Cordis, A. S., & Warren, P. L. (2014). Sunshine as disinfectant: The effect of state freedom of information act laws on public corruption. *Journal of Public Economics, 115,* 18–36.

Corrigan, T., & Gruzd, S. (2018). *Civil society participation in the open government partnership (OGP).* Washington, DC: United States Agency for International Development.

Criado, J. I. (2012). Interoperability of e government for building intergovernmental integration in the European Union. *Social Science Computer Review, 30*(1): 37–60.

Cucciniello, M., Porumbescu, G. A., & Grimmelikhuijsen, S. (2017). Twenty-five years of transparency research: Evidence and future directions. *Public Administration Review, 77*(1), 32–44.

Curtin, D., & Meijer, H. (1995). The principle of open government in Schengen and the European Union: Democratic retrogression? *Common Market Law Review, 32*(2), 391–442.

Dai, X. (2005). Why comply? The domestic constituency mechanism. *International Organization, 59*(2), 363–398. https://doi.org/10.1017/S0020818305050125

Danida. (n.d.). *Denmark's development cooperation.* Ministry of Foreign Affairs of Denmark. http://myanmar.um.dk/en/danida-en/

D'Artigues, K. (2016). 16 días para cambiar a México. *El Universal,* April 12, 2016. https://web.archive.org/web/20160415134505/https://www.eluniversal.com.mx/entrada-de-opinion/columna/katia-dartigues/nacion/2016/04/12/16-dias-para-cambiar-mexico

David-Barrett, E., & Okamura, K. (2016). Norm diffusion and reputation: The rise of the extractive industries transparency initiative. *Governance, 29*(2), 227–246.

De Blasio, E., & Selva, D. (2016). Why choose open government? Motivations for the adoption of Open Government policies in four European countries. *Policy & Internet, 8*(3), 225–247.

de Bruijn, H. D., & Dicke, W. (2006). Strategies for safeguarding public values in liberalized utility sectors. *Public Administration, 84*(3), 717–735.

De Búrca, G., Keohane, R. O., & Sabel, C. (2014). Global experimentalist governance. *British Journal of Political Science, 44*(3), 477–486. https://doi.org/10.1017/S0007123414000076

De Graaf, G., Huberts, L., & Smulders, R. (2016). Coping with public value conflicts. *Administration & Society, 48*(9), 1101–1127.

del Carmen Nava, M. (2014). Parlamento abierto en México: Un recuento. *Animal Politico,* September 9, 2014. https://www.animalpolitico.com/vision-legislativa/parlamento-abierto-en-mexico-un-recuento/

Demortain, D. (2004). Public organizations, stakeholders and the construction of publicness. Claims and defence of authority in public action. *Public Administration, 82*(4), 975–992.

Denhardt, J. V., & Denhardt, R. B. (2015). The new public service revisited. *Public Administration Review, 75*(5), 664–672.

Denhardt, R. B., & Denhardt, J. V. (2000). The new public service: Serving rather than steering. *Public Administration Review, 60*(6), 549–559.

Development Gateway, Inc., & Opening Contracting Partnership. (2017). *Open contracting scoping study: Ghana country report.* Washington, DC: Development Gateway. https://developmentgateway.org/wp-content/uploads/2020/10/Open-Contracting-West-Africa-Ghana-Development-Gateway.pdf

Dey, N., & Roy, A. (2013). India in open government and open government in India. *Stanford Social Innovation Review.* Sponsored supplement, 14.

DiMaggio, P. J., & Powell, W. W. (Eds.). (1991). *The new institutionalism in organizational analysis* (vol. 17, 1–38). Chicago: University of Chicago Press.

Downs, G. W., Rocke, D. M., & Barsoom, P. N. (1996). Is the good news about compliance good news about cooperation? *International Organization, 50*(3), 379–406.

Drayton, J. (2017). *Trinidad and Tobago end-of-term report 2014–2016.* [IRM Report]. Open Government Partnership, August 4, 2017. https://www.opengovpartnership.org/wp-content/uploads/2017/08/Trinidad-Tobago_EOTR_2014-2016.pdf

Dressel, B., & Bonoan, C. R. (2019). Southeast Asia's troubling elections: Duterte versus the rule of law. *Journal of Democracy, 30*(4), 134–148.

Drezner, D. W. *All politics is global: Explaining international regulatory regimes.* Princeton, NJ: Princeton University Press, 2007.

Dufief, E., Dorward, N., Simons, R., & Welford, K. (2017). With publication comes responsibility: Using open data for accountability in Benin and Tanzania—A discussion paper. Publish What You Fund, October 2017. http://www.publishwhatyoufund.org/wp-content/uploads/2017/09/With-Publication-Brings-Responsibility-A-discussion-paper.pdf

Duncan, J. (2015). *Global food security governance: Civil society participation in Committee on World Food Security*. London: EarthScan Routledge.

Dunleavy, P., & Hood, C. (1994). From old public administration to new public management. *Public Money & Management, 14*(3), 9–16.

Dunleavy, P., Margetts, H., Bastow, S., & Tinkler, J. (2006). New Public Management is dead—Long live digital-era governance. *Journal of Public Administration Research and Theory, 16*(3), 467–494.

Durant, R. F. (2008). Sharpening a knife cleverly: Organizational change, policy paradox, and the "weaponizing" of administrative reforms. *Public Administration Review, 68*(2), 282–294.

Dussauge Laguna, M. I. (2011). The challenges of implementing merit-based personnel policies in Latin America: Mexico's civil service reform experience. *Journal of Comparative Policy Analysis, 13*(1) 51–73. https://doi.org/10.1080/13876988.2011.538541

Eaves, D. (2012). The opportunities and challenges of the Open Government Partnership. Open Government Partnership, April 23, 2012. https://www.ogp.am/en/news/item/2012/04/23/brasilia2012/

Economist [editorial]. (2011a). A transparency conspiracy? America's latest bid for global dominance? September 30, 2011. https://www.economist.com/democracy-in-america/2011/09/30/a-transparency-conspiracy

Economist. [editorial]. (2011b). The parting of the red tape. October 8, 2011. https://www.economist.com/international/2011/10/08/the-parting-of-the-red-tape

Economist. (2015). Mexico and its NGOs: The new movers and shakers. May 2, 2015. https://www.economist.com/the-americas/2015/05/02/the-new-movers-and-shakers

Eisenstadt, T. A. (2004). *Courting democracy in Mexico: Party strategies and electoral institutions*. Cambridge: Cambridge University Press.

Elkins, D. J., & Simeon, R. (1979). A cause in search of its effect, or what does political culture explain? *Comparative Politics, 11*(2), 127–145.

Ellington, T. C. (2019). Transparency under Trump: Policy and prospects. *Public Integrity, 21*(2), 127–140. https://doi.org/10.1080/10999922.2018.1463837

El Norte. (2015). Alerta ONG regresión en apertura de datos. February 24, 2015.

Emerson, K., & Nabatchi, T. (2015). *Collaborative governance regimes*. Washington, DC: Georgetown University Press.

Esmark, A. (2016). Maybe it is time to rediscover technocracy? An old framework for a new analysis of administrative reforms in the governance era. *Journal of Public Administration Research and Theory, 27*(3), 501–516.

European Union, European Commission. (2016). *eGovernment in Norway*. [Country Profile]. https://joinup.ec.europa.eu/sites/default/files/inline-files/eGovernment%20in%20Norway%20-%20February%202016%20-%2013_0_v1_00.pdf

Evans, A. M., & Campos, A. (2013). Open government initiatives: Challenges of citizen participation. *Journal of Policy Analysis and Management, 32*(1), 172–185.

Excell, C. (2012). *Why the green crowd should care about the Open Government Partnership*. Washington, DC: Access Initiative.

Falla, R. (2017). Why OGP commitments fall behind. Open Government Partnership. https://www.opengovpartnership.org/sites/default/files/IRM_Technical-Paper_Failure_Dec2017.pdf

Falla, R. (2021). Effective, efficient, and equitable: How open government can deliver on vaccines. Open Government Partnership, March 15, 2021. https://www.opengovpartnership.org/stories/effective-efficient-and-equitable-how-open-government-can-deliver-on-vaccines/

Farrell, H., & Newman, A. (2018). Linkage politics and complex governance in transatlantic surveillance. *World Politics, 70*(4): 515–554.

Feldman, J. G., & Teberg, R. L. (1965). Beneficial ownership under section 16 of the Securities Exchange Act of 1934. *Western Reserve Law Review, 17*, 1054–1097.

Ferčíková, I. (2018). Peer Exchanges as a core element for pushing OGP reforms. Open Government Partnership, January 9, 2018. https://www.opengovpartnership.org/stories/peer-exchanges-as-a-core-element-for-pushing-ogp-reforms/

Finnemore, M., & Sikkink, K. (1998). International norm dynamics and political change. *International Organization, 52*(4), 887–917.

Forrer, J., Kee, J. E., Newcomer, K. E., & Boyer, E. (2010). Public–private partnerships and the public accountability question. *Public Administration Review, 70*(3), 475–484.

Fountain, J. E. (2004). *Building the virtual state: Information technology and institutional change*. Washington, DC: Brookings Institution Press.

Fox, J. (2007). *Accountability politics, power and voice in rural Mexico*. Oxford University Press, 2007.

Fox, J. A. (2015). Social accountability: What does the evidence really say? *World Development, 72*, 346–361. https://doi.org/10.1016/j.worlddev.2015.03.011

Francesco, F. D. (2012). Diffusion of regulatory impact analysis among OECD and EU member states. *Comparative Political Studies, 45*(10): 1277–1305.

Fraundorfer, M. (2017). The Open Government Partnership: Mere smokescreen or new paradigm? *Globalizations, 14*(4), 611–626.

Fraundorfer, M. (2018). *Rethinking global democracy in Brazil*. London: Rowman & Littlefield.

Frederickson, H. G. (1976). The lineage of new public administration. *Administration & Society, 8*(2), 149–174.

Freedom House. (2015). *Nations in transit: Macedonia*. Washington, DC: Freedom House. https://freedomhouse.org/sites/default/files/NIT_2015_Macedonia.pdf

FreedomInfo.org. (2011a). Brazil agrees to co-chair international FOI effort. FreedomInfo.Org, April 22, 2011. http://www.freedominfo.org/2011/04/brazil-agrees-to-co-chair-international-foi-effort

FreedomInfo.org. (2011b). Open government effort officially begun at NYC event. FreedomInfo. Org, September 20, 2011. http://www.freedominfo.org/2011/09/open-government-effort-officially-begun-at-nyc-event

FreedomInfo.org. (2011c). Some ineligible OGP countries ask how to join. FreedomInfo.Org. September 30, 2011. http://www.freedominfo.org/2011/09/some-ineligible-ogp-countries-ask-how-to-join

FreedomInfo.org. (2015a). OGP CSO leaders criticize Mexico over FOI legislation. February 21, 2015. http://www.freedominfo.org/2015/02/ogp-cso-leaders-criticize-mexico-over-foi-legislation/

FreedomInfo.org. (2015b). Mexican Senate approves new access legislation. March 19, 2015. http://www.freedominfo.org/2015/03/mexican-senate-approves-new-access-legislation

Frey, L., (2014). Memo: Financial contributions to the Open Government Partnership. Open Government Partnership, May 27, 2014. https://www.opengovpartnership.org/wp-content/uploads/2019/06/OGP-Memo-to-Participating-Countries-27-May.pdf

FUNDAR. (2014). Alianza para el parlamento abierto en México. September 22, 2014. http://fundar.org.mx/alianza-para-el-parlamento-abiero-en-mexico/

FUNDAR. (2015). Urgente que la Alianza para el Gobierno Abierto se convierta en una plataforma efectiva para ayudar a resolver los grandes problemas que enfrenta México. October 28, 2015. http://fundar.org.mx/urgente-que-la-alianza-para-el-gobierno-abierto-se-convierta-en-una-plataforma-efectiva-para-ayudar-a-resolver-los-grandes-problemas-que-enfrenta-mexico/

FUNDAR. (2016). La importancia del parlamento abierto para el combate a la corrupción. October 31, 2016. https://fundar.org.mx/la-importancia-del-parlamento-abierto-para-el-combate-a-la-corrupcion/

Fung, A. (2013). Infotopia: Unleashing the democratic power of transparency. *Politics & Society*, *41*(2), 183–212.

Fung, A., Graham, M., & Weil, D. (2007). *Full disclosure: The perils and promise of transparency*. Cambridge: Cambridge University Press.

García, A. G. (2016). Transparency in Mexico: An overview of access to information regulations and their effectiveness at the federal and state level. Wilson Center Mexico Institute. https://www.wilsoncenter.org/publication/transparency-mexico-overview-access-to-information-regulations-and-their-effectiveness

Garduño, S. (2015). Reprochan activistas exclusión de cumbre. *Reforma*, October 30, 2015. https://busquedas.gruporeforma.com/reforma/Libre/VisorNota.aspx?id=5806668|InfodexTextos&md5=f826f175025faa01aba51bf4897d6125

Gehring, T., & Faude, B. (2014). A theory of emerging order within institutional complexes: How competition among regulatory international institutions leads to institutional adaptation and division of labor. *Review of International Organizations, 9*(4), 471–498. https://link.springer.com/article/10.1007/s11558-014-9197-1

Gerring, J. (2011). *Social science methodology: A unified framework*. Cambridge: Cambridge University Press.

Gerson, P., & Nieto, F. (2016). Opening government? The Case of Mexico in the Open Government Partnership. Global Integrity, January 2016. https://www.globalintegrity.org/wp-content/uploads/2018/12/Mexico-final.pdf

Gingrich, J. (2015). Varying costs to change? Institutional change in the public sector. *Governance*, *28*(1), 41–60.

Global Integrity. (2011). Our role in the Open Government Partnership. July 19, 2011. http://www.globalintegrity.org/2011/07/our-role-in-ogp

Global Integrity. (2012). Assessing OGP action plans. June 21, 2012. https://www.globalintegrity.org/2012/06/ogp-action-plan-assessments/

Global Integrity. (2016). Learning to open government. Washington, DC: Global Integrity. https://www.globalintegrity.org/wp-content/uploads/2018/12/Learning-to-Open-Government-full.pdf

Global Open Data Index. (2014). United Kingdom. [Data Set]. http://2015.index.okfn.org/place/united-kingdom/2014/

Gogidze, Lasha. (2018). *Georgia end-of-term report 2014–2016* [IRM report]. Open Government Partnership, January 30, 2018. https://www.opengovpartnership.org/documents/georgia-end-of-term-report-2014-2016/

Gómez, R. (2012). Avala bancada del PRD plan para eliminar SSP y SFP. *El Universal*, November 12, 2012. http://archivo.eluniversal.com.mx/notas/882547.html

Gonzalez-Zapata, F., & Heeks, R. (2015). The multiple meanings of open government data: Understanding different stakeholders and their perspectives. *Government Information Quarterly*, *32*(4), 441–452.

Government of Albania (2015). Albania Second Action Plan for 2014–2016. Open Government Partnership.

Government of Costa Rica. (2013). Costa Rica action plan 2013–2014. Open Government Partnership. https://www.opengovpartnership.org/documents/costa-rica-action-plan-2013-2014/

Government of Malta. (2012). Malta action plan 2012–2013. Open Government Partnership. https://www.opengovpartnership.org/members/malta/commitments/MT0001/

Government of Norway. (2015). *Independent reporting Mechanism (IRM) progress report 2013–2014*. Washington, DC: Open Government Partnership. https://www.opengovpartnership.org/wp-content/uploads/2001/01/IRMReport_Norway_Final_Eng_0.pdf

Government of South Korea. (2014). South Korea second action plan for 2014–2016. Open Government Partnership, June 24, 2014. https://www.opengovpartnership.org/documents/south-korea-second-action-plan-for-2014-2016/

Government of the Republic of Croatia. (2015). Croatia's "E-citizens" voted best open government project in Europe. October 30, 2015. https://vlada.gov.hr/news/croatia-s-e-citizens-voted-best-open-government-project-in-europe/18030

Government of the United States. (2016). *United States of America midterm self-assessment report for the Open Government Partnership. Third open government national action plan, 2015–2017*. Washington, DC: Open Government Partnership. https://open.usa.gov/assets/files/nap_3_self_assessment_final.pdf

Green, J. E. (2010). *The eyes of the people: Democracy in an age of spectatorship*. Oxford: Oxford University Press.

Green, J. F. (2014). *Rethinking private authority: Agents and entrepreneurs in global environmental governance*. Princeton, NJ: Princeton University Press.

Greve, C. (2015). Ideas in public management reform for the 2010s. Digitalization, value creation and involvement. *Public Organization Review, 15*(1), 49–65.

Grimmelikhuijsen, S. G., & Feeney, M. K. (2017). Developing and testing an integrative framework for open government adoption in local governments. *Public Administration Review, 77*(4), 579–590.

Guedhami, O., & Pittman, J. A. (2011). The choice between private and public capital markets: The importance of disclosure standards and auditor discipline to countries divesting state-owned enterprises. *Journal of Accounting and Public Policy, 30*(5), 395–430.

Guerzovich, F., & Moses, M. (2016). *Learning to open government: Findings and reflections on how the Open Government Partnership is playing out, in practice, in five countries*. Washington, DC: Global Integrity.

Guillán Montero, A., & Taxell, N. (2015). *Open government reforms: The challenge of making public consultations meaningful in Croatia*. Bergen: Anti-Corruption Resource Centre.

Hafner-Burton, E. M., & Tsutsui, K. (2005). Human rights in a globalizing world: The paradox of empty promises. *American Journal of Sociology, 110*(5), 1373–1411.

Haggard, S., & Simmons, B. A. (1987). Theories of international regimes. *International Organization, 41*(3), 491–517.

Hale, T. (2016). "All hands on deck": The Paris Agreement and nonstate climate action. *Global Environmental Politics, 16*(3), 12–22.

Hale, T. (2020). Catalytic cooperation. *Global Environmental Politics, 20*(4), 73–98. https://doi.org/10.1162/glep_a_00561

Hall, P. A., & Taylor, R. C. (1996). Political science and the three new institutionalisms. *Political Studies, 44*(5), 936–957. https://doi.org/10.1111/j.1467-9248.1996.tb00343.x

Hansson, K., Belkacem, K., & Ekenberg, L. (2015). Open government and democracy: A research review. *Social Science Computer Review, 33*(5), 540–555.

Hardy, K., & Maurushat, A. (2017). Opening up government data for Big Data analysis and public benefit. *Computer Law & Security Review, 33*(1), 30–37.

Harrison, T. M., & Sayogo, D. S. (2014). Transparency, participation, and accountability practices in open government: A comparative study. *Government Information Quarterly, 31*(4), 513–525.

Heinrich, C. J. (2012). How credible is the evidence, and does it matter? An analysis of the Program Assessment Rating Tool. *Public Administration Review, 72*(1), 123–134.

Heller, N. (2011). *What the South African secrecy bill means for the Open Government Partnership.* Washington, DC: Global Integrity, November 29, 2011. https://www.globalintegrity.org/2011/11/29/south-africa-and-ogp/

Heller, N. (2016). Making the case for adding sub-national governments to the Open Government Partnership. Results for Development, January 12, 2016. https://www.r4d.org/blog/making-case-adding-sub-national-governments-open-government-partnership/

Herrero, A. (2017). *OGP as a framework for change: The experience of Buenos Aires.* Washington, DC: Open Government Partnership.

Hood, C. (1991). A public management for all seasons? *Public Administration, 6,* 3–19. https://doi.org/10.1111/j.1467-9299.1991.tb00779.x

Hood, C. (1995). The "New Public Management" in the 1980s: variations on a theme. *Accounting, Organizations and Society, 20*(2–3), 93–109.

Hood, C. (2007). What happens when transparency meets blame-avoidance? *Public Management Review, 9*(2), 191–210.

Hood, C. (2010). Accountability and transparency: Siamese twins, matching parts, awkward couple? *West European Politics, 33*(5), 989–1009.

Hood, C., & Peters, G. (2004). The middle aging of New Public Management: Into the age of paradox? *Journal of Public Administration Research and Theory, 14*(3), 267–282.

Howard, A. (2015). Mexico misses an opportunity to address corruption and press freedom. *Huffington Post,* October 29, 2015. https://www.huffingtonpost.co.uk/entry/mexicoopengovernment_us_56324e44e4b0631799115896

Howard, A., & Wonderlich, J. (2017). *Trump administration commits to participating in Open Government Partnership.* Washington, DC: Sunlight Foundation.

Hughes, T. (2015). Launching the NAP review: Conclusions. Open Government Partnership Blog, December 17, 2015. https://www.opengovpartnership.org/stories/launching-the-nap-review-conclusions/

Iakobidze, T. (2017). 2016 statistics on telephone surveillance and secret investigation in Georgia. Institute for Development of Freedom of Information, February 3, 2017. https://idfi.ge/en/statistical_data_on_phone_conversation_surveillance

Ingrams, A. (2017a). The legal-normative conditions of police transparency: A configurational approach to open data adoption using qualitative comparative analysis. *Public Administration, 95*(2), 527–545.

Ingrams, A. (2017b). *Open government performance: An analytical framework for organizational design* (PhD dissertation, Newark, NJ, Rutgers University-Graduate School).

Ingrams, A. (2018). Democratic transition and transparency reform: An fsQCA analysis of access to information laws in twenty-three countries. *Government Information Quarterly*, *35*(3), 428–436.

Ingrams, A. (2020). Administrative reform and the quest for openness: A Popperian review of open government. *Administration & Society*, *52*(2), 319–340.

Ingrams, A., Piotrowski, S. J., & Berliner, D., (2020). Learning from our mistakes: Public management reform and the hope of open government. *Perspectives on Public Management and Governance*, *3*(4), 257–272.

Jaeger, P. T., & Bertot, J. C. (2010). Transparency and technological change: Ensuring equal and sustained public access to government information. *Government Information Quarterly*, *27*(4), 371–376.

Janssen, M., & Estevez, E. (2013). Lean government and platform-based governance—Doing more with less. *Government Information Quarterly*, *30*(S1), S1-S8.

Jørgensen, T. (1999). The public sector in an in-between time: Searching for new public values. *Public Administration*, *77*(3), 565–584.

Jørgensen, T. B., & Bozeman, B. (2007). Public values: An inventory. *Administration & Society*, *39*(3), 354–381.

Judd, N. (2011). The semi-open development of an Open Government Plan. TechPresident, August 23, 2011. https://web.archive.org/web/20120209081102/http://techpresident.com/blog-entry/semi-open-development-open-government-plan

Kahler, M. (2018). Global governance: Three futures. *International Studies Review*, *20*(2), 239–246. https://doi.org/10.1093/isr/viy037

Kaimal, S., & González, A. A. (2015). OGP civil society co-chairs statement on the general transparency law in Mexico. Open Government Partnership, February 21, 2015. https://www.opengovpartnership.org/stories/ogp-civil-society-co-chairs-statement-on-the-general-transparency-law-in-mexico/

Kassen, M. (2014). Globalization of e-government: Open government as a global agenda; benefits, limitations and ways forward. *Information Development*, *30*(1), 51–58.

Keohane, R. O. (1984). *After hegemony: Cooperation and discord in the world political economy*. Princeton, NJ: Princeton University Press.

Keohane, R. O., & Martin, L. L. (1995). The promise of institutionalist theory. *International Security*, *20*(1), 39–51.

Keohane, R. O., & Victor, D. G. (2011). The regime complex for climate change. *Perspectives on Politics*, *9*(1), 7–23.

Kettl, D. F. (2000). The transformation of governance: Globalization, devolution, and the role of government. *Public Administration Review*, *60*(6), 488–497.

Kettl, D. F. (2006). Modernising government: The way forward—A comment. *International Review of Administrative Sciences, 72*(3), 313–317.

Kingdon, J. W. (1984). *Agendas, Alternatives, and Public Policies.* London: Longman.

Kitschelt, H. P. (1986). Political opportunity structures and political protest: Anti-nuclear movements in four democracies. *British Journal of Political Science, 16*(1), 57–85. https://doi.org/10.1017/S000712340000380X

Koremenos, B., Lipson, C., & Snidal, D. (2001). The rational design of international institutions. *International Organization, 55*(4), 761–799. https://doi.org/10.1162/002081801317193592

Korunovska, N. (2017). *Macedonia: 2014–2016 end-of-term report.* [IRM Report]. Washington, DC: Open Government Partnership. July 12, 2017. https://www.opengovpartnership.org/documents/macedonia-end-of-term-report-2014-2016/

La Porte, T. M., Demchak, C. C., & De Jong, M. (2002). Democracy and bureaucracy in the age of the web: Empirical findings and theoretical speculations. *Administration & Society, 34*(4), 411–446.

Lathrop, D., & Ruma, L. (2010). *Open government: Collaboration, transparency and participation in practice.* Cambridge, MA: O'Reilly.

Levitsky, S., & Way, L. A. (2006). Linkage versus leverage. Rethinking the international dimension of regime change. *Comparative Politics, 38*(4), 379–400. https://doi.org/10.2307/20434008

Lewis, J. R. (2000). Electronic access to public records. *Public Administration and Public Policy, 77*, 197–214.

Light, P. C. (1998). *The tides of reform: Making government work, 1945–1995.* New Haven, CT: Yale University Press.

Lindner, R., & Riehm, U. (2011). Broadening participation through e-petitions? An empirical study of petitions to the German Parliament. *Policy & Internet, 3*(1), 1–23.

Liu, H. K. (2017). Crowdsourcing government: Lessons from multiple disciplines. *Public Administration Review, 77*(5), 656–667.

Lodge, M., & Gill, D. (2011). Toward a new era of administrative reform? The myth of post-NPM in New Zealand. *Governance, 24,* 141–166.

Lynn, L. E., Jr. (2001). The myth of the bureaucratic paradigm: What traditional public administration really stood for. *Public Administration Review, 61*(2), 144–160.

Lynn, L. E., Jr. (2006). *Public management: Old and new.* London: Routledge.

Magaloni, B. (2006). *Voting for autocracy: Hegemonic party survival and its demise in Mexico.* Cambridge: Cambridge University Press.

Makinana, Z. (2013). Zuma sends secrecy bill back for fixing. *Mail & Guardian,* September 12, 2013. https://mg.co.za/article/2013-09-12-zuma-sends-secrecy-bill-back-for-fixing/

Manin, Bernard, Przeworski, Adam, & Stokes, Sustan. (1999). Introduction; elections and representation. In A. Przeworski, S. Stokes, & B. Manin (Eds.), *Democracy, accountability, and representation* (pp. 1–54). Cambridge: Cambridge University Press.

Marczak, B., & Scott-Railton, J. S. (2016). The million dollar dissident: NSO group's iPhone zero-days used against a UAE human rights defender. CitizenLab, August 24, 2016. https://citizenlab.ca/2016/08/million-dollar-dissident-iphone-zero-day-nso-group-uae/

Marczynski, A. (2018). It's time to make ambitious anti-corruption commitments to the OGP. *Voices for Transparency*, July 18, 2018. https://voices.transparency.org/its-time-to-make-ambitious-anti-corruption-commitments-in-the-ogp-a14489b02dc6

McCarthy, J. D., & Zald, M. N. (1977). Resource mobilization and social movements: A partial theory. *American Journal of Sociology*, *82*(6), 1212–1241. https://doi.org/10.1086/226464

McDermott, P. (2010). Building open government. *Government Information Quarterly*, *27*(4), 401–413.

McIntosh, T. (2011). India withdraws from Open Government Partnership. Freedominfo.org, July 12, 2011. http://www.freedominfo.org/2011/07/india-withdraws-from-open-government-partnership/

McIntosh, T. (2012). Open data, FOI communities show signs of convergence. Freedominfo.org, September 14, 20123. http://www.freedominfo.org/2012/09/open-data-foi-communities-show-signs-of-convergence/

McKenzie, J. (2014). Near 3-year mark, Open Government Partnership success still unclear. *techPresident*, May 29, 2014. https://web.archive.org/web/20160324094101/http://techpresident.com/news/wegov/25084/near-three-year-mark-ogp-success-still-unclear

McLean, C. (2020). COVID-19: What is the role of open government? Open Government, April 30, 2020. https://www.opengovernment.org.uk/2020/04/30/covid-19-what-is-the-role-of-open-government/

Mearsheimer, J. J. (1994). The false promise of international institutions. *International Security*, *19*(3), 5–49.

Meijer, A. J. (2009). Understanding modern transparency. *International Review of Administrative Sciences*, *75*(2), 255–269.

Meijer, A. J., Curtin, D., & Hillebrandt, M. (2012). Open government: Connecting vision and voice. *International Review of Administrative Sciences*, *78*(1), 10–29. https://doi.org/10.1177/0020852311429533

Mendeš, I. (2016). *Croatia: 2014–2016 end-of-term report*. Open Government Partnership, May 17, 2016. https://www.opengovpartnership.org/wp-content/uploads/2001/01/Croatia_EOTR_2014-2016_for-pub-comment_ENG.pdf

Mergel, I. (2015). Opening government: Designing open innovation processes to collaborate with external problem solvers. *Social Science Computer Review*, *33*(5), 599–612.

Mergel, I., & Desouza, K. C. (2013). Implementing open innovation in the public sector: The case of Challenge.gov. *Public Administration Review, 73*(6), 882–890.

Meyer, J. W., Boli, J., Thomas, G. M., & Ramirez, F. O. (1997). World society and the nation-state. *American Journal of Sociology, 103*(1), 144–181.

Meyer, M., & Hinojosa, G. (2018). WOLA report: Mexico's national anti-corruption system. Washington Office on Latin America, May 17, 2018. https://www.wola.org/analysis/wola-report-mexico-national-anti-corruption-system/

Michener, G. (2011a). FOI laws around the world. *Journal of Democracy, 22*(2), 145–159. https://doi.org/10.1353/jod.2011.0021

Michener, G. (2011b). The Open Government Partnership—A new direction for US foreign policy? *Christian Science Monitor*, July 13, 2011. https://www.csmonitor.com/World/Americas/Latin-America-Monitor/2011/0713/The-Open-Government-Partnership-a-new-direction-for-US-foreign-policy

Michener, G. (2019). Gauging the impact of transparency policies. *Public Administration Review, 79*(1), 136–139.

Michener, G., & Bersch, K. (2013). Identifying transparency. *Information Polity, 18*(3), 233–242.

Michener, G., & Pereira, C. (2011). Is Brazil fit to lead the Open Government Partnership? Secrecy vs. transparency and the ambivalence of Brazil's presidents. Brookings, July 18, 2011. https://www.brookings.edu/opinions/is-brazil-fit-to-lead-the-open-government-partnership-secrecy-vs-transparency-and-the-ambivalence-of-brazils-presidents

Michener, G., & Ritter, O. (2017). Comparing resistance to open data performance measurement: Public education in Brazil and the UK. *Public Administration, 95*(1), 4–21.

Milewicz, K., & Goodin, R. (2016). Deliberative capacity building through international organizations: The case of the Universal Periodic Review of Human Rights. *British Journal of Political Science, 48*(2) 1–21.

Millard, J. (2015). Open governance systems: Doing more with more. *Government Information Quarterly, 35*(4), S77–S87.

Miranda, D. (2019). Enhanced accountability: Reshaping the IRM together. Open Government Partnership, August 19, 2019. https://www.opengovpartnership.org/stories/enhanced-accountability-reshaping-the-irm-together/

Montalvo, T. L. (2014). Senadores hacen a un lado propuesta civil y cambian la Ley de Transparencia de último momento. *AnimalPolitico*, December 5, 2014. https://www.animalpolitico.com/2014/12/senadores-presentan-ley-de-transparencia-con-un-articulo-que-sanciona-la-apertura-de-informacion/

Montero, A. G., & Taxell, N. (2015). *Open government reforms: The challenge of making public consultations meaningful in Croatia*. U4 Anti-Corruption Resource Centre. December, No. 3, 1–46. https://www.u4.no/publications/open-government-reforms-the-challenge-of-making-public-consultations-meaningful-in-croatia

Montes, J. (2018). Mexico's multibillion-dollar airport project is well under way. It may be canceled. *Wall Street Journal*, April 27, 2018. https://www.wsj.com/articles/mexicos-multibillion-dollar-airport-project-is-well-under-way-it-may-be-canceled-1524821401

Moon, M. J., & Ingraham, P. (1998). Shaping administrative reform and governance: An examination of the political nexus triads in three Asian countries. *Governance, 11*(1), 77–100.

Moravcsik, A. (2000). The origins of human rights regimes: Democratic delegation in postwar Europe. *International Organization, 54*(2): 217–252.

Moses, M. (2016). Opening government? The case of Albania in the Open Government Partnership. Global Integrity, January 31, 2016. https://www.globalintegrity.org/resource/log-albania/

Moulton, S. (2009). Putting together the publicness puzzle: A framework for realized publicness. *Public Administration Review, 69*(5), 889–900.

Mueller, M. L. (2010). *Networks and states: The global politics of internet governance.* Cambridge, MA: MIT Press.

Mural. (2015). Llaman ONG a no retroceder en transparencia. February 24, 2015.

Murillo, M. J. (2015). Evaluating the role of online data availability: The case of economic and institutional transparency in sixteen Latin American nations. *International Political Science Review, 36*(1), 42–59.

Nalbandian, J. (2005). Professionals and the conflicting forces of administrative modernization and civic engagement. *The American Review of Public Administration, 35*(4), 311–326.

Nava Campos, G. (2018). *Mecanismo de Revisión Independiente (MRI): Informe de Avances de México 2016–2018.* Washington, DC: Open Government Partnership Independent Reporting Mechanism. https://www.opengovpartnership.org/wp-content/uploads/2018/04/Mexico_Mid-Term_Report_2016-2018_for-public-comment.pdf

Newman, A., & Posner, E. (2016). Structuring transnational interests: The second-order effects of soft law in the politics of global finance. *Review of International Political Economy, 23*(5), 768–798.

Ninua, T. (2016). Breaking down iron doors: Why opening up Soviet archives matters. Open Government Partnership, March 21, 2016. https://www.opengovpartnership.org/stories/breaking-down-iron-doors-why-opening-soviet-archives-matters

Notimex. (2014a). México encabeza acción en pro de la transparencia: Ministro británico. July 30, 2014.

Notimex. (2014b). México recibe premio en nombre de Alianza para el Gobierno Abierto. November 6, 2014.

Notimex. (2018). INAI realizará Cumbre de Gobierno Abierto. March 27, 2018.

Noveck, B. S. (2009). *Wiki government: How technology can make government better, democracy stronger, and citizens more powerful.* Washington, DC: Brookings Institution Press.

Noveck, B. S. (2017). Rights-based and tech-driven: Open data, freedom of information, and the future of government transparency. *Yale Human Rights & Development Law Journal, 19*(1).

Núcleo de la Sociedad Civil para el Gobierno Abierto en México. (2017a). Mexican civil society statement for OGP steering committee. Open Government Partnership, May 23, 2017. https://www.opengovpartnership.org/sites/default/files/Mexican_Letter_Civil-Society_May23-2017.pdf

Núcleo de la Sociedad Civil para el Gobierno Abierto en México. (2017b). September 2017 letter from Mexican civil society to the Steering Committee. Open Government Partnership, September 19, 2017. https://www.opengovpartnership.org/documents/september-2017-letter-from-mexican-civil-/

Ocejo Rojo, A. (2016). *Mecanismo de Revisión Independiente: México Informe de Fin de Término 2013–2015*. Washington, DC: Open Government Partnership Independent Reporting Mechanism.

O'Donnell, G. A. (1998). Horizontal accountability in new democracies. *Journal of Democracy*, 9(3), 112–126.

OECD and GovLab. (2021). *Open data in action: Initiatives during the initial stage of the COVID-19 pandemic*. New York: OECD and GovLab. https://www.oecd.org/gov/digital-government/use-of-open-government-data-to-address-covid19-outbreak.htm

OGP Support Unit. (n.d.). OGP support unit, accessed May 21, 2019. https://www.opengovpartnership.org/about/about-ogp/ogp-support-unit

OGP Support Unit (2017). Open Government for improving public services in Asia. Open Government Partnership, August 4, 2017. https://www.opengovpartnership.org/stories/open-government-for-improving-public-services-in-asia/

OGP Support Unit. (2018). The Kingdom of Morocco joins Open Government Partnership, April 26, 2018. https://www.opengovpartnership.org/news/the-kingdom-of-morocco-joins-open-government-partnership/

Ohemeng, F. L., & Ofosu-Adarkwa, K. (2015). One way traffic: The open data initiative project and the need for an effective demand side initiative in Ghana. *Government Information Quarterly*, 32(4), 419–428.

Open Contracting Partnership. (2019). Open contracting in Mexico. https://web.archive.org/web/20170606041128/http://www.open-contracting.org/why-open-contracting/worldwide/mexico/

Open Data Barometer. (2017). *Quantitative datasets*. 4th ed. World Wide Web Foundation: Washington, DC.

Open Government Partnership. [Webpage] (n.d.). Governance. Accessed January 18, 2019. https://www.opengovpartnership.org/about/who-we-are/

Open Government Partnership (2012a). Second European outreach and support meeting. October 16, 2012. https://www.opengovpartnership.org/stories/update-from-the-second-ogp-european-outreach-and-support-meeting-in-dubrovnik/

Open Government Partnership. (2012b). OGP independent reporting mechanism concept note. December 4, 2012. https://www.opengovpartnership.org/documents/irm-proposal-approved

Open Government Partnership. (2012c). Ministerial level steering committee meeting minutes. London, December 4, 2012. https://www.opengovpartnership.org/wp-content/uploads/2019/10/SC-Minutes-Dec-4-2012-Final_0.pdf

Open Government Partnership. (2012d). *Self-assessment report Mexico*. December 14, 2012. https://www.opengovpartnership.org/wp-content/uploads/2019/06/14Dic2012_Self-AssessmentReport_ENG-1.pdf

Open Government Partnership. (2013a). *More inclusive and meaningful public engagement on laws in Croatia*. [Case study]. January 1, 2013. https://www.opengovpartnership.org/sites/default/files/Inspiring%20Story%20-%20Croatia.pdf

Open Government Partnership. (2013b). Draft national action plan for the Republic of Ghana. January 2013. https://www.opengovpartnership.org/wp-content/uploads/2001/01/Ghana_Action%20Plan%202013_2014_final.pdf

Open Government Partnership. (2013c). *Mecanismo de Revisión Independiente: México Informe de Avance 2011–2013*. Open Government Partnership Independent Reporting Mechanism. https://www.opengovpartnership.org/wp-content/uploads/2001/01/Mexico%20for%20Public%20Comment.pdf

Open Government Partnership. (2014a). Four-year strategy, 2015–2018. https://www.opengovpartnership.org/wp-content/uploads/2001/01/4YearAP-Online.pdf

Open Government Partnership. (2014b). *Outcome statement of the OGP high-level event: Citizen action, government responsiveness*. Washington, DC: Open Government Partnership.

Open Government Partnership. (2015a). Criteria & Standards Subcommittee meeting minutes, Open Government Hub, Washington, DC, USA. March 9–10, 2015. https://www.opengovpartnership.org/wp-content/uploads/2019/10/Minutes-9-10-March-Meeting.pdf

Open Government Partnership. [Webpage] (2015b). *Open Government Partnership: Articles of governance* (April 2015 update). https://www.opengovpartnership.org/wp-content/uploads/2019/06/OGP_Articles-Gov_Apr-21-2015.pdf

Open Government Partnership. (2016a). Featured commitment—Georgia. March 1, 2016. https://www.opengovpartnership.org/stories/featured-commitment-georgia.

Open Government Partnership. (2016b). *São Paulo action plan*. Washington, DC: Open Government Partnership. https://www.prefeitura.sp.gov.br/cidade/secretarias/upload/Sao_Paulo_Subnational_Action_Plan2016_ENG.pdf

Open Government Partnership. (2017a). #OGP15: Giorgi Kldiashvili, Institute for Development of Freedom of Information, March 30, 2017. YouTube video, 2:10. https://www.youtube.com/watch?v=8HGd4yUnmOg&list=UUCDhqc6Xx5a-VKZNo6q_8aQ&index=77

Open Government Partnership. (2017b). Open Government Partnership statement on domestic OGP developments in Mexico. May 25, 2017. https://www.opengovpartnership.org/stories/open-government-partnership-statement-on-domestic-ogp-developments-in-mexico/

Open Government Partnership. (2017c). Statement from OGP steering committee co-chairs on recent withdrawal by Mexican civil society from national OGP platform. June 14, 2017. https://www.opengovpartnership.org/sites/default/files/OGP-SC-co-chair-Mexico-statement_%20June2017.pdf

Open Government Partnership. (2017d). OGP steering committee working level meeting minutes. June 27 and 28, 2017. https://www.opengovpartnership.org/sites/default/files/OGP_SC-Working-Level-Mtg_Minutes_June2017.pdf

Open Government Partnership. (2017e). Mongolia: 2014–2016 end-of-term report. Washington, DC: Open Government Partnership.

Open Government Partnership. (2018a). FAQs on the OGP multi donor trust fund. February 20, 2018. https://www.opengovpartnership.org/ogp-multi-donor-trust-fund/faqs-on-the-ogp-multi-donor-trust-fund/

Open Government Partnership. (2018b). OGP steering committee meeting. December 5–6, 2018—Washington DC: Open Government Partnership.

Open Government Partnership. [Webpage] (ca. 2018). Finances and budget. https://www.opengovpartnership.org/about/transparency-financial-information/#budget

Open Government Partnership. (2018c). OGP participation and co-creation toolkit. https://www.opengovpartnership.org/stories/ogps-participation-and-co-creation-toolkit-from-usual-suspects-to-business-as-usual/

Open Government Partnership. (2018d). Open Government Partnership SU-IRM budget—2018. https://www.opengovpartnership.org/wp-content/uploads/2019/07/OGP_SU-IRM-Budget_2018.pdf

Open Government Partnership (2019a). *Open Government Partnership global report: Democracy beyond the ballot box*. Washington, DC: Open Government Partnership Secretariat.

Open Government Partnership. (2019b). Mexico resumes national Open Government process. March 5, 2019. https://www.opengovpartnership.org/documents/mexico-resumes-national-open-government-process-march-5-2019/

Open Government Partnership. (2019c). OGP global summit 2019: Ottawa, Canada. May 29, 2019. https://www.opengovpartnership.org/events/ogp-global-summit-2019-ottawa-canada/

Open Government Partnership. (2019d). Articles of governance. June 17, 2019. https://www.opengovpartnership.org/about/about-ogp/governance/articles-of-governance.

Open Government Partnership. (2019e). Argentina and the B team's Robin Hodess take helm of International Partnership on Open Government. October 1, 2019. https://www.opengovpartnership.org/news/argentina-and-the-b-teams-robin-hodess-take-helm-of-international-partnership-on-open-government/

Open Government Partnership (2020a). IRM refresh approved by the OGP steering committee. February 2020. https://www.opengovpartnership.org/wp-content/uploads/2020/06/IRM-Refresh-Approved-by-the-OGP-Steering-Committee-February-2020.pdf

Open Government Partnership. (2020b). Why join OGP Local? May 2020. https://www.opengovpartnership.org/wp-content/uploads/2020/05/OGP-Local_Why-Join_20200528.pdf

Open Government Partnership. (2020c). A guide to open government and the Coronavirus: Open response, open recovery. August 25, 2020. https://www.opengovpartnership.org/documents/a-guide-to-open-government-and-the-coronavirus/

Open Government Partnership. (2020d). 56 local jurisdictions join global partnership to promote open government. October 20, 2020. https://www.opengovpartnership.org/news/56-local-jurisdictions-join-global-partnership-to-promote-open-government/

Open Government Partnership. (2020e). *Open Government Partnership Handbook*. Washington, DC: OGP.

Open Government Partnership. (2022). OGP values check assessment. March 20, 2022. https://www.opengovpartnership.org/process/joining-ogp/eligibility-criteria/

OpenTheGovernment. (2011). Is a blog with e-mail public participation? August 16, 2011. https://www.openthegovernment.org/is-a-blog-with-e-mail-public-participation

Organisation for Economic Cooperation and Development (2019). OECD public governance reviews, open government in Argentina. Paris: Organisation for Economic Cooperation and Development.

Osborne, D., & Gaebler, T. (1992). *Reinventing government: How the entrepreneurial spirit is transforming government*. Reading, MA: Adison Wesley.

Osborne, S. P. (2010a). Delivering public services: Time for a new theory? *Public Management Review*, 12(1), 110. https://doi.org/10.1080/14719030903495232

Osborne, S. P. (ed.). (2010b). *The new public governance: Emerging perspectives on the theory and practice of public governance*. London: Routledge.

Pandey, S. K., Davis, R. S., Pandey, S., & Peng, S. (2016). Transformational leadership and the use of normative public values: Can employees be inspired to serve larger public purposes? *Public Administration*, 94(1), 204–222.

Park, S. M., & Joaquin, M. E. (2012). Of alternating waves and shifting shores: the configuration of reform values in the US federal bureaucracy. *International Review of Administrative Sciences*, 78(3), 514–536.

Partlow, J., & Martinez, G. (2015). Halfway through his term, Mexico's Peña Nieto has tumbled in polls. *Washington Post*, September 2, 2015. https://www.washingtonpost.com/world/the_americas/halfway-through-his-term-mexicos-pena-nieto-has-tumbled-in-polls/2015/09/02/9e09082c-50f1-11e5-b225-90edbd49f362_story.html

Pérez, H. (2013). Alianza para el Gobierno Abierto: Una oportunidad para México. FUNDAR, April 1, 2013. https://fundar.org.mx/alianza-para-el-gobierno-abierto-una-oportunidad-para-mexico/

Perlroth, N. (2017). Spyware's odd targets: Backers of Mexico's soda tax. *New York Times*, February 11, 2017. https://www.nytimes.com/2017/02/11/technology/hack-mexico-soda-tax-advocates.html

Petersen, G. (2020). Early democratization, corruption scandals and perceptions of corruption: Evidence from Mexico. *Democratization*, 28(2), 333–352. https://doi.org/10.1080/13510347.2020.1819246

Pierson, P. (1993). When effect becomes cause: Policy feedback and political change. *World Politics, 45*(4), 595–628. https://doi.org/10.2307/2950710

Pimentel, T. (2018). Achieving compliance despite the shifting political tides. Open Government Partnership, April 12, 2018. https://www.opengovpartnership.org/stories/achieving-compliance-despite-the-shifting-political-tides/

Piotrowski, S. J. (2007). *Governmental transparency in the path of administrative reform*. Albany, NY: SUNY Press.

Piotrowski, S. J. (ed.) (2010). *Transparency and secrecy: A reader linking literature and contemporary debate*. Lanham, MD: Lexington Books.

Piotrowski, S. J. (2014). Transparency: A regime value linked with ethics. *Administration & Society, 46*(2), 181–189. https://doi.org/10.1177/0095399713519098

Piotrowski, S. J. (2017). The "Open Government Reform" movement: The case of the Open Government Partnership and U.S. transparency policies. *American Review of Public Administration, 47*(2), 155–171. https://doi.org/10.1177/0275074016676575

Piotrowski, S. J., Rosenbloom, D. H., Kang, S., & Ingrams, A. (2018). Levels of value integration in federal agencies' mission and value statements: Is open government a performance target of U.S. federal agencies? *Public Administration Review, 78*(5), 705–716. https://doi.org/10.1111/puar.12937

Piotrowski, S. J., & Van Ryzin, G. G. (2007). Citizen attitudes toward transparency in local government. *American Review of Public Administration, 37*(3), 306–323.

Piscopo, A., Siebes, R., & Hardman, L. (2017). Predicting sense of community and participation by applying machine learning to open government data. *Policy & Internet, 9*(1), 55–75.

Pollitt, C., & Bouckaert, G. (2011). *Continuity and change in public policy and management*. London: Edward Elgar Publishing.

Pollitt, C., & Dan, S. (2011). *The impacts of the New Public Management in Europe: A meta-analysis*. Rotterdam: Coordinating for Cohesion in the Public Sector of the Future.

Pollitt, C., & Hupe, P. (2011). Talking about government: The role of magic concepts. *Public Management Review, 13*(5), 641–658.

Porumbescu, G. A., Cucciniello, M., & Gil-Garcia, J. R. (2020). Accounting for citizens when explaining open government effectiveness. *Government Information Quarterly, 37*(2), [101451]. https://doi.org/10.1016/j.giq.2019.101451

Porumbescu, G. A., Piotrowski, S. J., & Mabillard, V. (2020). Performance information, racial bias, and citizen evaluations of government: Evidence from two studies, *Journal of Public Administration Research and Theory, 31*(3), 523–541. https://doi.org/10.1093/jopart/muaa049

Pousadela, I. (2019). *The road to genuine co-creation: Insights from Argentina*. Washington, DC: Open Government Partnership. https://www.opengovpartnership.org/stories/the-road-to-genuine-co-creation-insights-from-argentina/

Power, S. (2015). Keeping the Open Government Partnership vital, innovative, and true to its founding principles. U.S. Department of State, October 28, 2015. https://2009-2017.state.gov/p/io/rm/248934.htm

Pozen, D. (2018). Transparency's ideological drift. *Yale Law Journal, 128*, 100–165.

Prakash, A., & Potoski, M. (2007). Collective action through voluntary environmental programs: A club theory perspective. *Policy Studies Journal, 35*(4), 773–792.

Proceso. (2016). INAI: 23 estados se han sumado a iniciativa de Gobierno Abierto. August 2, 2016. https://web.archive.org/web/2016*/https://www.proceso.com.mx/449505/inai-23-estados-se-han-sumado-a-iniciativa-gobierno-abierto

Proceso. (2018). ONG a AMLO: Sólo regímenes autocráticos ven a la sociedad civil como amenaza. April 11, 2018. https://web.archive.org/web/20191003031314/https://www.proceso.com.mx/529430/ong-a-amlo-solo-regimenes-autocraticos-ven-a-la-sociedad-civil-como-amenaza

Pyo, S., Reggi, L., & Martin, E. G. (2020). The potential role of open data in mitigating the COVID-19 pandemic: Challenges and opportunities. Health Affairs, November 2, 2020. https://www.healthaffairs.org/do/10.1377/hblog20201029.94898/full/

Raat, C. (2016). *Netherlands: 2013–2014 end of term report.* [Final Report]. Washington, DC: Open Government Partnership. February 1, 2016. https://www.opengovpartnership.org/documents/nederland-2013-2014-eindrapport/

Radaelli, C. M. (2003). *The open method of coordination: A new governance architecture for the European Union?* Stockholm: Swedish Institute for European Policy Studies.

Rainey, H. G., & Jung, C. S. (2014). A conceptual framework for analysis of goal ambiguity in public organizations. *Journal of Public Administration Research and Theory, 25*(1), 71–99.

Randma-Liiv, T. (2008). New public management versus neo-Weberian state in Central and Eastern Europe. *NISPAcee Journal of Public Administration and Policy, 1*(2), 69–81.

Rashchupkina, Y. (2015). The European Union's role in networks on removal of fossil fuel subsidies and disclosure of climate change information. *Contemporary Politics, 21*(3), 354–366.

Raymond, M., & DeNardis, L. (2015). Multistakeholderism: Anatomy of an inchoate global institution. *International Theory, 7*(3), 572–616.

Reforma. (2015a). Plantean acotar transparencia; Pide Presidencia 82 cambios a proyecto de ley. February 10, 2015.

Reforma. (2015b). Anuncian medidas sobre rendición de cuentas: Asegura Presidente que transparencia es el antídoto contra la corrupción. October 29, 2015.

Reforma. (2017). Rompen acuerdo en transparencia. May 24, 2017.

Reinsberg, B., & Westerwinter, O. (2021). The global governance of international development: Documenting the rise of multi-stakeholder partnerships and identifying underlying theoretical explanations. *The Review of International Organizations, 16*, 59–94. https://doi.org/10.1007/s11558-019-09362-0

Reynaers, A. M. (2014). Public values in public–private partnerships. *Public Administration Review*, *74*(1), 41–50.

Rhodes, R. A. (2016). Recovering the craft of public administration. *Public Administration Review*, *76*(4), 638–647.

Ríos, V. (2016). Mexico wins: Anti-corruption reform approved. Wilson Center, July 12, 2016. https://www.wilsoncenter.org/article/mexico-wins-anti-corruption-reform-approved

Ríos, V. (2017). How Mexico's anti-corruption fight went off-track. *Americas Quarterly*, September 18, 2017. https://www.americasquarterly.org/content/how-mexicos-anti-corruption-fight-went-track

Rivoir, A., & Landinelli, J. (2017). New pathways for citizen agency: Open government national action plans in Uruguay. IT for Change. https://opendocs.ids.ac.uk/opendocs/bitstream/handle/123456789/13011/Research-Brief-Uruguay.pdf?sequence=2&isAllowed=y

Roberts, A. (2006). *Blacked out: Government secrecy in the information age*. Cambridge: Cambridge University Press.

Robinson, K. (2021). The case for open contracting and the COVID-19 vaccine. Open Contracting Partnership, February 18, 2021. https://www.open-contracting.org/2021/02/18/the-case-for-open-contracting-the-covid-19-vaccine/

Rodea, F. (2019). 5 estados mostraron desinterés hacia plan de gobierno abierto en 2018: INAI. *El Financiero*, January 1, 2019. https://web.archive.org/web/20210128084759/https://www.elfinanciero.com.mx/nacional/5-estados-mostraron-desinteres-hacia-plan-de-gobierno-abierto-en-2018-inai/

Roelofs, P. (2019). Transparency and mistrust: Who or what should be made transparent? *Governance*, *32*(3), 565–580. https://doi.org/10.1111/gove.12402

Roldán, N. (2015). El Sistema Nacional Anticorrupción, ¿un triunfo de la sociedad civil? *Animal Politico*, February 27, 2015. https://www.animalpolitico.com/2015/02/el-sistema-nacional-anticorrupcion-un-triunfo-de-la-sociedad-civil/

Romzek, B. S., & Dubnick, M. J. (1987). Accountability in the public sector: Lessons from the *Challenger* tragedy. *Public Administration Review*, *47*(3), 227–238.

Rooney, B. (2013). Open government and open data are not the same thing. *Wall Street Journal*, August 15, 2013. https://www.wsj.com/articles/BL-TEB-5696

Rosenbloom, D. H. (2000). Retrofitting the administrative state to the Constitution: Congress and the judiciary's twentieth-century progress. *Public Administration Review*, *60*(1), 39–46.

Ruelas, A. C. (2015). Mexico: OGP leader faking transparency. FreedomInfo.org, February 19, 2015. http://www.freedominfo.org/2015/02/mexico-ogp-leader-faking-transparency/

Ruelas, A. C., & Mora, D. (2015). Notes of the Mexican Transparency System reform. FreedomInfo.org, April 29, 2015. http://www.freedominfo.org/2015/04/notes-of-the-mexican-transparency-system-reform/

Ruelas Serna, A. C. (2016). La transparencia en México: Un trabajo colectivo. *Fundación Friedrich Ebert en México*. http://rendiciondecuentas.org.mx/wp-content/uploads/2016/03/Analisis_Ana-Cristina-Ruelas.pdf

Ruggie, J. G. (2002) The theory and practice of learning networks: Corporate social responsibility and the global compact. *Journal of Corporate Citizenship*, 5, 27–36.

Ruggie, J. G. (2007). Business and human rights: The evolving international agenda. *American Journal of International Law*, 101(4), 819–840.

Rushton, S., & Williams, O. (Eds.). (2011). *Partnerships and foundations in global health governance*. Basingstoke: Palgrave Macmillan.

Sabatier, P. A. (1991). Toward better theories of the policy process. *PS: Political Science & Politics*, 24(2), 147–156. https://doi.org/10.2307/419923

Schedler, A. (1999). Conceptualizing accountability. In A. Schedler, L. Diamond, & M. F. Plattner (Eds.), *The self-restraining state: Power and accountability in new democracies* (pp. 13–28). Boulder, CO: Lynne Rienner Publishers.

Schillemans, T., Van Twist, M., & Van Hommerig, I. (2013). Innovations in accountability: Learning through interactive, dynamic, and citizen-initiated forms of accountability. *Public Performance & Management Review*, 36(3), 407–435.

Schmidthuber, L., Hilgers, D., Gegenhuber, T., & Etzelstorfer, S. (2017). The emergence of local open government: Determinants of citizen participation in online service reporting. *Government Information Quarterly*, 34(3), 457–469.

Schneider, J. (2015). Bringing government data into the light: Slovakia's open data initiative, 2011–2015. Innovations for Successful Societies, Princeton University, http://successfulsocieties.princeton.edu/

Schnell, S. (2015). Mimicry, persuasion, or learning? The case of two transparency and anti-corruption policies in Romania. *Public Administration and Development*, 35(4), 277–287.

Schnell, S. (2018). Cheap talk or incredible commitment? (Mis)calculating transparency and anti-corruption. *Governance*, 31(3), 415–430.

Scott-Railton, J., Marczak, B., Guarnieri, C., & Crete-Nishihata, M. (2017a). Bitter sweet: Supporters of Mexico's soda tax targeted with NSO exploit links. CitizenLab, February 11, 2017. https://citizenlab.ca/2017/02/bittersweet-nso-mexico-spyware/

Scott-Railton, J., Marczak, B., Razzak, B. A., Crete-Nishihata, M., & Deibert, R. (2017b). Reckless exploit: Mexican journalists, lawyers, and a child targeted with NSO spyware. CitizenLab, June 19, 2017. https://citizenlab.ca/2017/06/reckless-exploit-mexico-nso/

Sedacca, M. (2021) A key tool in COVID Tracking: The Freedom of Information Act. *New York Times*, April 21, 2021. https://www.nytimes.com/2021/04/14/insider/freedom-of-information-covid.html

Selakovic, B. (2018). *Political will is still key to transformative changes*. Belgrade: United Nations Development Program.

Shkabatur, J. (2012). Transparency with(out) accountability: Open government in the United States. *Yale Law & Policy Review, 31*(1), 79–140.

Simmons, B. (2000). International law and state behavior: Commitment and compliance in international monetary affairs. *American Political Science Review, 94*(4), 819–835. doi:10.2307/2586210

Simmons, B. (2009). *Mobilizing for human rights: International law in domestic politics*. Cambridge: Cambridge University Press.

Simmons, B. (2010). Treaty compliance and violation. *Annual Review of Political Science, 13,* 273–296.

Simmons, B., & Danner, A. (2010). Credible Commitments and the International Criminal Court. *International Organization, 64*(2), 225-256. doi:10.1017/S0020818310000044

Simmons, B. A., & Martin, L. L. (2002). International organizations and institutions. In W. Carlsnaes et al. (Eds.), *Handbook of international relations* (pp. 192–211). London: Sage.

Slaughter, A. M. (2009). *A new world order*. Princeton, NJ: Princeton University Press.

SocialTIC. (2015). Urgente que la Alianza para el Gobierno Abierto se convierta en una plataforma efectiva para ayudar a resolver los grandes problemas que enfrenta México. October 28, 2015. https://socialtic.org/blog/urgente-que-la-alianza-para-el-gobierno-abierto-se/

Stamati, T., Papadopoulos, T., & Anagnostopoulos, D. (2015). Social media for openness and accountability in the public sector: Cases in the Greek context. *Government Information Quarterly, 32*(1), 12–29.

Steibel, F., Alves, M., & Konopacki, M. (2017). Fighting corruption alone: Civic participation in OGP anti-corruption commitments. *International Journal of Open Governments, 6,* 1–32. https://ojs.imodev.org/?journal=RIGO&page=article&op=view&path%5B%5D=205

Stone, D. (2004). Transfer agents and global networks in the "transnationalization" of policy. *Journal of European Public Policy, 11*(3): 545–566.

Stone, D. (2019). Transnational policy entrepreneurs and the cultivation of influence: Individuals, organizations and their networks. *Globalizations, 16*(7), 1128–1144. https://doi.org/10.1080/14747731.2019.1567976

Stone, R. W. (2013). Informal governance in international organizations: Introduction to the special issue. *Review of International Organizations, 8*(2), 121–136. https://doi.org/10.1007/s11558-013-9168-y

Susha, I. (2015). Participation in open government. *Orebro studies in informatics* 8. Orebro University School of Business, Orebro University, Sweden.

Tallberg, J., Sommerer, T., Squatrito, T., & Jönsson, C. (2013). *The opening up of international organizations*. Cambridge: Cambridge University Press.

ten Oever, N. (2019). Productive contestation, civil society, and global governance: Human rights as a boundary object in ICANN. *Policy & Internet, 11*(1), 37–60.

Terrazas, R. (2015). Gobierno abierto local, ¿más que una moda? *Animal Político*, May 29, 2015. https://www.animalpolitico.com/blogueros-res-publica/2015/05/29/gobierno-abierto-local-mas-que-una-moda/

Terry, L. D. (2005). The thinning of administrative institutions in the hollow state. *Administration & Society*, 37(4), 426–444.

Timberman, D. G. (2016). The vote in the Philippines: Elite democracy disrupted? *Journal of Democracy*, 27(4), 135–144. https://doi.org/10.1353/jod.2016.0069

Tisné, M. (2014a). The ambition of Open Government Partnership. Tisné.org, May 27, 2014. https://tisne.org/2014/05/27/the-ambition-of-open-government-partnership/

Tisné, M. (2014b). "What can OGP do for me?" Open Government Partnership, September 24, 2014. https://www.opengovpartnership.org/stories/what-can-ogp-do-for-me/

Tisné, M. (2015). OGPx—Going local for global impact. Open Government Partnership, October 27, 2015. https://www.opengovpartnership.org/stories/ogpx-going-local-for-global-impact/

Tisné, M. (2016). The magic in the room: How the Open Government Partnership can inspire and go to scale. Tisné.org, September 20, 2016. https://tisne.org/2016/09/20/the-magic-in-the-room-how-the-open-government-partnership-can-inspire-and-go-to-scale

Transparencia Mexicana. (2015a). Letter from Mexican CSOs to the Tripartite Technical Secretariat. February 3, 2015. https://www.tm.org.mx/wp-content/uploads/2015/02/Letter-from-Mexican-CSO-to-the-TTS-Feb-3.15.pdf

Transparencia Mexicana. (2015b). Mexican CSO warn of possible regressions on access to information. February 17, 2015. https://www.tm.org.mx/mexican-cso-warn-possible-regressions-access-information/

Transparencia Mexicana. (2016). Mensaje al Senado de la República con motivo de la dictaminación de la Iniciativa Ciudadana de Ley General de Responsabilidades Administrativas "Ley3de3." June 13, 2016. https://www.tm.org.mx/mensaje-al-senado-la-republica-motivo-la-dictaminacion-la-iniciativa-ciudadana-ley-general-responsabilidades-administrativas-ley3de3-2/

Treisman, L. (2019). New at the OGP Summit: OpenOwnership and UK Government launch a major collective action platform, and we scale up our help for implementers. Open Ownership, May 2019. https://www.openownership.org/news/new-at-the-ogp-summit-openownership-and-uk-government-launch-a-major-collective-action-platform-and-we-scale-up-our-help-for-implementers/

Trend News Agency. (2012). Int'l organizations' opinions considered while preparing national action plans in Azerbaijan. September 6, 2012. https://en.trend.az/azerbaijan/politics/2062493.html

Trubek, D. M., & Trubek, L. G. (2005). Hard and soft law in the construction of social Europe: The role of the open method of co-ordination. *European Law Journal*, 11(3): 343–364.

Twaweza Ni Sisi. (n.d.) About Twaweza. Accessed March 2, 2022. https://www.twaweza.org/go/about-us

Ubaldi, B. (2013). *Open government data: Towards empirical analysis of open government data initiatives* (OECD Working Papers on Public Governance, no. 22). Paris: OECD Publishing. https://doi.org/10.1787/5k46bj4f03s7-en

UK Cabinet Office (2013). PM speech at Open Government Partnership 2013. Accessed March 22, 2022. https://www.gov.uk/government/speeches/pm-speech-at-open-government-partnership-2013

United Nations (2015). *The sustainable development goals*. New York. United Nations. https://sdgs.un.org/goals/goal16

United Nations Framework Convention on Climate Change. (n.d.) Transparency of support under the Paris Agreement. https://unfccc.int/topics/climate-finance/workstreams/transparency-of-support-ex-post/transparency-of-support-under-the-paris-agreement

United Nations Framework Convention on Climate Change. (2015). *The Paris Agreement*. (FCCC/CP/2015/L.9/Rev.1). New York: United Nations. https://unfccc.int/files/essential_background/convention/application/pdf/english_paris_agreement.pdf

Universidad Panamericana. (2016). Analizan rol de la sociedad civil en Sistema Nacional Anticorrupción. August 11, 2016. http://www.up.edu.mx/es/noticias/29709/analizan-rol-de-la-sociedad-civil-en-sistema-nacional-anticorrupcion

Vabulas, F., & Snidal, D. (2013). Organization without delegation: Informal intergovernmental organizations (IIGOs) and the spectrum of intergovernmental arrangements. *Review of International Organizations, 8*(2), 193–220.

van Zyl, A. (2014). How civil society organizations close the gap between transparency and accountability. *Governance, 27*(2), 347–356. https://doi.org/10.1111/gove.12073

Verzosa, N. (2017). Insights on the Philippines' 4th national action plan: Co-creating our governance outcomes. Open Government Partnership Blog, August 10, 2017. https://www.opengovpartnership.org/stories/insights-on-the-philippines-4th-national-action-plan-co-creating-our-governance-outcomes/

Vila, S., & Wilson, C. (2013). Open thread: The second Open Government Partnership summit. TechPresident, November 5, 2013. https://web.archive.org/web/20140327022029/http://techpresident.com/ogpsummit

Volintiru, C., & Osuna Olivas, J. J. (2018). *Preventing corruption at local and regional level in South Mediterranean countries*. Brussels, Belgium: European Committee of the Regions (CoR). http://eprints.lse.ac.uk/90170/1/Olivas-Osuna_Preventing%20corruption_2018.pdf

von Bertele, K. (2015, December 15). Calling all subnational reformers! Open Government Partnership (website), December 15, 2015. https://www.opengovpartnership.org/stories/calling-all-subnational-reformers

von Stein, J. (2005). Do treaties constrain or screen? Selection bias and treaty compliance. *American Political Science Review, 99*(4), 611–622. http://www.jstor.org/stable/30038968

Vossler, L., & Foti, J. (2018). When more is more: Toward higher impact OGP commitments. *Open Government Partnership Independent Reporting Mechanism.* https://www.opengovpartnership.org/sites/default/files/IRM_Analysis-Paper_Higher-Impact_20180327.pdf

Waldo, D. (2017). *The administrative state: A study of the political theory of American public administration.* New York: Routledge.

Webber, J. (2019). López Obrador takes on Mexico's institutions. *Financial Times.* July 30, 2019. https://www.ft.com/content/69bf2628-b1e1-11e9-bec9-fdcab53d6959

Weerakkody, V., Irani, Z., Kapoor, K., Sivarajah, U., & Dwivedi, Y. K. (2017). Open data and its usability: An empirical view from the citizen's perspective. *Information Systems Frontiers, 19*(2), 285–300.

Weinstein, J. (2013). Transforming multilateralism: Innovation on a global stage. *Stanford Social Innovation Review.* Sponsored supplement. 3–7.

Welch, E. W., & Wong, W. (2001). Effects of global pressures on public bureaucracy: Modeling a new theoretical framework. *Administration & Society, 33*(4), 371–402.

White House. (2010a). Fact sheet: U.S. support for open government. September 23, 2010. https://obamawhitehouse.archives.gov/the-press-office/2010/09/23/fact-sheet-us-support-open-government

White House. (2010b). Remarks by the president to the United Nations General Assembly. September 23, 2010. https://obamawhitehouse.archives.gov/the-press-office/2010/09/23/remarks-president-united-nations-general-assembly

White House. (2011). Opening remarks by President Obama on Open Government Partnership. Waldorf Astoria Hotel, New York City, New York. https://obamawhitehouse.archives.gov/the-press-office/2011/09/20/opening-remarks-president-obama-open-government-partnership

Wijnhoven, F., Ehrenhard, M., & Kuhn, J. (2015). Open government objectives and participation motivations. *Government Information Quarterly, 32*(1), 30–42.

Williams, S. (2018). *How the Catholic Church is fighting the drug war in the Philippines.* New York: America Magazine. https://www.americamagazine.org/politics-society/2018/01/25/how-catholic-church-fighting-drug-war-philippines

Wilson, C. (2020). The socialization of civic participation norms in government? Assessing the effect of the Open Government Partnership on countries' e-participation. *Government Information Quarterly, 37*(4), 101476.

Wilson, C. (2021). Multi-stakeholder initiatives, policy learning and institutionalization: the surprising failure of open government in Norway. *Policy Studies, 42*(2), 173–192.

Wilson, W. (1887). The study of administration. *Political Science Quarterly, 2*(2), 197–222. https://doi.org/10.2307/2139277

Winters, M. S. (2014). Targeting, accountability and capture in development projects. *International Studies Quarterly, 58*(2), 393–404. https://doi.org/10.1111/isqu.12075

World Bank. (2015). *Indonesia—Country partnership framework for the period FY16–20*. (Report No. 99172). Washington, DC: World Bank Group. http://documents.worldbank.org/curated/en/195141467986374707/text/99172-REVISED-World-Bank-Indonesia-Country-Partnership-Framework-2016-2020.txt

Worthy, B. (2015). *United Kingdom progress report 2013–2015*. [IRM Second Progress Report]. Washington, DC: Open Government Partnership. March 30, 2015. https://www.opengovpartnership.org/documents/united-kingdom-progress-report-2013-2015/

Wotipka, C. M., & Tsutsui, K. (2008). Global human rights and state sovereignty: State ratification of international human rights treaties, 1965–2001. *Sociological Forum, 23*: 724–754. https://doi.org/10.1111/j.1573-7861.2008.00092.x

Yavuz, N., & Welch, E. W. (2014). Factors affecting openness of local government websites: Examining the differences across planning, finance and police departments. *Government Information Quarterly, 31*(4), 574–583. https://doi.org/10.1016/j.giq.2014.07.004

Yeung, R. L. K. (2005). Public enterprise governance: KRC corporation and its governance controversies. *Public Management Review, 7*(4), 565–587. https://doi.org/10.1080/14719030500362579

Yu, H., & Robinson, D. G. (2012). The new ambiguity of open government. *UCLA Law Review Discourse, 59*, 178.

Zagdragchaa, B., & Tserenjav, D. (2017). *Mongolia end-of-term report 2014–2016*. Open Government Partnership, August 4, 2017. https://www.opengovpartnership.org/documents/mongolia-end-of-term-report-2014-2016/

Zahariadis, N. (2008). Ambiguity and choice in European public policy. *Journal of European Public Policy, 15*(4), 514–530. https://doi.org/10.1080/13501760801996717

Zeitlin, J. (2009). The open method of coordination and reform of national social and employment policies. In M. Heidenreich and J. Zeitlin (Eds.), *Changing European employment and welfare regimes: The influence of the open method of coordination on national reforms* (pp. 214–245). New York: Routledge.

Zeleti, F. A., Ojo, A., & Curry, E. (2016). Exploring the economic value of open government data. *Government Information Quarterly, 33*(3), 535–551. https://doi.org/10.1016/j.giq.2016.01.008

Zuiderwijk, A., & Janssen, M. (2014). Open data policies, their implementation and impact: A framework for comparison. *Government Information Quarterly, 31*(1), 17–29. https://doi.org/10.1016/j.giq.2013.04.003

Index

Note: Figures and tables are indicated by a "f" and "t," respectively, following the page number. Endnotes are indicated by an "n" and note number following the page number.

Abbott, K. W., 72, 73–74, 76
Access to information. *See also* Freedom of information laws; *and specific countries*
Access Info Europe, 40, 104
Access Initiative, 163
access to information criterion, 104
Accountability policies, 46–49
Action plans. *See* National Action Plans
Administrative State, The (Waldo), 54
African Union, collaboration with OGP, 168
Africa OGP Convention, 170
Agency-based approaches to institutional design, 73, 74–75
Albania
  anticorruption initiatives, 134
  local engagement with OGP values, 141–142
Amnesty International, 146
Andonova, L. B., 73
Anticorruption initiatives, 44, 48, 133
"Anti-Corruption Open Data Principles" (Group of 20), 155
Aquino, Benigno, 91, 98, 165
Argentina
  domestic coalition impacts, 164
  as member of OGP, 102, 159

Ministry of Modernization, 165
public participation amidst political transitions, 27, 171
response to COVID-19, 226
subnational models, 160–161, 162
Article 19 (Universal Declaration of Human Rights), 40, 42–43, 185, 187, 193
Articles of Governance, 15–17, 110, 111
Asian Development Bank, 168
Australia, beneficial ownership registries, 156
Automated decision making, 51
Azerbaijan, National Action Plans, 110

Bacon, Francis, 37
Bantay Kita, 171
Basel Institute on Governance, University of Basel, Switzerland, 110
Beneficial ownership, 157–159
Beneficial Ownership Transparency Network, 156
Bentham, Jeremy, 12–13, 38
Berliner, D., 17, 74, 77
Berners-Lee, Tim, 91
Biden, Joe, 223
Boin, A., 66
Bolsonaro, Jair, 223

Bond Anti-Corruption Group, 133
Borrás, S., 64
Bozeman, B., 62
Brandeis, Louis, 38
Brazil
  democratic disruption in, 2
  Document Management Policy, 142
  as founding member of OGP, 1, 84–85, 87, 90
  National Action Plans, 107
  response to COVID-19, 226
  subnational models, 159
Brockmyer, B., 69, 71
B Team, 102
Budget and expenditures, 100–101, 101t
Bureaucracy and the modern state, history of, 38–40

Calderón Hinojosa, Felipe, 181, 182
Cameron, David, 120–121
Canada, National Action Plans, 107
Casa Blanca scandal, 200, 201
Centre for Law and Democracy, 40, 104
Chr. Michelsen Institute, 135
CIDAC (Centro de Investigacion para el Desarrollo, A.C.), 187
Citizen participation
  citizen innovation, 45
  Citizen Lab, 202
  citizen participation principle, 107
  citizen sourcing, 45
  civic engagement criterion, 104
Civicus, 3
Civil Society Core Group (Nucleo de la Sociedad Civil), 187, 205–206, 210
Civil society organizations. *See also* Mexico, pathways of change (case study); *specific organizations*
  approach to institutional design, 74
  commitment outcomes, 132–134, 137, 141, 157–159, 161, 163–165, 171–172
  drawbacks to involvement of, 136
  early concerns of, 91–93
  as members of OGP, 1, 3
  National Action Plans and, 6, 25–27, 109–110
Classical public administration, 53–54
Clinton, Bill, 50
Clinton, Hillary, 88–89
Collaborative democracy, 45
Colombia, as member of Contracting 5, 155
Commitments, types of, 129–130, 130f, 235n
Competing policy actors, as political conflicts, 67–68
Computer-mediated transparency, 49, 50
Conflict-based approaches to institutional design, 73–74, 75
Constituency support, 45
Contracting 5, 155
Corruption Perceptions Index (Transparency International), 165, 182
Costa Rica, modernization of postal service, 142
Country researchers, 111, 114
Country Support group, 103
COVID-19 pandemic, 224–226
Croatia
  Access to Information Act (2013), 134–135
  held OGP European Outreach and Support meetings, 169
  leverage of civil society, 164
  National Action Plans, 107
  open data initiatives, 134–135
  Public Consultation Code (2009), 134–135
Cross-country relevance, as implementation risks, 60
Crowdsourcing, 50
Cultura Ecologica, 187
Culture of co-creation concept, 159
Curtin, D., 11, 13, 35

Dan, S., 60
Data.gov, 41

De Graaf, G., 62
De Jong, M., 57–58
Demchak, C. C., 57–58
Democratic values criterion, 104
DeNardis, L., 69
Denmark, open government initiatives, 143, 156
Design-reality gaps, as implementation risks, 59
Digital-era governance, 57
Direct pathways of change, 120–148, 173–175
  commitment-and-comply focus, 4
  components of, 17–18, 17f, 28t, 122f
  evaluation of, 28–30, 231–233
  expectations of, 19, 19t
  Independent Reporting Mechanism, 123, 124–126, 147–148
  limitations of, 20–23
  mixed performance outcomes, 128–147, 130f
  National Action Plans, 123, 126–127
  OGP commitment-level outcomes, 124–126, 125t
  OGP commitment statistics (2011–2019), 126–127, 127t
  as positive performance trend, 127–128, 128f
Domestic network resources, 162–163
Dominican Republic, National Action Plans, 107
Duncan, J., 229
Duterte, Rodrigo, 223

Economic and technological developments, as structural barriers, 65–66
e-government, 21, 46, 49–50, 134, 144–145
Ehrenhard, M., 45
Elkins, D. J., 121–122
Enlightenment principles, in open government, 36–37
Esmark, Anders, 57

European Convention on Human Rights, 43
European Union (EU)
  collaboration with OGP, 168
  Open Method of Coordination, 21, 230
  Support for Improvement in Governance and Management initiative, 167
Extractive Industries Transparency Initiative (EITI), 71, 91, 143, 156–157

Faddism and short-term perspectives, 66–67
Faude, B., 73
Financial Transparency Coalition, 155
Finland, Freedom of Information laws, 39
Finnemore, M., 152
Fiscal openness policies, 48
Fiscal transparency criterion, 104
Flops, as commitment type, 130f, 131, 145–147, 235n
Ford Foundation, 16
Fountain, Jane, 231
Fox, J. A., 69, 71, 149
Fox Quesada, Vicente, 181
France, open government initiatives, 27, 155, 171
Fraundorfer, M., 157–158
Frederickson, H. G., 54
Freedom House, 136
Freedom of Information Act (1966) (US), 39–40
Freedom of information laws, *See also* Access to information; *and specific countries*
  anticorruption initiatives and, 44
  assessment of, 104
  democratic rights and, 12
  open government and, 13, 171–172
  requirements of founding members, 90
  technology and, 11
Functionalist approach to institutional design, 72, 74
FUNDAR, 185, 187
Funding sources, 165–167
Fung, A., 49

Gaebler, Ted, 55
García, A. G., 211
Gehring, T., 73
Georgia (country), open government initiatives, 132–133, 166
Gerson, P., 184, 191
GESOC (Gestion Social y Cooperacion), 187
Ghana, open government initiatives, 138–139
Gill, D., 56–57
Gingrich, Jane, 64
Global Fund Against AIDS, Tuberculosis, and Malaria, 80
Global Integrity, 165
Global Open Data Index (2013–2016), 153, 154t, 165
Global power influences, as structural barriers, 64–65
Global Summits (OGP)
  London (2013), 114, 120–121, 153
  Mexico (2015), 116, 179, 196–197, 200–201
  Ottawa (2019), 110
  Paris (2016), 155
Goal ambiguity, 61–63
Gore, Al, 55
Government Information Locator System, US, 50
Graham, M., 49
Grand challenges, of action plans, 106–107
Green, J. F., 72–73
Greve, C., 57
Group of 7, 168
Group of 20
  "Anti-Corruption Open Data Principles," 155
  open data principles, 168
  "Principles for Promoting Integrity in Public Procurement," 155
Grupo Oaxaca, 181, 236n6
Guerzovich, F., 165

"Guide to Implementing Beneficial Ownership Transparency, A" (Beneficial Ownership Transparency Network), 156
"Guide to Open Government and the Coronavirus, A: Open Response, Open Recovery" (OGP), 225

Hage, Jorge, 87, 91
Hale, T., 73
Heller, Nathaniel, 81
Herrero, Alvaro, 162
Hewlett Foundation, 16, 110
Hillebrandt, M., 11, 13, 35
Hivos, 16, 110
Hodess, Robin, 102
Hollowed-out state institutions, 60, 154–155
Hood, C., 11, 47
Huberts, L., 62
Human rights advocacy, 40
Human Rights Watch, 146–147

IA Pro (software), 163
Ibrahim, Mo, 91
IMCO (Instituto Mexicano para la Competitividad—Mexican Institute for Competitiveness), 183, 187, 202–203, 236n5
Implementation problems, 59–61
INAI (Instituto Nacional de Acceso a la Informacion), 186, 206, 207, 208
Independent Reporting Mechanism. *See also* National Action Plans; Steering Committee
  budget, 101
  country assessment reports, 105, 112, 114–116, 133, 134–145, 184–185, 189, 193–195
  country researchers, 111, 114
  criteria and standards subcommittee oversight, 113, 115
  International Experts Panel, 103, 112, 113–114, 115

key findings on direct pathway of change, 147–148
nongovernmental actor role in, 109–110
as part of direct pathway of change, 123, 124–126, 147–148
program management team, 112–113
revisions to process of, 107–108
roles of, 103, 111–116
India, as founding member of OGP, 84–85, 94–95
Indirect pathways of change, 148–175, 221–234
beneficial ownership, 156–157
components of, 17f, 28t, 151f
evaluation of, 28–30
evaluation of process-based dynamics, 227–233
expectations of, 19, 19t
future of open government, 222–227
institutional collaboration, 167–169
key findings, 172–173
linkages and coalitions, 26–27, 167
new norms and policy models, 148–161
norms and policy models, 24–25
open contracting, 154–156
open data movement, 153, 154t
participatory processes, 157–159
as process-driven mechanisms, 4, 18
resources and opportunities, 25–26, 161–167
subnational open government model, 159–161
transnational and domestic nongovernmental linkages, 170–172
transnational governmental linkages, 169–170
Indonesia
Corruption Perceptions Index ranking, 182
environmental initiatives, 137–138
as founding member of OGP, 1, 84–85

public participation amidst political transitions, 27
subnational models, 159, 160, 161
Infocip, 141
INFOMEX, 183
Ingrams, A., 17
Inherent value ambiguities, 61–62
Institute for Democracy and Mediation (IDM), 141
Institutional crises, as political conflicts, 66
Institutional forces, as structural barriers, 64
Insufficient resources, as implementation risks, 60
Interdepartmental discrepancies, 63
Intergovernmental organizations, 70
International Budget Partnership, 104
International Campaign to End Landmines, 80
International Convention on Civil and Political Rights, 42–43
International Experts Panel, 103, 112, 113–114, 115
International institutions, 7–9, 69
International organizations, National Action Plans and, 110–111
Internet, impact on open government, 40–41, 50
Interorganizational complexity, 62–63
IRM Refresh, 112, 115, 139, 215
Israel, National Action Plans, 107

Joaquin, M. E., 56
Jordan, National Action Plans, 107
Jørgensen, T. B., 62

Kant, Immanuel, 38
Kelsey, Tim, 41
Keohane, R. O., 72–73
Kettl, Donald, 61
Kingdon, J. W., 67
Kldiashvili, Giorgi, 166
Koremenos, B., 72
Kuhn, J., 45

La Porte, T. M., 57–58
Late Modern Technocracy, 57
Late Modern Technocracy (Esmark), 57
Lean dynamism, as goal of OGP, 1–2
Learners' Tier, 159
Levitsky, S., 149–150
Light, Paul, 51–52, 67
Linkages and coalitions, 26–27, 167, 169–172
Lipson, C., 72
Lodge, M., 56–57
Logics of administrative change, 64
Low-dose interventions, 149
Low-hanging fruit, as commitment type, 130–131, 130f, 141–145, 235n
Lynn, L. E., Jr., 54

Maassen, Paul, 103
Magic concept, 44
Malicious flops, 146–147
Malta, environmental initiatives, 142
Marván, María, 183
Mass digital surveillance, 51
McCarthy, Julie, 88
McIntosh, Toby, 94, 171–172
Meijer, H., 11, 13, 35
Mexican Open Government Partnership, 198
Mexico
   civil society organizations in, 25, 26, 27
   Corruption Perceptions Index ranking, 182
   democratic disruption in, 2
   Digital Strategy National Coordinating Office, 191–192, 193, 196–197
   as founding member of OGP, 1, 84–85, 180–181
   IFAI (Instituto Federal de Acceso a la Informacion y Proteccion de Datos), 181–182, 186–187, 189, 198
   Joint Declaration for the Implementation of Actions for an Open Government, 207
   as member of Contracting 5, 155

Ministry of Public Administration, 185, 186, 191, 201, 203, 205–206
National Anticorruption System, 211, 213
public participation amidst political transitions, 27, 171
reversal of progress, 22
Right to Information Ratings, 211
Mexico, pathways of change (case study), 177–220
   background and context, 181–183
   evaluation of pathways of change, 213–219, 214t, 217t
   formation of STT, 186–190
   General Law on Transparency and Access to Public Information, 197–199, 209–210
   government surveillance and civil society withdrawal, 200–206
   initial phase of OGP membership, 183–199
   legislative developments, 209–213
   Ley 3 de 3 campaign, 212
   methodology and case selection, 179–181
   National Action Plans, 177, 179, 184–185, 192–195, 196, 203, 205–206, 214, 214t, 216
   as Steering Committee Chair and Global Summit host, 195–197
   subnational developments, 24, 206–209
Mexico City airport, 197
Michener, G., 149
Mill, John Stewart, 12–13
Mixed coalitions, 80
Mjaft! Movement, 141
Modern reforms, history of, 51–58
Moldova, National Action Plans, 107
Mongolia, open government initiatives, 137, 145
Morena party (Mexico), 205
Moses, M., 165
Multiple streams theory, 67
Multistakeholderism, defined, 69–70
Myth of bureaucratic paradigm, 54

Naïve realism, 123
National Action Plans. *See also* Independent Reporting Mechanism; *specific countries*
  civil society organizational input, 6, 25–27, 109–110
  commitments of, 2–3, 14–16, 20–22, 107–108, 122–123
  components of, 106–109
  initial plans, 90–91
  lack of enforcement of plans, 6
  low-hanging fruit in, 141
  nongovernmental actor input, 109–111
  as part of direct pathway of change, 123, 126–127
  reviews by Independent Reporting Mechanism, 7, 16, 20, 21, 31
  as two-year plans, 25, 105
National Citizens' Observatory (Observatorio Nacional Ciudadano), 194–195
Netherlands, Change Attitudes and Procedures Through Smarter Working and Public Servant, 138
New Public Administration, 54–55
New public governance, 56, 63, 65
New Public Management (NPM)
  effects of local factors on, 65
  legacy of, 36
  limitations of direct pathways of change, 232
  post-NPM reforms, 10–11, 55–57, 60, 62–63
  public accountability and, 47
  seen as panacea for prior approaches, 66
  transparency theory and, 43–44
New public service, 57
Nieto, F., 184, 191
Nigeria, subnational models, 161
North Macedonia, open government initiatives, 135–136, 140–141
Norway, open government initiatives, 1, 84–85, 144
Noveck, Beth, 11, 41
NSO Group, 202

Obama, Barack
  focus on transparency, 50
  influence on growth of OGP, 96, 97, 98
  on open government, 2
  Open Government Directive, 10, 41–42, 78, 81–82
  at UN General Assembly (2011), 91
Obrador, Andrés Manuel López, 197, 205, 217, 220, 223
OGP commitment statistics (2011–2019), 126–127, 127t
OGP Explorer (website), 116, 124
Omidyar, Pierre, 91
Omidyar Network, 16, 41
Open contracting, 154–156
Open Contracting Data Standard, 155–156, 197
Open Contracting Partnership, 25, 71
Open Data Barometer, 24, 156
Open Data Charter, 25
Open Data Index, 24
Open data movement, 153, 154t
Open government, defined, 4–5, 12–14
Open Government Declaration, 104
Open Government Partnership (OGP), 1–34. *See also* Direct pathways of change; Indirect pathways of change; Support Unit
  Articles of Governance, 15–17, 110, 111
  critiques of, 2–3, 22–23
  evaluation of impacts of, 5–12
  founding of, 1–5, 14–17, 41–42
  impacts on public sector reform, 30–32
  members of, 2–3, 14, 15t, 22, 40, 103
  open government, defined, 4–5, 12–14
  two pathways to impact, 17–19, 17f, 19t
Open Government Partnership (OGP), as international institution, 69–117
  budget and expenditures, 100–101, 101t
  Independent Reporting Mechanism, 111–116
  multistakeholder initiatives, 70–77
  National Action Plans, 106–109

Open Government Partnership (OGP) (cont.)
  national level membership, 103–106
  nongovernmental actors in Action Plan cycles, 109–111
  structure and leadership, 101–103
  subnational governments, 116–117
Open Government Partnership (OGP), origin story, 77–100
  early concerns of members, 91–95
  emergence of idea for, 78–80
  member eligibility criteria, 88–91, 104–106
  membership growth before launch, 95–98
  motivations and methodology, 77–78
  NSC efforts, 80–82
  path to White House, 82–85
  White House summit meeting (2013), 85–88
Open Government Partnership Global Report (2019), 154–155, 157–158
Open Government Partnership Handbook, 105
Open Government Partnership Local initiative, 14, 100, 103, 116–117, 159
OpenOwnership, 156, 157
Open Society Foundations (formerly Open Society Institute), 16, 40, 41
  Justice Initiative, 104
Openwashing, 14, 135
O'Reilly, Tim, 41
Organisation for Economic Co-Operation and Development (OECD), 24, 65, 165, 167, 168
Organizational ecology approach, to institutional design, 72–73
Orthodox public administration, 53–54
Osborne, David, 55
Otero, Maria, 95

Pardinas, Juan, 162, 183, 202–203
Paris Climate Agreement, 19, 21, 169, 230
Park, S. M., 56

Participation. *See also* Citizen participation
  participation policies, 44–46
Partido Acción Nacional, 181
Partido Revolucionario Institucional, 181, 191
Pathways of change, overview, 17–19, 17f, 19t, 119–120. *See also* Direct pathways of change; Indirect pathways of change
Pegasus (software), 202, 206
Peña Nieto, Enrique
  approval ratings, 200
  corruption scandals associated with, 182, 201
  open data agenda, 194, 196–197, 209
  presidential election of, 181, 191–192
Pendleton Civil Service Act (1883) (US), 38
Pérez, Haydeé, 189
Performing governance, 62
Peru, leverage of civil society, 164
Philippines
  Corruption Perceptions Index ranking, 182
  Dagyaw program of virtual town hall meetings, 158
  democratic disruption in, 2
  as founding member of OGP, 1, 84–85, 98
  Freedom of Information laws, 223
  leverage of OGP awards and recognition, 165
  National Action Plans, 110–111
  People's Watch (Masa Masid), war on drugs, 146–147
  public participation amidst political transitions, 27, 171
  subnational governments, 171
Piotrowski, S. J., 17
Pipe dreams, as commitment type, 130, 130f, 135–141, 235n
Policy entrepreneurs, 73
Policy windows, 67
Policy-window successes, 131–132
Political conflicts, 66–67
Political efficacy, 121–122

Political influence, as implementation risks, 60–61
Pollitt, C., 60
Popper, Karl, 39
Populism, rise of, 223
Pousadela, Inés, 158–159
Powell, Joe, 108
Power, Samantha, 78, 81, 83, 84, 116
Pradhan, Sanjay, 103
Prakash, A., 74, 77
President's Task Force for Twenty-First-Century Policing (US), 162–163
"Principles for Promoting Integrity in Public Procurement" (Group of 20), 155
Privacy rights, 44
Private sector, role in global summits, 110
Proper governance, 62
Public accountability principle, 107
Public asset disclosure criterion, 104
Public choice theories, 55, 56
Public education, 45–46
Public management reform, history of, 35–68
  accountability policies, 46–49
  bureaucracy and the modern state stage and, 38–40
  examples of open government initiatives, 43t
  history of competing visions, 51–58
  industrialization and liberalism stage and, 37–38
  influence of the Enlightenment on, 36–37
  mass media, democratization, and Internet impacts on, 40–41, 50
  participation policies, 44–46
  reforms and risks, 58–67, 58f
  technology policies, 49–51
  transparency policies, 42–44
Public sector reform literature, 9–12
Public values, 53, 54, 63

Radaelli, C. M., 64
Raymond, M., 69
Reagan, Ronald, 55

Reforms and risks, 58–67
  goal ambiguity, 61–63
  implementation problems, 59–61
  internal vs. external foci, 58f
  political conflicts, 66–67
  structural barriers, 64–66
Reinsberg, B., 72, 73
Reinventing Government (Osborne and Gaebler), 55
Responsive governance, 62
Right to Information Ratings, 211
Robinson, D. G., 3
Roger, C. B., 73
Rosenbloom, David, 39
Rousseau, Jean-Jacques, 37
Rousseff, Dilma, 88, 90
Ruelas Serna, Ana Cristina, 211
Rushton, S., 229

Sabatier, Paul, 149, 228
Sanctions, in accountability policies, 47
São Paulo, Open Government Agents training program, 142–143
Schnell, S., 76
Serbia, as member of OGP, 158
Sida, 110
Sikkink, K., 152
Simeon, R., 121–122
Simon, Herbert, 54
Slovakia, open government initiatives, 156, 163
Smart city initiatives, 46
Smulders, R., 62
Snidal, D., 72, 73–74, 76
SNV, 110
SocialTic, 187, 202
South Africa, open government initiatives, 1, 2, 84–85, 107–108, 163–164
South Korea, public disclosure initiatives, 137
Stanford Social Innovation Review, 78, 80
Stars, as commitment type, 108–109, 130, 130f, 131–135, 235n

Steering Committee
  appointment of International Experts Panel, 113
  approval of IRM Refresh, 112
  chairs of, 16, 191, 198–199
  civil society organizations and, 216
  formation of fact-finding mission to Mexico, 204–205
  founding members of, 83
  Policy on Upholding the Values and Principles of Open Government Partnership, 106
  stakeholder roles, 71
  subcommittees of, 102
Structural barriers, 64–66
STT (Secretariado Tecnico Tripartita—Tripartite Technical Secretariat)
  collapse of, 206
  drafting of General Law of Transparency, 210
  roles and stakeholders of, 186–190, 191, 194–195, 203, 213
  working groups, 192–193
Study of Administration, The (Wilson), 38
Subnational Government Pilot Program, 159–161, 173
Subnational governments, 24, 116–117, 142–143, 171
Support Unit
  efforts regarding Mexico's withdrawal, 204
  focus of National Action Plans, 21
  peer exchanges, 170
  staff and goals of, 16, 99, 103
  standards and guidelines, 216
  working paper by Basel Institute on Governance, 110
Sweden
  Freedom of Information laws, 37, 39
  New Public Management policies, 55
Symbolic and political resources, 163–165

Tallberg, J., 19
Tanzania, open government initiatives, 3, 110, 160
Targeted transparency, 49
Technology and innovation principle, 107
Technology policies, 49–51
t'Hart, P. T., 66
Thatcher, Margaret, 55
Tisné, Martin, 83, 85, 88, 108–109, 159
Transnational and domestic nongovernmental linkages, 170–172
Transnational governmental linkages, 169–170
Transnational multistakeholder initiatives, 69
Transparencia Mexicana, 198
Transparency and Accountability Initiative, 80–81, 82–84, 88, 141–142
Transparency International, 158, 187
  Corruption Perceptions Index, 165, 182
Transparency policies, 42–44, 43t, 47
Transparency principle, 107
Transparency theory, 43–44
Trinidad and Tobago, civil society organizations in, 137
Triparte Technical Secretariat. *See* STT (Secretariado Tecnico Tripartita—Tripartite Technical Secretariat)
Trump, Donald, 223
Turek, Helen, 170
Twaweza, 110

Ukraine, open government initiatives, 132, 144–145, 155, 156, 158, 236n3
United Kingdom (UK)
  anticorruption initiatives, 133
  democratic disruption in, 2
  Department for International Development (DFID), 110
  as founding member of OGP, 1, 84–85, 87, 120–121
  as member of Contracting 5, 155

open data initiatives, 153
Open Government Network, 172
subnational models, 159, 160
transparency initiatives, 140
United Nations (UN)
  Ad Hoc Working Group transparency guidelines, 169
  charter of, 43
  climate change open data initiatives, 168–169
  collaboration with OGP, 168
  Convention against Corruption, 168
  Development Programme, 170
  as entrepreneurs, 73
  Global Compact, 74, 77
  Global Compact and Extractive Industries Transparency Initiative, 18–19, 26
  National Security Council, 78, 80–82, 88
  Sustainable Development Goals, 168, 195, 230
  Universal Periodic Review, 19, 229–230
United States (US)
  civil service, 38
  democratic disruption in, 2
  as founding member of OGP, 1, 84–85
  Freedom of Information laws, 37, 39–40
  leverage of civil society, 164
  National Performance Review, 55
  New Public Management policies, 55
  President's Task Force for Twenty-First-Century Policing, 162–163
  response to COVID-19, 226
  subnational models, 159, 160
United States Agency for International Development, Facilitating Public Investment project, 110–111
Universal Declaration of Human Rights, Article 19, 40, 42–43, 185, 187, 193
Uruguay, National Action Plans, 109–110
U.S. Support for Open Government (fact sheet), 82

Values of public governance (Jørgensen and Bozeman), 62
Varieties of Democracy project, 104
Vision and voice concept, 11, 13, 35–36, 44–45

Waldo, Dwight, 54
Way, L. A., 149–150
Web 2.0 technologies, 41
Weber, Max, 54
Web of Science, 167, 237n1
Weil, D., 49
Weinstein, Jeremy, 78, 80, 81, 83, 85
Westerwinter, O., 72, 73
Wijnhoven, F., 45
Williams, O., 229
Wilson, Woodrow, 38
Window-dressing institutions, 8–9, 20, 76–77, 136
World Bank
  on barriers of poor governance and corruption, 138
  as entrepreneurs, 73
  OGP trust fund, 26, 166
  path dependency and, 65

Yu, H., 3

Zuma, Jacob, 164